From Achilles to Superman

"Dr. Joseph McInerney has done a remarkable service in making the profound historical analysis of Alasdair MacIntyre accessible and applicable for a wide audience. In our age of confused and often simplistic discussions of moral questions, this book is an invaluable introduction to thinking well about what it means to not only be a good leader, but simply a good human being."

—**Patrick E. Kelly**, supreme knight, Knights of Columbus

"Dr. McInerney brilliantly synthesizes the wisdom of timeless ethical principles of the ancient Greeks with the leadership traits of today's most successful leaders. Drawing from Alasdair MacIntyre's masterful work, *A Short History of Ethics*, McInerney weaves a fascinating story of the positive developments and corruptions in the history of ethics, offering clear presentations of the most significant ethical thinkers and leaders."

—**William E. Lori**, archbishop of Baltimore

"An essential read for leaders, *From Achilles to Superman* masterfully illuminates the evolution of ethical thought from ancient Greece to modern times as a practical guidebook for leaders seeking to elevate the standards, virtues, and values that define their organizational culture, while also enhancing their own decision-making. A beacon of clarity for those striving to lead with wisdom, character, and principle amidst the chaos and ambiguity of our present times."

—**Ryan Bernacchi**, director of leadership and character development, retired, United States Naval Academy

"Sometimes you don't realize you need something until you get it: that is the case with Captain Joseph McInerny's book, *From Achilles to Superman*. We are drowning in books on leadership, but so few of them connect leadership to the intellectual tradition that produces men and women of virtue like this one does. The only remedy to our cynicism about our leaders—their character, their effectiveness, their good for us—is for us to be able to recognize people of character. This book tells the story we need to hear to help bring clarity back to our vision of leadership at this urgent moment."

—**Joseph E. Capizzi**, dean, The Catholic University of America

From Achilles to Superman
A Leader's Guide to MacIntyre's History of Ethics

Joseph J. McInerney

CASCADE *Books* • Eugene, Oregon

FROM ACHILLES TO SUPERMAN
A Leader's Guide to MacIntyre's History of Ethics

Copyright © 2025 Joseph J. McInerney. All rights reserved. Except for brief quotations in critical publications or reviews, no part of this book may be reproduced in any manner without prior written permission from the publisher. Write: Permissions, Wipf and Stock Publishers, 199 W. 8th Ave., Suite 3, Eugene, OR 97401.

Cascade Books
An Imprint of Wipf and Stock Publishers
199 W. 8th Ave., Suite 3
Eugene, OR 97401

www.wipfandstock.com

PAPERBACK ISBN: 979-8-3852-2699-3
HARDCOVER ISBN: 979-8-3852-2700-6
EBOOK ISBN: 979-8-3852-2701-3

Cataloguing-in-Publication data:

Names: McInerney, Joseph J.

Title: From Achilles to Superman : a leader's guide to MacIntyre's history of ethics / Joseph J. McInerney.

Description: Eugene, OR : Cascade Books, 2025 | Includes bibliographical references and index.

Identifiers: ISBN 979-8-3852-2699-3 (paperback) | ISBN 979-8-3852-2700-6 (hardcover) | ISBN 979-8-3852-2701-3 (ebook)

Subjects: LCSH: MacIntyre, Alasdair C. | MacIntyre, Alasdair C.—Criticism and interpretation. | History of philosophy, philosophical traditions. | Ethics and moral philosophy.

Classification: B1647.M124 M35 2025 (paperback) | B1647.M124 (ebook)

VERSION NUMBER 07/21/25

For Ellen

Contents

Acknowledgments | ix

Introduction: How This Book Came to Life | 1

1 Why Should We Bother to Examine the History of Ethics? | 9
2 The Beginnings of Our Ethical History | 18
3 Sophistry and the Wisdom of Socrates | 29
4 Plato's Description of the Good | 41
5 Politics and The Moral Psychology of Plato's *Republic* | 52
6 Plato's Description of Desire and Habit in Relation to Morality | 63
7 Aristotle's Impact on Greek Ethics | 71
8 Classical Ethics, Modern Contrasts, Stoics, and Epicureans | 92
9 Christian Morality as the Bridge Between Ancient and Medieval Ethics | 111
10 Re-Thinking Ethics in the Post-Medieval Era | 126
11 The Ethics of Rights and Freedom in the Marketplace | 145
12 Eighteenth-Century British Ethics | 157
13 Ethics in Eighteenth-Century France | 174
14 The Ethics of Immanuel Kant | 189

15 Hegel, Marx, and the Historical Nature of Ethics | 205
16 Nineteenth-Century Utilitarianism | 222
17 Danish and German Ethics in the Nineteenth Century | 238
18 Twentieth-Century Ethics and Twenty-First-Century Leadership | 258

Bibliography | 277

Index | 283

Acknowledgments

THIS BOOK, LIKE MANY others, could not have been written without the help of a community. If there is one thing I have learned in reading the work of Alasdair MacIntyre it is that wisdom is always the product of a community and a tradition over time. If there is any wisdom in the pages that follow it is the result of so many wonderful conversations and insights that have been given to me through the gifts of my family, friends, and colleagues. I have to offer the typical disclaimer that any mistakes in the following pages are mine, because that is, of course, the truth. St. Paul tells us that we should not boast because anything that we have is purely a gift from God, and the insights I have been able to record in these pages are truly God's gift to me, given through so many wonderful people.

I would also like to embark on the dangerous task of thanking some of those friends by name in the hope I do not overlook anyone. I must first mention Ian Shaw and James Anthony, whose intellectual curiosity started the conversation that produced this book. Other early collaborators include Danny McInerney, Jess Valerino, Kevin Mullaney, Rev. Jim Corkery, SJ, Gwen Pattison, Amy Zaleski, Liam McInerney, Rev. Luke Ballman, Mike Donnelly, Harry Fulton, Patrick McInerney, and Jonathan Driesslein. I also owe a debt of gratitude to Chris Eberle who is always a source of guidance and encouragement to me. Jeff Fitzgerald and Steve Means are likewise friends of great wisdom and constant encouragement. Encouragement also came from enthusiastic work colleagues, who include Brian Gedicks, George Silos, and John Marella. Saving the best for last is my enduring thanks to my wife Ellen, whose love, painstaking assistance, and constant example of excellence is the source of so much that is good in my life. God has shown his light through the beauty of these many friends, and I am truly thankful to all of them.

Introduction
How This Book Came to Life

WHY SHOULD A LEADER read about the history of ethics, of all things? That cannot be answered until we understand why someone would write a book about the history of ethics. Here is how this project came to life. I had the good fortune to teach ethics and leadership at the US Naval Academy in Annapolis for almost a decade. Towards the end of my tenure, I was approached by two of my midshipmen students who both wanted to know more about ethics. They wanted to know if I could recommend a good book. Apparently, they went to the wrong person because I gave them a bad recommendation. They were both really bright, one a straight-A student in robotics engineering and the other a former Rhodes Scholar finalist. So, I suggested a book I had read a few years back as a graduate student, *A Short History of Ethics* by a philosopher named Alasdair MacIntyre. I remembered MacIntyre's work as a tough read, but worth the effort.

    I offered my suggestion in the month of December; the following February I checked in with both of them to see how they were doing. Not well. They had both put the book down because it was too dense, too technical. It seemed a real shame since my memory was that MacIntyre had put together a compelling breakdown of all the major ethical players, from the pre-Socratic literature of the ancient Greeks to twentieth-century moral philosophy. I had greatly benefited from reading his work. Then I picked up the book again and recalled what a tough read it was. I was able to get through his writing only after years of studying philosophical and theological texts. His writing was intended for a student in the field of philosophy or an especially motivated and well-prepared lay reader. With my refresher on MacIntyre, though, I also became more convinced that he would be a worthwhile read for my students, so I suggested reading him together at the end of the semester when we all had a little more time. When summer arrived, it took us a few weeks to get into a groove with our discussion. I would translate MacIntyre's technical language for the students, and then we would talk about it. Six months and many enjoyable discussions later, we finished the book.

By the time we finished, I had written eighty pages of notes. Writing those notes had been the best ethics education activity I had ever experienced, and they became the inspiration for this book. My goal is to share the many ethical insights we discovered reading and thinking about MacIntyre's history[1] and link those insights to the important moral challenges that confront leaders today.

MacIntyre's book helps to answer the ethical challenges of the fast-paced, morally complicated world of twenty-first-century America. He gives us a starting point in our reading about ethics and how to make sense of moral ideas. MacIntyre's history is a guide to understanding the tradition of ethics that stretches from the ancient Greeks to the twentieth century. One might think it's absurd for me to provide a guide to the guide, but given the great contribution MacIntyre makes and the difficulty reading his contribution entails, it actually makes sense.

---

1. Over the course of this study, we will see that history is central to MacIntyre's approach to ethics. Indeed, he says you cannot think about morality accurately without reference to history, especially the history of the way communities and cultures have thought about moral topics. Because history has been essential to MacIntyre's entire intellectual endeavor over the last seventy years (he is still alive today) the history he describes in this book, written in the mid-1960s, is different from his thinking later in life. Were MacIntyre to write a history of ethics today, it would be a much different book. During a later interview MacIntyre describes his thought of the period in his life when he wrote *A Short History of Ethics* as "messy and fragmented," but he also notes that he learned a lot through that messiness. Although MacIntyre's *Short History of Ethics* represents his thinking when it was far from its maturity decades later, others have described the book as "a significantly novel, and synthetic achievement." Given this background I ask my reader to keep two things in mind. First, when MacIntyre's history is mentioned in the text of this book that phrase refers to his *Short History of Ethics* published in 1966 and does not refer to his later writing, which is also centered on the history of ethics. Second, his historical work from the mid-1960s may not represent his most mature thinking, but it is certainly worth our consideration and study. We can learn through the "messiness" of MacIntyre's earlier thinking just as he did.

MacIntyre's thinking is really helpful in two ways. First, his level of education is remarkable, which enables him to direct us through the massive history of moral thinking in the Western tradition. He dramatically reduces the work of determining the most important ethics books to read. So, MacIntyre provides us a superb place to begin. We don't have to read every ethical book ever written to figure out who the important thinkers are and identify their important ideas about morality. MacIntyre has done this work for us, and he is a trustworthy guide through that body of thought. The second benefit of MacIntyre's education is that he is able to place the points made by writers like Plato or Machiavelli in context, and he can provide criticism of the important, but not well-thought-out, ideas. Our discussion group often found it entertaining that MacIntyre was able to criticize some of the greatest thinkers in history as if they were students in his own class. We didn't always agree with MacIntyre's analysis, but we were always edified by it. What MacIntyre's writing shows is that just because a concept is formulated by a great thinker, it doesn't mean the idea itself is great, even though oftentimes those ideas are enormously influential. His criticism is a great help to seeing both the strengths and weaknesses of our ancestors and is also a great aid in our work to formulate our own views about ethics.

Given MacIntyre's significance to twentieth-century moral philosophy, as well as this book, it is important to provide some biographical details on his life and career. MacIntyre was born in 1929 in Glasgow, Scotland, the only child of two physicians. His family moved to London shortly after he was born, and there he grew up, attended college, and earned a bachelor's degree in classics from the University of London in 1949. He earned a master's degree in philosophy two years later and then began a long career in teaching. MacIntyre's intellectual influences were unique in a number of ways. He was a student and product of modern philosophy, but he was also interested in and shaped by his reading of Irish literature, having been taught the Gaelic language by his aunt at an early age. Modern philosophy was a tradition built on intellectual theories, while Celtic literature was a landscape filled with stories and narratives.[2] In addition to these two disparate influences, MacIntyre was also shaped early on by Christianity and the Marxist critique of liberal individualism. MacIntyre abandoned his Christian faith and wrote as an atheist from the early 1960s through the mid-1970s. *A Short History*

---

2. MacIntyre, "Interview with Giovanna Borradori," 255.

of Ethics, published in 1966, came almost in the middle of MacIntyre's sojourn as an atheist. MacIntyre emigrated to the United States in 1969 and shifted to an Aristotelian view of philosophy roughly eight years after arriving in North America.[3] He wrote his most influential book, *After Virtue*, in 1981 and converted to Catholicism in 1984 after an in-depth engagement with the thought of St. Thomas Aquinas.[4] MacIntyre has taught at almost as many universities (thirteen in Britain and the United States) as he has written books (nineteen). At the time of this writing, he is a senior research fellow at London Metropolitan University's Centre for Contemporary Aristotelian Studies in Ethics and Politics and a professor emeritus at the University of Notre Dame in South Bend, Indiana. MacIntyre has led an extraordinary academic life over the last seventy years and will surely be remembered as one of the most important moral philosophers of the twentieth century.

MacIntyre is worth reading, but as I've noted, his writing is hard to understand for the lay reader, which is a challenge this book is meant to address. My own encounter with MacIntyre's work is relevant in setting the stage for this book. I started studying theology and philosophy in my late twenties without having studied those fields at all when I was in college. By the time I entered graduate school, I had accumulated several years of experience as a naval officer and was a few years older than many of my peers. Those extra years, however, did not give me the conceptual tools that a few pertinent undergrad courses could have provided. I was an enthusiastic student, having done some reading on my own, but my start in the classroom was not smooth. I had not even heard of the words we were using in class (terms like hermeneutics and hypostatic union are not the words of daily conversation), and once I got familiar with the terminology, I still struggled to understand many of the abstractions. Over time, however, I developed the skills to understand what I read and came to the somewhat obvious conclusion that the great thinkers are called great for a reason. Their ideas are worth thinking about, even for the typical person without a philosophical background. As a result, I decided to become a translator and guide. I wanted to capture the ideas of influential thinkers—in whose company I would put MacIntyre—and communicate them to leaders who have not had the time to undertake these studies. That is the objective of this book: to put some of the most

3. Lutz, "Alasdair Chalmers MacIntyre."
4. Cornwell, "MacIntyre on Money."

important ideas about ethics and morality into words that will resonate with twenty-first-century leaders.

I have also had the good fortune to study great ethical thinkers in the context of my experience as an officer in the United States Navy. I am blessed to have developed as a leader within an institution whose tradition of leadership is long and storied. This tradition not only boasts some of the most accomplished leaders in American history—John Paul Jones, Oliver Hazard Perry, David Glasgow Farragut, and Chester W. Nimitz, to name a few—but it is also an intellectual tradition that is alive and kicking within the ranks of the twenty-first-century Navy. As imperfect as the US Navy is, it takes leadership seriously. It invests in leadership thought and education, it evaluates people on the basis of leadership, and leadership is a topic that is continuously discussed and debated. As I matured as a leader and as a student of ethics, I began to realize that the two halves of my professional life were intimately related. To be honest, as a young officer in my twenties I paid little attention to the relationship between ethics and leadership. But as I studied and gained experience as an officer in the Navy, it became obvious to me that leadership was and is an intrinsically moral endeavor. Having read leadership scholarship, I must admit that this last assertion is controversial. Not everyone thinks leadership is linked to ethics, and the great thing about MacIntyre's history is that he points out the thinkers whose writing supports a separation between ethics and leadership. This is not my view, however, and I hope the pages of this book will make clear that leadership is not only an ethical undertaking, but it may be the most important ethical undertaking a person ever pursues. What I also hope to accomplish is to show how high moral standards on the part of leaders are the surest way to empower followers and organizations to achieve their mission.

And so, that is why I wrote this book. The further question is, "Why should a leader read it?" Let me start with the bad news: leadership seems to be in sad shape in contemporary American culture. Respect for our leadership elites has never been lower. All we need to do is peruse the latest headlines to see leadership failures that happen daily or read the national surveys by the Pew Research Center and others that track a decades-long decline in trust of American leaders and institutions.[5] Political pundit David Brooks summarized the plight of contemporary

---

5. Pew Research Center, "Public Trust in Government: 1958–2023." Cf. Edelman, "Edelman Trust Barometer." for an international survey that examines trust in leaders specifically.

leadership succinctly when he asserted, "The leadership class is fundamentally self-dealing."[6] Prominent authors in the leadership education industry—the industry that is supposed to develop good leaders—agree with his assessment too. A series of authors have recently written books not only documenting the precipitous decline of respect for leaders in almost every aspect of American culture, but they even point a finger at themselves as being part of the problem.[7] The last four decades have seen the leadership education industry grow exponentially, with corporations, government entities, and universities spending billions of dollars per year on leadership development. Yet, the resulting improvement for leadership performance has been too meager to measure in any significant sense.

What gives? Is there any way to correct our downward leadership trajectory? While the answer to such a broad question must of its nature be complex, I think a significant and even a fundamentally important aspect of this downward trajectory is the fact that our culture does not promote a good understanding of ethics. Contemporary moral thinking, our moral thinking, has gotten worse over the last few centuries rather than better. One reason for this (among many) is that we are ignorant of many important ethical principles. And our understanding of the moral principles with which we are familiar is far too superficial. This ignorance affects our leaders. Leaders will face difficult moral dilemmas. Sometimes those dilemmas are complicated, but more often they are difficult because they require an inner strength to overcome, which is something many leaders lack. And one reason they lack such strength is they are unaware of the ethical resources offered to them by the three-thousand-year-old tradition of ethics to which we are all heirs. One action necessary for us to reverse our course, therefore, is to examine how the ethical ideas in this three-thousand-year tradition have developed. By tracking and understanding that development, we can critically appraise, rethink, and reshape the moral ideas that have led to the sorry shape of ethics and leadership bemoaned by so many in our own society. Through the critical examination of our moral tradition, we can begin to reform ourselves and prepare the next generation of leaders for the moral challenges they will inevitably face.

---

6. Brooks, "Who Is James Johnson?"

7. Cf. Kellerman, *End of Leadership*, Pfeffer, *Leadership BS*, and Kolditz et al., *Leadership Reckoning*, for three recent books offering critiques of the contemporary leadership education industry and prescriptions to help tackle the problems with the industry.

Here is my plan of attack to achieve that goal. In each chapter of this book, I will provide the pertinent data from the historical period that MacIntyre is addressing in his book to set the context for MacIntyre's reading of that history. Following the historical data, I will provide a summary of MacIntyre's most important points regarding the moral thought of that time period. Lastly, after each summary, I will identify one of the moral principles covered in that chapter and discuss how it applies to the practice of leadership. The last chapter will tie some of the most important themes together and offer insights into how we can apply those ideas to make the contemporary practice of leadership better.

My hope is that this study will be a beginning, and the reader won't stop with this guide, or even MacIntyre's guide, but will go on to engage with Homer, Hobbes, Hume, and all the other figures that have shaped the most important moral ideas that come down to us through the centuries. My hope is that studying this body of thought will help you to become the best person and leader you can be.

A last point regarding our tradition and history of ethics concerns the quality of that tradition. Why would turning to the Western European tradition of ethics not immediately raise concerns? After all, isn't the Western tradition the source of the moral failure to which so many of our leaders fall prey? If we look to Homer's Achilles and Nietzsche's Ubermensch, or Superman, will we not be looking at the alpha and omega of our moral leadership deficits? Both are moral monsters that haunt the Western ethical tradition. C. S. Lewis tells us that, "Homer's Achilles knows nothing of the demand that the brave should also be the modest and merciful. He kills men as they cry for quarter, or takes them prisoner to kill them at leisure."[8] The Ubermensch of Nietzsche is not the Superman of American comic books. Rather, he is the nineteenth-century belligerent that looms behind the great moral catastrophes and the crimes against humanity we have seen time and again in recent history. The Ubermensch is the superior human, the great leader who lives to express power and knows neither love nor mercy. For Nietzsche, the expression of power is intrinsically adversarial. He says, "It is . . . absurd to ask strength not to express itself as strength, not to be a desire to overthrow, crush, become master, to be a thirst for enemies, resistance and triumphs as it is to ask weakness to express itself as strength."[9] Are these

---

8. Lewis, "Necessity of Chivalry."
9. Nietzsche, *On the Genealogy of Morality*, 1.13.

not the very ideas, the very archetypes, that have led us down our dark path of immoral leadership?

Luckily there is more, much more to the Western story of ethics than these two unfortunate characters. Between these two ogres is a litany of insights, both good and bad, that can truly enlighten us and make us wise in the ways of morality. But we have to develop the intellectual skill to unlock these insights—that's the challenge. To hone our ethical learning, we must work, and we must work hard. We must study. We must persevere in our effort to understand the moral complexities of life. Why must we do this? Because our followers, including our children and all the people we love, are depending on us to not only make that effort, but to be successful in our endeavor. We must aspire to wisdom and moral excellence if we are to play the leadership roles necessary for our communities and our culture to flourish. So, let's turn to history, our history, to discover the great moral principles of our tradition and become the ethical leaders our world so desperately needs.

1

Why Should We Bother to Examine the History of Ethics?

"It is by our own folly that the enemy will defeat us," cried Boromir. "How it angers me! Fool! Obstinate fool! Running willfully to death and ruining our cause. If any mortals have claim to the Ring, it is the men of Númenor, and not Halflings. It is not yours save by unhappy chance. It might have been mine. It should be mine. Give it to me!"[1]

WITH THOSE WORDS, THE character Boromir attacks his friend Frodo in J. R. R. Tolkien's epic, *The Lord of the Rings*. Although the good guys had the fortune of finding the ring of power, the most potent weapon of their enemy, things are not going well for them at this point in the plot. The fellowship traveling with the ring bearer is struggling for survival and hopelessly outnumbered. Boromir argues that the fellowship, which is defending the innocent against the cruel aggression of their enemy, should take the opportunity to use the enemy's weapon against him. Yet Frodo, guided by the opinions of others, wants to take the ring into the enemy's stronghold without any backup in an attempt to destroy it. For Boromir, the plan is utter folly. Given the strength of the enemy and the fellowship's weakness, it is a fool's errand with almost no hope of success. It also makes no sense since the ring can give the fellowship and its allies

1. Tolkien, *Fellowship of the Ring*, 520.

the power they desperately need to fight the enemy whose military might is overwhelming. Why is Frodo pursuing this path? Frodo's position only makes sense in the context of what has been communicated at the beginning of the story. The ring, although powerful, is the product of its maker who is utterly corrupt. The corrupting power of the ring will turn to evil whatever good a person might initially desire to do (which is demonstrated poignantly when Boromir attempts to take the ring from Frodo by force). In addition, for those powerful enough to wield the ring, it holds a further danger. The desire for power and the corruption latent in the ring (perhaps a metaphor for the corruption associated with leadership power?) would make a person capable of wielding it into another tyrant. The danger of the enemy's aggression could not be eliminated without destroying the ring itself. Thus, Frodo's actions only make sense if you understand the background that was told at the beginning of the story. The same is true for our understanding of ethics; if we really want to make sense of contemporary moral dilemmas, we need to start at the beginning of the story and trace it through time to our current situation.

MacIntyre begins his story of ethics by providing his rationale for studying the history of ethics before he dives into the actual history. He asserts that if we want to understand ethics, we must look at the intellectual environments where ethical ideas have been formulated and reformulated over long periods of time. In MacIntyre's view, there are two aspects of moral philosophy that require an examination of history. One is the fact that moral concepts change over time,[2] and the second is the impact that a society has in shaping moral concepts and the resulting impact society has on the behavior of individual people.[3] Although these assertions might initially strike a reader as reasonable, it is important to note that both positions are controversial. Not everyone agrees on these issues, especially philosophers. Let's take a look at each assertion to see what MacIntyre means by them and why others might disagree.

Moral Concepts Change Over Time and Place

In the discussion group that I mentioned in the introduction, our conversation was plunged into controversy after reading page one of *A Short*

---

2. MacIntyre, *Short History of Ethics*, 1. Referred to as *SHE* hereafter.

3. Cf. *SHE*, 5, where MacIntyre asserts that societal changes impact not only the way moral behavior is viewed in society, but even the moral concepts used to communicate these ideas.

History of Ethics. On page one, MacIntyre simply asserts, "Moral concepts change as social life changes."[4] Having read that, the participants in our discussion concluded that MacIntyre was a relativist. For some, that was seen as a good thing, and for others it was a bad thing. MacIntyre has often been accused of being a moral relativist, an accusation he denies. In making the assertion that ethical concepts change, MacIntyre is offering a historical observation that was particularly important to his thinking when he wrote *A Short History of Ethics*. An examination of history shows us that moral ideas such as justice and duty do vary over time. This reality and MacIntyre's focus on it have led scholars to describe MacIntyre at this point in his career as a historicist and a relativist. It is important to note that although MacIntyre's later thinking maintains its focus on history, he also asserts that a historical approach to ethics need not be relativistic.[5]

Returning to his assertion about the relationship between ethics and social life, in studying MacIntyre's history we will see that there is little doubt that the human understanding of moral principles is different from time to time and place to place, and that those differences are not just the product of the separation between cultures. The differences in the understanding of moral ideas can be a product of historical evolution within a relatively homogenous culture over time and can also be a product of the historical interaction between different moral cultures. MacIntyre makes his point somewhat abstractly at first, but then provides numerous examples throughout the rest of the book. We will start here with the abstract explanation and then move into the historical examples in our succeeding chapters.

The fact that ideas change over time does not apply to all concepts. There are some ideas that are quite stable over time and even between cultures. MacIntyre places these stable ideas into two categories. The first are specialized concepts within a specific field, such as the principles of geometry, or mathematics more broadly.[6] The idea that two plus two equals four does not change over time or in different locations. The

---

4. SHE, 1.

5. Cf. Weinstein, *On MacIntyre*, 18, and Stern, "MacIntyre and Historicism," 146 for insight regarding how historicism and relativism impact MacIntyre's thinking and its reception by others. Cf. Vainio, "After Relativism," 315–30, and Lutz, *Tradition in the Ethics of Alasdair MacIntyre* for descriptions of how MacIntyre later becomes a Thomistic realist who denies that a historicist approach to ethics must also be relativistic.

6. SHE, 2.

second category of unchanging concepts MacIntyre mentions are the ideas necessary to the function of human language. For example, all languages use the ideas represented by the English words "and," "or," and "if" to communicate human thought.[7]

Moral ideas, on the other hand, fall into neither of these categories.[8] They are more complex and admit a great deal of ambiguity. Aristotle asserts that we cannot expect the field of ethics to admit the same clarity as theoretical fields such as mathematics.[9] Abstract fields of knowledge are of a different nature than an applied field such as ethics. We have little choice but to recognize the complexity and ambiguity of ethics. This is not to say that genuine moral knowledge is impossible. Rather, this position merely implies that moral knowledge is different than the knowledge of abstract sciences. Ambiguity, complexity, and change are products of this difference, and the fact that moral concepts change is clearly evident by examining the texts of different time periods during which such concepts are used. Although there is continuity between the idea of justice in ancient Greece and twenty-first-century America, there are also significant differences between the two. MacIntyre notes that the Greek term for justice, *dikaiosune*, "combines notions of fairness in externals with that of personal integrity."[10] Justice, in the view of twenty-first-century America (as defined in *The Merriam-Webster Dictionary*), means "The administration of what is just especially by the impartial adjustment of conflicting claims or the assignment of merited awards and punishments."[11] No doubt there is continuity between the two formulations, but there is also difference, one might say even significant difference.[12]

It is important for us to examine the similarities and differences for a couple of reasons. First, it provides a context to better understand contemporary moral ideas. For example, the Christian virtue of humility in

7. *SHE*, 2.
8. *SHE*, 2.
9. Aristotle, *Nicomachean Ethics*, 1104a7.
10. *SHE*, 11.
11. Merriam-Webster Dictionary Online, "Justice (n.)."
12. That difference can be seen as the product of historical evolution. Reference to justice as a character trait is missing in the modern definition, a likely result of Enlightenment/Modern ethics, which shifted away from the ancient Greek context for morality in which the virtues, which are morally excellent character traits, play a central role. The contemporary focus of justice on reward and punishment can also be attributed to contemporary philosophers such as John Rawls who made reward/punishment concerns a significant part of his theory of distributive justice. Cf. Rawls, *Theory of Justice*.

centuries gone by was often described as an excellent moral habit with a particular focus on the lowliness of the humble person. In Marxist philosophy (and other modern thinkers such as David Hume and Friedrich Nietzsche), humility is a vice, simply a bad moral habit that maintains an unsatisfactory status quo.[13] In contemporary psychology, humility is often seen as an accurate self-view that is able to appreciate not only a person's weaknesses but one's strengths as well.[14] Knowing those different perspectives on the ideal of humility enriches our understanding of humility, which enables us to apply the idea in a more accurate and intentional manner, whether that be in our thought or, more importantly, in the way we behave. Second, knowing that there can be different conceptions of moral ideas can make us more humble (there's that word again) and more thoughtful. For example, we might find it surprising that there's more than one way to think about justice. Recognition of that fact might make us think about justice, and not just in a different way, but to think about it at all. The idea that there might be more than one notion of an idea like justice or other moral concepts, such as freedom, was not presented to me until I was well into adulthood, and I found the idea unsettling. My first reaction was, "Well if there's more than one idea of (insert the moral term) then that means mine is right and there are a bunch of wrong/bad ideas floating around out there." After a little reflection, though, I started to realize that my own ideas, although not necessarily wrong, could be enriched and clarified, and sometimes corrected. So, the realization that more than one version of a particular moral concept exists can produce the happy result that one can refine, clarify, and understand that concept better by comparing and contrasting what other people and intellectual traditions have to say about that idea.

MacIntyre's point about the changing nature of moral concepts presents a challenge to many moral philosophers, however. The challenge lies in MacIntyre's observation that many moral philosophers seem to be ignorant of the fact that moral concepts change over time or that they are unwilling to see that change as significant. Many philosophers write as if moral ideas are unchanging and timeless.[15] The impact of moral concepts being viewed as unchanging is that the history of ethics is rarely discussed. Yet history is crucial to understanding ethical principles because history is the stage on which these ideas have their effect, and examining that

---

13. Marx, "Communism of the Paper Reinischer Beobachter," 268–69.
14. Cf. Owens et al., "Expressed Humility in Organizations," 1518.
15. *SHE*, 1.

effect furthers our understanding of those principles. For example, when studying history, we can see that altering moral concepts threatens to alter human behaviors. This reality can be seen through the actions of people fighting against the possibility of changed behavior. MacIntyre highlights the Athenians executing Socrates, English Parliament condemning Hobbes's *Leviathan*, and the Nazi philosophical book burnings as examples of people recognizing that moral thinking affects moral behavior. Thus, those in power act to prevent the spread of ideas that might undermine their power and position in society.[16] Changes in moral thinking can undermine the status quo, and the people that want to maintain the status quo have frequently used their power to prevent change.

Another brief example of a historical change in moral philosophy can be seen in the thinking of Karl Marx. Returning to the idea of humility, we see Marx disparage notions of humility, which he saw as a drain on the revolutionary drive that he sought to inspire in the proletariat. He saw Christian humility as an impediment to the pride and courage through which the working class could assert its independence.[17] Marx criticized the idea of humility. He changed its characterization. He said humility was bad and not good, as it had been described by the Jewish and Christian moral traditions for millennia. For Marx, humility was bad because it was a moral roadblock to the goal of revolution. Whether you agree with Marx's analysis or not, it is difficult to argue against the impact his ideas have had not only on individuals, but also on the moral frameworks of entire societies, with correspondingly dramatic impact on behavior. Thus, we can conclude two things. First, moral ideas do change, and second, those changes are significant to the behavior of individuals and even entire societies. The changes in moral ideas that happen over time, requires us to examine the history of evolving moral frameworks and the impact those frameworks have had on both individuals and the communities in which they lived.

The Impact of Society on Shaping and Changing Moral Ideas

Before moving into the actual history of ethics, we need to cover one more observation MacIntyre makes that is crucial to understanding ethics and that again points us toward evaluating the history of ethics. Returning to

---

16. *SHE*, 1.
17. Marx, "Communism of the Paper Reinischer Beobachter," 268–69.

his assertion that "moral concepts change as social life changes," we see MacIntyre pointing to the unavoidable relationship between the ethics of individuals and the moral contexts established by communities or societies. Ethical principles change over time because societies change over time. Moral concepts, MacIntyre asserts, "are embodied in and are partially constitutive of forms of social life."[18] A quick example from United States history can help us understand his point. At the end of the eighteenth century, the Declaration of Independence asserted the equality of humans, and the Constitution established the nation as a democratic republic. Yet voting rights, which had been delegated to the states for regulation, were restricted to a small group of white men. Over time, the American understanding of equality as articulated in the Declaration would change those voting restrictions, opening the right to vote to all citizens of a certain age, regardless of gender or race. The result was not only a change in political structure, but a change in how Americans understood equality. Where an eighteenth-century American might be entirely comfortable with an idea of equality that prevented women or people of other races from voting, such a view would not only be rejected by twenty-first-century Americans, but it is almost unimaginable for someone to openly advocate for the disenfranchisement of women or minority groups. The idea of equality and its application has changed over the history of the United States, and knowledge of that history enables a person to understand why it should have changed and how that changed notion of equality is important to other cultural issues. This is an example of a dynamic that we will observe repeatedly as MacIntyre guides us through the history of moral cultures—ancient, medieval, and modern.

Leadership Reflection: Leadership Ethics and the Impact on Organizations

The idea that moral principles change over time and that communities shape ethical concepts is enormously important to leadership. If moral principles change in societies, that means they can also change in organizations, and leaders can have a hand in that process. MacIntyre's analysis asserts that the culture of a community impacts the ethical thinking and behavior of an individual, and the ethical thinking and behavior of the individual impacts the community as well. Examining the impact

18. *SHE*, 1.

individuals have on a community, we can see that a leader's influence is particularly powerful. The words—and more importantly, the behavior—of a leader have an enormous effect on what followers think is acceptable behavior. What the leader says and does authorizes the same behavior in her or his followers. Here's a quick example from recent military history. In 2003, a US army lieutenant colonel serving in Iraq fired a pistol next to the head of a prisoner in order to scare the prisoner into providing much needed intelligence about the enemy's movements.[19] Despite serving an otherwise honorable career, the officer was fined and discharged from the army. We might ask why. Why, after serving honorably and effectively for twenty years, would the army discharge a person who was trying to support the military mission and did not even hurt the enemy in the process? The answer to that lies in the moral power of a leader's example. If the army had not punished that officer, every member of his organization (and typically a lieutenant colonel is in charge of roughly five hundred to eight hundred people) would have thought that behavior was acceptable. The army would have risked having hundreds of soldiers thinking that firing a weapon next to the head of a prisoner to get intelligence was appropriate. Given the principles of the Geneva Conventions concerning the treatment of prisoners and the importance of respecting prisoner rights in any war effort (much less the obvious safety concerns), this was not a risk US fighting forces could afford to take.

In the wake of such an incident, we see the power a leader's example can have on the moral culture of his or her organization. To put it another way, the leader's example impacts the moral thinking and behavior of his or her followers. This is both good and bad news. To focus on the bad first, there are few people in an organization that can corrupt an organization's moral culture more efficiently and effectively than its leader. If a leader is willing to cheat, lie, or engage in otherwise immoral behavior, we should not be surprised to see his or her followers following that example.[20] On the other side of the ledger, we can also assert that leaders are uniquely positioned to improve the moral culture of an organization. Recent social science confirms that ethical leadership promotes good moral behavior on the part of followers[21] and can even be the primary factor that leads

19. Cf. LA Times Archive, "Officer Says He Threatened Iraqi."

20. Cf. Chandler, "Perfect Storm of Leaders' Unethical Behavior," 69–93, for an overview of the detrimental effect unethical leaders can have on an organization.

21. Cf. Mayer et al., "How Does Ethical Leadership Flow?," 1–13, for one empirical study that identifies a link between the good moral behavior of leaders and followers.

to greater organizational productivity.[22] Corrupting the moral culture of an organization is likely easier work than improving it, but the leader's importance and role in either process is crucial and, to a large extent, unavoidable. Such is the moral power and responsibility all leaders have within their organizations. The only question is whether they will use that power for good or ill.

---

22. Cf. Obicci, "Effect of Ethical Leadership on Employee Performance in Uganda," 52.

2

The Beginnings of Our Ethical History

When Agamemnon intends to steal the slave girl Briseis from Achilles, Nestor says to him, "Do not, **agathos** though you be, take the girl from him."[1]

WHY START THIS CHAPTER with a line from an ancient poem few of us have read and highlight a word in a foreign language? The short answer is that it draws attention to MacIntyre's method. MacIntyre looks not only at the ethical thinking of philosophers, but also considers other writing and genres that communicate the moral ideas in the history of a society. So, despite the fact that ethics is often considered a branch of philosophy, we will also examine religious, literary, and political writing in our search to understand morality.[2] And when it comes to examining Greek moral thought prior to the classical period of Socrates, Plato, and

---

1. *SHE*, 8, referring to Homer, *Iliad* 1:275.
2. Some would criticize *SHE* for its weak focus on Jewish and Christian morality. MacIntyre no doubt covers Christian religious thinkers (to include Aquinas, Luther, and Calvin), but that emphasis is light and he barely mentions the Jewish tradition when he goes to great depth covering the moral thought of ancient Greece. Given the long history of Christian thought and its significance to the history of Europe and the Western Hemisphere, this is a significant omission, although it does have the benefit of limiting and narrowing a discussion that can be almost infinite.

Aristotle, MacIntyre has little choice but to examine literature, as there are no strictly "philosophical texts" available to examine.[3]

MacIntyre starts at the dawn of Greek as a written language, with the initial written works of *The Iliad* and *The Odyssey*, the epic poems of Homer. There is little historical evidence about Homer himself, but the scholarly consensus dates his life to the eighth century BCE (there are third-party references to *The Iliad* dating to roughly 730 BCE).[4] It is during this time that the Greek alphabet and written language come into use. By writing the *Iliad* and *Odyssey*, Homer is credited with recording an oral tradition that was likely hundreds of years old at the time. In these writings, we can see ethical principles at work. Like other works of literature, they articulate and record moral ideals and ethical norms in the context of a powerful narrative. We will see that the power of those ideas survives and even outlives the civilization that gave birth to them. By the sixth century (500s) BCE, Greek literature is using the moral terms of the Homeric period (which by then was a significantly distant past) in different ways. This use causes confusion, which gives rise to the need for a philosophy of ethics—a systematic and intentional definition of moral terms so that people (Greek people in this case) can figure out how to live good lives.[5] We see the philosophical examination of these ideas emerge in the dialogue between Socrates and the Sophists in the fifth century (400s) BCE. Our task in this chapter will be to look at the transition of meaning in moral terms in Greek literature between the eighth and sixth centuries so that in the next chapter we can address the debate these changes caused in the fifth century.[6]

Agathos and *Areté* in the Epics of Homer and the Theognid Literature

MacIntyre highlights the different uses of moral terms between eighth- and sixth-century-BCE Greece by comparing the works of the Theognid

---

3. Cf. *SHE*, 24 where MacIntyre notes that it is Socrates who raises the key philosophical questions for ethics, thus implying the historical transition in Greek culture where a philosophy of ethics, or an attempt to systematically define and describe ethical ideas, is pursued.

4. Silk, in Homer, *Iliad*, 3.

5. *SHE*, 5.

6. *SHE*, 5. MacIntyre traces the transition from the writings of Homer through the Theognid literature to the Sophists rather than marking the transition in centuries.

literary corpus to those of the earlier Homeric writings. Theognis of Megara, like Homer, was a person from ancient Greece (sixth century, or the 500s BCE) about whom we know very little. His name (again like Homer's) is applied to a body of poems that likely had different individual authors and comes down to us from this later time period.[7] MacIntyre focuses on these poems as important because it is through them that we can see how the meanings of Greek moral terms were changing compared to the earlier usage in Homer's time.[8]

Approaching the ethical ideas articulated in Homer's writing, we quickly see the importance a society has in shaping moral concepts. MacIntyre observes that the community in the background of Homer's writing makes its most important judgments about individual people based on the way individuals fulfill their assigned roles in society. Those roles, whether it be that of a judge, a warrior, a shepherd, or a king, carried with them expectations of performance. Terms such as courageous, clever, or authoritative were used to describe the qualities necessary for a person to fulfill a specific role well.[9] The word *agathos* (a Greek word we translate as good) initially described performance in the role of a nobleman. To say that a nobleman was *agathos* was to say that the person had the character traits to be successful as a nobleman in peace and war, whether they were the traits necessary for economic success or the bravery necessary in combat.[10] Cleverness, courage, cunning, and other important characteristics of ruling-class members were covered by the idea of *agathos* because those were the traits a person needed to be successful specifically in the role of nobleman. *Agathos*, however, cannot be simply equated to the English term "good." The English word "good" can be used to describe the traits of bravery and cleverness without reference to a role—that is, by using the word "good" in English we can indicate characteristics such as bravery and cleverness detached from any role for which those traits might be useful. The word *agathos* did not function for the Greeks of the Homeric period in the same way. It is only used when it describes a person who has those traits in the context of the role of a nobleman and because of this it connoted those characteristics that were good for

---

7. Figueira and Nagy, *Theognis of Megara*, 1.
8. *SHE*, 9.
9. *SHE*, 5.

10. *SHE*, 6. MacIntyre cites W. H. Adkins (a former professor of classical language and literature at the University of Chicago) from his work *Merit and Responsibility in Greek Ethics*, 32–33 for this characterization.

a nobleman to possess. *Agathos* is interchangeable with these traits, so to say it about a king but not mean that the person is kingly, courageous, or cunning would be a contradiction for the members of Homeric culture.[11] In addition, *agathos* was not applied to shepherds or warriors because it was not applicable to those societal roles.

Furthermore, the description *agathos* provides can be seen as a factual description because it can only be applied to a person who has acted on these traits in the past. As a result, it is also a predictive description since a person who has acted bravely in the past is likely to be able to act bravely in the future.[12] The Greeks are saying the opposite of what our mutual fund managers tell us about their financial products. For the Greeks, past performance *is* indicative of future behavior, and unlike the difficulties of predicting the stock market, there is broad philosophical consensus that a person's moral character is predictive of the moral choices she or he will make in the future.

The idea of *agathos*, then, is applied only in the context of the role a person plays in Greek society at the time. Another moral term of the Homeric period with ties to a societal role is the word *areté*, a word whose closest English equivalent is virtue, understood as morally excellent characteristics. *Areté* is applied to a person who is excellent at fulfilling her or his social role. *Areté* therefore differs between people who play different roles in society.[13] The *areté* of a lawyer includes cleverness and speaking skill, while that of a warrior includes physical courage, and that of a physician includes compassion for the pain of others. Later in the Homeric period, *agathos* is applied to more roles than that of the nobleman and indicates a person who has the *areté*, the excellence, necessary to fulfill his or her assigned role well. This helps us make sense of Nestor's admonition to Agamemnon at the beginning of the chapter. Agamemnon can remain *agathos* even if he does something bad, like stealing from another person, because *agathos* refers to how Agamemnon plays his role as King of Mycenae. Agamemnon can retain the *areté* of his role as king, which includes bravery, cunning, and authoritativeness, while at the same time stealing from others.

The importance of role performance in the judgment of a person's character can also be seen in a negative correlate of *agathos/areté*, which is *eidos*, the Greek term for shame. Shame for the Greeks of this time is the

11. *SHE*, 6.
12. *SHE*, 6.
13. *SHE*, 8.

emotion that a person should feel at failing to fulfill her or his allotted role. Shame is the awareness that you ought to be criticized because you failed to perform in your role the way the community expects you to perform.[14] Here we see the background for the admonition of Spartan mothers to their sons as they set out for war, "Come back with your shield or on it." For Spartan infantry soldiers marching together, the shield played the twofold role of protecting the soldier and his comrade next to him. If a Spartan returned from war with his shield, it meant he had been successful in battle, and he had kept faith with his fellow soldiers by maintaining his shield as a protection not only of himself, but for them as well. If he came back on his shield that meant he had died a glorious death in battle. If he came back without his shield, however, that meant he had broken faith with his fellow soldiers by losing the shield (or by throwing it down in cowardice) that would serve to protect the other soldiers. This failure to perform the task expected in the role of the infantry soldier was accompanied by shame, not just for the soldier, but for his family as well.[15]

One of MacIntyre's observations at this point (which will be an issue we discuss later in the book) is the fact that the ancient Greek practice of judging people on the basis of factual premises, such as a person's role in society, is rejected by many modern philosophers. Those philosophers assert that you cannot get a moral "ought" from a factual "is."[16] It is difficult to make sense of this modern position outside of the dramatic differences between the society of Homer's time and that of Europe in the 1700s (when this idea was explicitly formulated), which brings us back to the fact that social setting is the driving force for the way Greeks of Homer's time understood moral terms.

When we turn to the poetry of the Theognid period in the sixth century (roughly two centuries after *The Iliad* and *The Odyssey* were written), we see changes in the functions of the words *agathos* and *areté*. Their definition has changed because that definition is no longer closely tied to role fulfillment. MacIntyre relates how one Theognid author writes, "The whole of *areté* is summed up in justice. Every man, Cyrnus, is *agathos* if he has justice."[17] Anyone, according to the author, can be *agathos* by being just. *Agathos* and *areté* are now functioning in a more general way, referring

---

14. SHE, 8.

15. Cf. French, "When Teaching the Ethics of War is Not Academic," for a discussion of the saying.

16. SHE, 6–7.

17. SHE, 9–10.

to personal characteristics that can exist outside of performance in a particular role. Greek society has changed over the course of two hundred years, and those changes are affecting the meaning of Greek moral concepts. The questions MacIntyre addresses next are, how did these changes come about and what are the ethical implications of the changes?

Historical Change Yields Moral Confusion

The change in the meaning of the terms is the result of changes in Greek society. The new meanings reflect the fact that history is marching on and the social structures of the Homeric period are breaking down. This breakdown happens over time and is an uneven process, which can be seen in cultural signs that the old structures persist and are even fighting for survival.[18] The cultural changes afoot can be seen against the background of Greek mythology and in the contacts between Greek society and other foreign societies that were becoming more and more frequent in sixth-century Greece.[19]

Anthropologists assert, as MacIntyre notes, that myths express and represent the social structures of a particular society.[20] This is a function played by Greek mythology, which at the time of Homer was considered sacred writing. The myths represented an order of necessity that reigned over gods and men that continued to be influential in the 500s BCE. An example of this influence can be seen in the fifth-century Greek concept of *hubris*, or pride. Pride was the sin of overstepping the moral order of the universe. It was a unique foolishness based on a person's overconfidence.[21] Given the changes in Greek society, however, the understanding of hubris was becoming more difficult because the understanding of the universe was changing. Can you blame a person for overstepping the order of the universe when your view of the universe is unclear or when that person might have an entirely different understanding of the universe? According to MacIntyre this understanding, the very order of the universe as expressed by the myths, was coming into question for two reasons. The first reason lay with the myths themselves and their relationship to historical Greek communities. The order in the myths was never perfectly copied by

18. *SHE*, 10.
19. *SHE*, 10.
20. *SHE*, 10.
21. *SHE*, 10.

an actual Greek society, so the myths raised the question about why the order of the universe, or the order of nature, and the order that could be observed in a real Greek community was so different. Why was the reality of a community such an imperfect manifestation of the ideal?[22] Reinforcing this question and giving it unprecedented urgency was the greater contact between Greek culture and radically different foreign cultures. The impact of colonization, increases in trade and travel, and Persian invasions highlighted the existence of societies and cultures vastly different than those of the Greeks.[23] The difference between what was good in Persia and what was good in Egypt and what was good in Athens challenged the notion latent in the Greek myths that there was a universal order. If justice in Egypt differs from justice in Athens, what does that mean for justice in general? Also, if justice is different in different places, what does it mean to say that *agathos* and *areté* are summed up in the meaning of justice? Are moral practices based on the customs of an individual community or are they based on universal human nature?

This series of questions had not been considered by the Greeks before and represents the divide between moral philosophy and moral practice. How people should understand moral concepts and how they apply those concepts to their own moral choices are separate but related questions. And again, it is clear from history that questions about ethical concepts are not just academic questions. They had significant impact on the moral decisions Greek people were trying to make. The ideas played out in both the domestic politics and the foreign relations of the time, and the confusion in concepts yielded confusion in moral thinking as well as the decisions based on that thinking. Writing in the fifth century, Thucydides records the confusion of moral language during a rebellion that takes place on the Greek island of Corfu. "The meaning of words no longer has the same relations to things, but was changed by them as they thought fit. Reckless doing was held to be loyal courage; prudent delay was the excuse of a coward; moderation was the disguise of unmanly weakness; to know everything was to do nothing."[24] The question regarding the nature of justice also rises in the different behaviors expected within Greek society and what was permissible when dealing with foreigners. Alcibiades, an Athenian statesman and general, was condemned when

---

22. *SHE*, 10.

23. *SHE*, 10.

24. Thucydides, *Peloponnesian War*, Benjamin Jowett, ed., Book III, 82:3–4, as cited in *SHE*, 12.

he did not observe the restraints of justice within the Athenian state. Yet when Athenian envoys ignored those same restraints in their dealings with other states—treachery and coercion being sanctioned tactics in dealing with foreigners—the laws of nature were used to justify those actions. The laws of nature, the Athenians asserted, were not made by them. They were merely abiding by those laws and doing what any other community would do if they had the power to act like the Athenians.[25]

Again, these historical developments raised significant moral questions for the Greeks, and a whole series of moral questions became urgent to Greek society. To begin with, the Greeks were asking what was the meaning of key moral terms? What did words like *agathos* and *areté* actually mean?[26] The good character traits for a nobleman in the warfare of the Homeric time frame, which were held to be boldness, cunning, and courage, were likely destructive in the courts and democratic assemblies of the fifth-century Greek city-state. The blood thirsty Achilles was *agathos* in a previous, more brutal age,[27] but was a monster to be feared in the relatively gentile courts and assemblies of the fledgling Greek democracies. Given these different societal contexts, how should what was morally good be understood or defined? In the context of these differences, what were the virtues necessary for the success of a Greek nobleman? And of particular import, what was the meaning of the word justice? In the background of the terminological question regarding justice is the specter of a moral question with which we still grapple today. Is morality local, based on the customs of a community, or is it universal, drawing its foundation from a human nature that is always and everywhere the same? These are the questions that Socrates and the Sophists tackled in fifth-century Greece, and it is to MacIntyre's account of this dialogue that we will turn in the next chapter.

Leadership Reflection: Excellence and the Ethics of Leadership

I'm a big believer in starting with high standards and raising them. We make progress only when we push ourselves to the highest level. If we don't progress, we backslide into bad habits, laziness and poor attitude.—Dan Gable[28]

---

25. Thucydides, *Peloponnesian War*, Benjamin Jowett, ed., Book V, 105:2, as cited in *SHE*, 12.
26. *SHE*, 12.
27. *SHE*, 17.
28. Gable, *Coaching Wrestling Successfully*, 15.

Every American wrestler in the last forty years has heard of Dan Gable. Revered as the greatest wrestler in American history, Gable only lost one match during his entire wrestling career, which turned out to be his last college match at the 1971 NCAA championships. His reaction to that loss? "Then I got good." The only thing more remarkable than Gable's career as an athlete was his career as a coach. The most striking among his accolades (which are too many to list) was leading the University of Iowa wrestling team in an unprecedented nine-year national championship streak between 1978 and 1986. Gable's pursuit of individual excellence spilled over to his pursuit of excellence as a leader, and no one would say the two were unrelated.

Gable, like the ancient Greeks, saw excellence as a function of habit. The practice of linking the idea of excellence to habit comes down to us from the depths of Greek history. The term *areté* emerges from prehistoric Greek culture as one of the key moral terms in the epics of Homer. It is an idea that gains strength in the classical tradition that is communicated to us through the thought of Socrates, Plato, and Aristotle. Later in the book, we will see *areté* presented as habitual excellence in such a compelling manner that its influence will be seen in the thinking of moral philosophers over the course of two thousand years. It is an idea still at work in the twenty-first century and is evident in the resurgence of virtue as an important concept in the fields of psychology, philosophy, political theory, and theology. In his book *Nicomachean Ethics,* Aristotle asserts that moral excellence is formed by habit, which is why the Greek word for habit, *ethos,* literally becomes the name for the classical approach to morality. For Aristotle and the Greek tradition, ethics is the science of morally excellent habits.[29] Humans, in this view, can become excellent through their moral choices, which give rise to morally excellent character traits. Ethics is therefore the pursuit of individual excellence, and the achievement of that excellence is indeed satisfying and even noble.

Yet for Aristotle, the achievement of individual excellence is not the greatest good available to humans. That good lies in the realm of politics rather than ethics because politics pursues the good of the community, a good that is greater than that of the individual. No doubt Aristotle values the excellence that can be achieved by individuals, but he asserts that the excellence of a community is the greatest good to be achieved.[30] To

---

29. Aristotle, *Nicomachean Ethics,* 1103a17–18.
30. Aristotle, *Nicomachean Ethics,* 1094b9–11.

rank the excellence of the community over that of the individual is not terribly controversial. After all, if the excellence of one person is valuable, it stands to reason that the excellence of many people would be more valuable. This is evident in the world of professional athletics. Individual athletes can become famous on the basis of their individual performance, but if they do not marry that performance to team championships, they are either almost forgotten, or if not forgotten, they are labeled as that great talent who could not win the big one. Dan Marino in football and Karl Malone in basketball reside in this category. On the other hand, Michael Jordan and Tom Brady are considered by many to be the greatest players in the history of their respective sports, and their title of GOAT (Greatest of All Time) is founded on their ability to lead their teams to the most championships and is not based primarily on their individual performance.

Yet to distinguish between the excellence of communities and that of individuals is not to say that they are unrelated. Excellent communities cannot exist without excellent individuals, and excellent individuals are always supported by relationships that communicate some prior excellence, whether it is through the love of parents for a child or the excellence of a school supporting the learning of a student. It is a bit of a chicken and egg relationship, and leadership plays a crucial role in that relationship. If ethics can be seen as the pursuit of individual excellence, leadership can be seen as the pursuit of organizational excellence by an individual who is the organization's leader. And leadership is crucial to organizational excellence, to the excellence of the community, in a few related ways. First, excellent individuals attract other excellent people to their organization. If you want to be the best, you have to train and work with the best. So talented people in a particular field will look to join organizations where their talent can be fostered and developed by leaders who are even more experienced and successful in that field. Second, individual excellence, the habitual excellence advocated by Aristotle and the Greek tradition, is the cornerstone of trust in the relationship between leaders and followers. Morally excellent people, people of integrity, are sought out for leadership positions because their excellence serves as the foundation of their influence as leaders. Followers trust and are therefore more effectively led by leaders of outstanding moral character than leaders who are known to be corrupt. This is why so many leaders are deposed when they prove themselves corrupt and therefore untrustworthy. Third, in addition to being excellent individuals, leaders must also pursue excellence for the sake of the organizations they lead and in service to the followers whose work actually accomplishes the mission. This is true because the purpose of a leader is to get a team to complete some task, to accomplish some mission. The idea of improvement, of betterment, of excellence, is intrinsic to the purpose of mission accomplishment. To put it bluntly, if the leader is not trying to achieve something good or make his or her organization better, that person has no business being its leader. The purpose of leadership is to pursue positive change. If the mission undertaken by a leader and his or her team does not improve the status quo in some manner, does not pursue excellence in some form, there is no point to their work.

Leadership as the pursuit of organizational excellence is therefore a natural product of an ethics of excellence. The individual excellence of a leader makes her or his leadership more effective, and the pursuit of moral excellence on the part of the leader naturally supports and even produces organizational excellence. There is perhaps no greater example of this dynamic than Dan Gable. As the greatest wrestler in history, he attracted the best talent when he turned to coaching. He soon realized that the one thing he enjoyed more than winning wrestling championships himself was coaching another athlete to do the same. His drive for individual excellence was the same drive that produced one of the greatest traditions of championship excellence in modern NCAA competition. Gable is the perfect example of a person dedicated to and benefitting from his own excellence, who was then able to parley that individual excellence into organizational excellence. It is a dynamic that can apply to any organization. The morally excellent leader knows that the pursuit of excellence is worth the effort, and that leader can become the catalyst for extraordinary team performance.

3

Sophistry and the Wisdom of Socrates

MOVING FROM SIXTH- TO fifth-century BCE Greece, we are introduced to one of the most famous names in the history of philosophy, Socrates (b. 470 BCE), and to the group with whom he often interacted, the Sophists. Examining the Sophists first, history tells us that they were a consortium of intellectuals who had significant influence on the Greek culture of that time. The title "Sophist" was taken from the Greek word for wisdom, *sophia*. The Sophists were thinkers who toured the Greek world teaching for pay on a wide range of subjects, but their emphasis was on the virtues necessary for success.[1] Chief among those virtues was the skill of rhetoric, understood as proficiency in public speaking and oral persuasion. Due to the increase in democratic government during the fifth century, improved skill in persuasion and argument became crucial to the success of citizens in their lives as members of the Greek city-state. Many of the Sophists were quite famous as prominent actors in Greek public affairs. Despite that prominence (or maybe because of it), they developed reputations as being dishonest, argumentative tricksters, and while they did not belong to schools or groups, they held a significant number of ideas in common.[2] Turning to Socrates, we see that he was a contemporary of the Sophists and appears as their chief antagonist in the dialogues of Plato. Socrates did not leave behind any written work,

---

1. Guthrie, *Sophists*, 35.
2. Taylor and Lee, "Sophists."

so present-day knowledge of his life is derived from the writings of his contemporary, Aristophanes, and his students, Plato and Xenophon.[3] It is in the dialogues of Plato that we often see Socrates engaging with the Sophists and addressing the pressing moral issues of the time. MacIntyre observes that there were two questions in the background driving the dialogue of nearly every debate between Socrates and the Sophists. The first concerned how key ethical ideas like the greatest good or moral excellence should be understood. The second question addressed the nature of justice. Was justice defined by local practices or did universal principles define the nature of justice?[4] We will look first to the Sophist answers to these questions, which happen to be answers many still believe today, and then examine the challenges Socrates offered to their views.

The Sophists on the Virtues of Success and the Varieties of Justice

MacIntyre begins his analysis by observing that Sophist thinking is marked by a strong cultural relativism. In Plato's dialogue, *Theaetetus*, Socrates quotes Protagoras (perhaps the most prominent Sophist) saying, "Man is the measure of all things."[5] Socrates explains the point of Protagoras by observing how a breeze is hot or cold only in relation to how it makes a person feel. The hotness or coolness of the breeze is defined by each individual person. It does not make sense to ask if the breeze is truly hot or cold; it is only as hot or as cold as the person perceiving it feels it to be. The Sophists approached the idea of justice and other moral concepts in a similar fashion. Although Protagoras does admit that there are some moral values necessary to the social life of any or all cities, the goal of the Sophists is to teach what is just in each city, recognizing that justice is defined differently in each location. For the Sophist, the question "What is justice?" cannot be asked. You can only ask, "What is justice in Athens or Corinth or Egypt?"[6]

---

3. Cf. *SHE*, 19 for the characterization MacIntyre provides concerning the different depictions of Socrates offered by each of these authors.

4. Cf. *SHE*, 15 and 24 for MacIntyre's comments on the ideas that Socrates and the Sophists were addressing at the time.

5. *SHE*, 15.

6. *SHE*, 16.

It is in this context that the Sophists define *areté* or virtue for the human person. The moral excellence of a person consists in a person's ability to function well in the Greek city-state, the *polis*, which is the dominant form of social life in fifth-century Greece. To function well in the *polis* is to be a successful citizen. The Sophists therefore define virtue in terms of success. How does one succeed in the *polis*? Success is defined as competing well in the courts and the democratic assembly. How does one do that? To be successful in those venues a person must study the customs of the city-state, what is good and just in the eyes of that community, adapt oneself to those customs, and then mold one's audience to see things as the speaker sees them on the basis of those customs.[7] For example, speakers wishing to win over an audience in New York City might reference aspects of city life in northeast America and make their pitch in the context of hustling in the city that never sleeps, while a speaker in a small town in the American south might appeal to agricultural metaphors and a cultural focus on hospitality. The ability to recognize the cultural touchpoints of a community and use them to the speaker's advantage is the skill that the Sophists teach. The Sophists figure out the important customs or values in each city-state and then show others how to articulate those ideas so they can convince the population of the local *polis* to go along with whatever the person doing the convincing wants. By winning in the courts and the assembly through argument and persuasion, a person would meet with success.

The Sophist answer to the question of universal moral principles, which is there are no such principles, is implied in their account of justice varying from city to city. MacIntyre notes that to the questions of "what am I to do?" or "how am I to live?" in general, the Sophists have no answer. They can only answer how-to live-in Corinth or Athens.[8] So, the simple question of where one should live becomes difficult because there are no overarching natural norms by which to judge different communities. The question of where one should live implies that there might be better or worse ways to organize a community, which the Sophists deny in their position that justice varies from place to place.

The Sophists are not entirely consistent on this issue, however, and do see a role for the concept of a universal nature in relation to how justice operates in a particular location. Since the norms of justice are developed

---

7. *SHE*, 14.
8. *SHE*, 16.

by each city, justice in their view is a convention, a construction of the human intellect in a specific time and place. And mutual self-interest requires the establishment of justice in every city in order to restrain the wayward desires that are natural to all humans. This is necessary, according to the Sophists, because when an individual person is left to her or his own natural desires, that person will be either a wolf or a sheep, predator or prey, an aggressor or one unjustly attacked. Justice is required to regulate the universal state of human nature as either predator or prey. Justice is needed to protect the sheep from the wolves. Without justice, the natural tendency of humans is to take whatever they desire; to devour one another and be devoured. In the Sophists' view, the natural person, a person free of the constraints placed upon her or him by society, will pursue power or pleasure, or more likely both. In this context, the ethical person is the person of convention, the person who abides by the law or rules of justice. The natural person, on the other hand, has no moral standards. The natural person stands outside of morality, existing simply as either predator or prey.[9] Human nature as pursuing its own interest (if not checked by the justice of a specific *polis*) is the one universal phenomenon recognized by the Sophists.

MacIntyre pauses at this point in his analysis to look at the impact of this notion of nature in relation to justice because it is highly influential on later European thought and is influential even to this day.[10] I have had the opportunity to teach the Sophist position to my students in college, and the large majority are initially convinced that the Sophists are right about justice and the selfishness of human nature. We will also reencounter a version of this idea in modern thinkers like Hobbes, who conceives of the state of nature as a nasty, brutish, self-serving, constant state of warfare. Morality in this context becomes a contest between the natural people who want to rape and pillage and those who do not want to be raped or pillaged.

MacIntyre pulls no punches in his criticism of this position. He asserts that the entire description of the natural person offered by the Sophists is a philosophical fairy tale, albeit one that is remarkably consistent and durable.[11] He makes that assertion for a number of reasons. First, the natural person presented by the Sophists is not really a natural person, by which they mean a person who stands completely outside of

9. *SHE*, 16–17.
10. *SHE*, 17.
11. *SHE*, 17.

a conventional society. The natural person they are describing expresses the social attitudes of the Homeric hero. The so-called natural person is merely the aggressive person from an earlier, defunct culture that no longer fits the description of *areté* in the fifth-century city-state.[12] This is true because describing a person as nasty, aggressive, and selfish, or as unselfish and mild cannot be done without a social setting.[13] The *agathos* (i.e., the good nobleman) of Homer's time is *agathos* (good) because she or he is aggressive, cunning, courageous, and even violent when necessary, which are character traits that were valued in the Homeric social context. However, this same person is seen as a brute in the Greek city-state of the fifth century because those combative characteristics are not the traits suitable for success in the democratic assembly. In either description, the social context provides the terms by which the description is made. It is impossible to describe the virtues or vices of a person outside of a social context because it is the social context that defines what traits are good or bad for a particular community.[14] The natural person of the fifth century has to be a person of another time/society because without the fifth-century society to define that person as bad (or the previous society to define the person as good), there are no terms through which to make the definition. MacIntyre's analysis also measures up to the reality that no human person has ever existed apart from a human society. A hermit can break away from a society, but his or her ability to be independent can only be achieved through a significant period of dependence on others. The independent adult is first a dependent child who can develop the skills necessary to be independent through that initial dependence on others. Humans are intrinsically social animals and the concept of a natural person that stands completely outside of society cannot account for that fact.[15]

Getting back to the Sophists, the implications of their view of the natural person is a conception where everyone has the impulses of the natural person, which are to get what one wants. And what everyone wants is power that enables pleasure. In society, however, the conventional person has to channel these desires into appropriate avenues of expression. The conventional person must acquire power and pleasure through the conventions of the society in which she or he is living. The

12. *SHE*, 17.
13. *SHE*, 17.
14. *SHE*, 18.
15. *SHE*, 18.

conventional person uses the moral vocabulary of the society as the tool to fulfill private/natural desires. That person must say what people want to hear in the assembly or in the courts so that people will put power into her or his hands. The *areté* of that person is to use the power of rhetoric to bend other people to his or her wishes. The conventional person of the Sophists, as MacIntyre puts it, "must take them by the ear before he takes them by the throat."[16] Socrates, on the other hand, has concerns with the Sophist approach to these issues. He seeks to present an alternative to this understanding of humanity and of ethics, so let's take a look at what he has to say.

Socrates, Knowledge, and the Important Questions About Ethics

MacIntyre tells us that Socrates found himself in a context where he distrusted the two primary intellectual camps of his day. He saw the position of moral conservatives problematic because their moral vocabulary (based on the ideals of the Homeric hero) had become incoherent in the face of the changed social roles that constituted the Greek city-state of the fifth century. This is despite the fact that Socrates generally honored moral conservatism and mocked ethical innovation. His instinct of suspicion for innovation led to a critical stance toward the Sophists as well, whose moral formulations Socrates saw as both troubling and ambiguous.[17]

So how do we get at the points Socrates is trying to make in his dialogue with the Sophists? There are two challenges to examining his thought, and both stem from the teaching methods of Socrates. First, since Socrates taught but did not write any books, we have to go to the writings of others to see what he has to say. Our primary understanding of his thought comes through the writing of his student, Plato (b. 428 BCE). Due to this arrangement, it is often difficult to see where the thinking of the teacher Socrates leaves off and that of the student Plato picks up. MacIntyre takes two steps in his attempt to see the thought of Socrates as clearly as possible. First, he turns to what Aristotle (b. 384 BCE) says about Socrates. As a student of Plato who never met Socrates, Aristotle reports on Socrates from a less personal and at times more critical perspective than does Plato. Second, MacIntyre examines Plato's

---

16. *SHE*, 18.
17. *SHE*, 19.

earlier dialogues where Plato's own teachings are less well developed, and therefore the views of Socrates can be seen more clearly.[18]

The second challenge to examining the thought of Socrates lies in the nature of his arguments, or better, the questions that Socrates employs to confound his audience. It appears as if Socrates is more interested in asking befuddling questions of the people listening to him than in providing them with authentic knowledge. MacIntyre asserts that this observation is more than just an appearance. Socrates, in his view, is trying to upset his audience rather than provide them with data.[19] The question then becomes, why? What good does that do? What is Socrates trying to achieve and what point, if any, does he have? In examining his method, we will see that Socrates is attempting to educate his audience but not in the normal manner of providing information to his listeners. As a result, his great contribution to ethics lies in the disruption he achieves in challenging the Sophist consensus and in the questions he raises for succeeding generations to pursue.[20]

MacIntyre observes (and many of us know) that the signature of Socratic dialogue is the ability to ask perceptive and difficult questions in the search for truth. The method takes its name from Socrates because he was an early example of a teacher using this method and because he was able to employ it so well. One might say he employed it too well because he rarely offered answers to the questions he posed. This is no accident, in MacIntyre's view. The purpose of Socrates's method was to stump his audience and not to provide answers. The rationale for such an approach makes sense in the context of another trait for which Socrates is famous, which is his intellectual humility. MacIntyre reminds us of this humility by repeating the observation of the Delphic oracle who said that Socrates was the wisest Athenian because he was the one thinker who recognized he knew nothing. So, Socrates's goal as a teacher was to increase the wisdom of his audience by leading them to recognize their own ignorance. Socrates hoped to produce a change in his listeners rather than to communicate knowledge to them. His purpose and method were to produce discomfort in his listeners by infuriating them with perplexing questions

---

18. Cf. *SHE*, 19 where MacIntyre cites Aristotle's *Metaphysics* that notes the focus of Socrates on excellences of character and in connection with them became the first person to inquire about the problem of universal definition.

19. *SHE*, 20.

20. *SHE*, 24.

in the hope that their discomfort would lead them to reconsider their thinking, to reconsider what they thought they knew.[21]

If convincing his listeners that they knew nothing was the main goal of Socrates, that does not mean he had no positive positions or contributions to make to the ethical thought of his time. One of his most significant positions was his assertion that having knowledge of what is good is the same as being virtuous. The fact that knowledge and virtue were so closely aligned for Socrates can be seen in the writing of both Plato and Aristotle. Aristotle maintains that Socrates believed that all the moral virtues were forms of knowledge in such a way that when a person knew what justice was, that person would make just or morally good choices by virtue of that knowledge alone.[22] The idea is stated in Plato's dialogue *Meno* where Socrates says, "People don't desire bad but what they think is good, though in fact it is bad; those who through ignorance mistake bad things for good obviously desire the good."[23] Where the Sophists would see what is good simply as getting what one wants, Socrates recognizes that what is good might be different from what one wants,[24] a significant moral insight missed by both the Sophists and many people today. His explanation for a person desiring what is bad is that the person has simply made a mistake. The critics of Socrates say this ignores the fact that humans often recognize what is good and knowingly choose something else. In Socrates's view, the answer to that challenge lies in the fact that our actions show us our real beliefs. Actions speak louder than words, so our words can contradict our actions, but our actions are the proof of what we truly believe. If, therefore, a person really knows what she or he ought to do, that person will do it. For Socrates, there is no power greater than knowledge that can prevent a person from doing what she or he knows ought to be done.[25] The writings of Plato largely support Socrates's position on the relation of knowledge to moral behavior, but we will see Aristotle later reject this formulation in the context of his own moral theory.

Despite the clarity Socrates offers in his view of knowledge and moral choice, MacIntyre finds the positive teachings of Socrates hard to pin down. Socrates many times doesn't answer his questions and some of his conclusions are ambiguous. Socrates would likely be comfortable with

21. *SHE*, 20.
22. *SHE*, 21.
23. Plato, *Meno*, 77d–e.
24. *SHE*, 22.
25. *SHE*, 23.

that description. After all, he was only trying to convince his listeners that they did not know what they were talking about. MacIntyre points out, however, that if we only focus on the ambiguity of Socrates's positions, we will miss his greatest contribution to moral philosophy. Socrates, unlike his contemporaries, was able to recognize the inconsistency and incoherence of the moral language of his time. Given that state of disrepair, he raises key questions for a philosophy of ethics in the hopes of overcoming that incoherence. The first of the key questions he raises is how do we understand the concepts we use in the moral decisions and the moral judgments that we make?[26] An example of how we might understand a moral concept can be seen in the distinctions we can make between similar moral attributes. There is a subtle but significant difference between the moral concepts of boldness (a willingness to take risks) and brashness (to be self-assertive in a rude and noisy manner), and moral philosophy does the work of making those subtle distinctions. Another question he raises is, what is the criteria that guide the good application of these moral concepts?[27] If we have clear definitions of boldness versus brashness, what are the rules of society that guide a person to use those ideas well? Although brashness as defined above would normally be considered a bad character trait, the infinity of possible circumstances can yield a situation where a generally bad character trait like brashness might be the right trait to exercise in a specific situation. Societies and communities provide criteria to determine when the application of a normally bad character trait like brashness can be used. It might be brash to assert oneself obnoxiously in the face another person, but if that person is a bully, it might be appropriate and even good to be brash. Lastly, Socrates raises questions about the inconsistency of the moral terminology at that time.[28] Are there moral concerns that are equally true in Athens and Corinth? How do we make sense of the fact that what is just in one city might be construed very differently in another?

The questions of Socrates push his followers to come to grips with the ambiguities and inconsistency of Greek moral terminology and to search for moral concepts that can reliably guide the practical decisions every person in their society had to make. To achieve this goal, a new investigation of morality had to be pursued, and this is what the heirs of Socrates set out to do. The most influential of that group is Plato, who

26. SHE, 24.
27. SHE, 24.
28. SHE, 24.

recognizes that moral concepts can only be understood in the context of a social order.[29] Plato's attempt to construct such an order and define ethics within that construct is up next for MacIntyre.

Leadership Reflection: Socrates as Leader

It might seem strange to highlight the figure of Socrates as a leader. One reason for this is that much of what we know about him is quite speculative, and the little that we do know does not point to him holding any significant leadership positions. In his early life, he was a foot soldier (a hoplite) in the Athenian army and not a leader. His father was a stoneworker, so he was not born of an aristocratic or influential family. He was not a writer, or even a teacher, refusing to be paid for the many intellectual interactions that he had with the citizens of Athens. In addition, his method of dialogue raised questions but seldom provided answers. How can someone who left a train of confusion be considered a leader?

Despite those characteristics, there are two distinct aspects that put him in the category of influential leader. First, there is no doubt that Socrates was an intellectual leader. The effect of his inquiries on the people of Athens were so significant that many authors—including Aristophanes (a comedian who wrote insultingly of Socrates), Xenophon, and most importantly Plato—captured the impact his words and ideas had on his audiences. His intellectual leadership was unique because Socrates was not a teacher in the typical sense. His goal was not to educate his listeners, but to jar them and challenge them so they might move away from their intellectual complacency. It was a goal that he seems to have been particularly effective in achieving, and it highlights one way a leader can have a significant impact on followers, which is to challenge their beliefs and even their behavior. The way Socrates challenged his audiences no doubt contributed to his legacy as an intellectual leader.

The manner in which Socrates challenged and even criticized his listeners is the second way we can discern his role as a leader. Challenging or criticizing one's audience is not a quick route to becoming popular as a leader (and it likely contributed to the execution of Socrates), but it often is a way to have a significant impact on one's followers over the long term. People generally do not like to be criticized, but when a challenge or a critique is delivered in an effective manner—that is, when it offers an

---

29. *SHE*, 25.

accurate (even if unwelcome) assessment to an individual and is communicated in a compelling way—it can have life-changing and enduring effects. I have to admit that I learned this lesson during my career as a high school wrestler. I was a good practice wrestler, but I was too nice during my actual matches, losing more often than I won. After one such loss, my coach (a man I admire to this day) was so disgusted with me he would not even talk to me. After he finally got over his anger, he said something gentle along the lines of "Why are you such a loser?" to me. Initially I was really angry. I had just lost. He should have been comforting me in my grief. Over time I realized, however, that I was good enough to win that match, and I needed to get tougher, even angry in my matches if I wanted to win. I went on to a successful high school career, and I am firmly of the opinion that I would not have reached the success I did without being challenged by my coach after that match.

Given the unpopularity of challenging followers about their own behavior or beliefs, how does a leader go about challenging them in an effective way? The behavior of Socrates demonstrates two crucial elements for effectively challenging followers, getting them to reflect on themselves rather than defending themselves in the face of the leader's criticism. The first is the fact that leaders can only challenge their followers in the context of the leader's own moral character. For leaders to challenge their followers effectively, they must exhibit integrity. In the face of criticism, people will first seek to defend themselves from criticism rather than see the truth in it. If followers know that the leader delivering the criticism, delivering the challenge, is a person of good will, a person of good character, and most importantly, not a hypocrite, then they may be open to examining their own behavior. Even in the context of a leader's integrity, however, followers may not be open to the challenge, and if the leader has significant moral failings, followers will likely turn a leader's criticism around and focus their own criticism on the moral failings of the leader. This was exactly the case in my relationship with my wrestling coach. He was a quiet man and a person of extraordinary integrity. I knew his criticism was given in good faith and reflected his effort to make me a better wrestler. It was painful to hear, but I was able to listen because of the respect I had for him. Reading the historical record regarding the moral character of Socrates, we can see that he was similarly well qualified to issue such challenges to his audiences. Plato's dialogues describe Socrates as a figure of extraordinary integrity, asserting that Socrates was "the noblest, the gentlest, and the best" of men.[30] The challenges of Socrates would have fallen on deaf ears if he had not backed them up with his own morally excellent behavior.

A second and related element is the leader's willingness to suffer. If you are going to challenge or criticize your audience, do not expect them to take it lying down. It is a risky way for a leader to influence his or her followers. Before they are convinced, followers are likely to lash out, and it may very well be the case that followers will attack a challenging leader without ever recognizing the wisdom the leader is trying to impart. The willingness to suffer can also be seen in the accounts describing Socrates's behavior in the face of his condemnation and execution at the hands of his fellow Athenians. Not only was he willing to suffer attacks as the result of the way he challenged others (Socrates was put on trial for irreverence to the gods and for corrupting the youth of Athens), he was not willing to abandon his own moral principles to save his life. He adhered to those principles even under the pain of death. Socrates asserts in Plato's dialogue *Crito* that ". . . it is never right to do wrong or to requite wrong with wrong, or when we suffer evil to defend ourselves by doing evil in return."[31] For Socrates, these principles meant that he could not flee the lawful judgment of the Athenian jury without breaking the law and thus corrupting the youth of the city as he had been charged. He therefore submitted himself to the execution meted out by the jury. Extraordinary integrity and a willingness to suffer provide the backdrop for Socrates's teaching and leadership. Those two elements, combined with the high quality of his thought, has made Socrates one of the most important intellectual leaders in the history of western civilization.

---

30. Plato, *Phaedo*, 116c.
31. Plato, *Crito*, 49d.

4

Plato's Description of the Good

THE INFLUENCE OF SOCRATES on Greek thought and on his student Plato was enormous. Few scholars, however, would hesitate to say that the influence of Plato on the history of philosophy and European thought was even greater. Part of that greater influence stems from the fact that unlike Socrates, Plato wrote, and he wrote a lot. But it is not just the fact that he wrote, nor the volume of his writing that makes Plato so significant. Rather, it is his extraordinary abilities as both writer and thinker that propel Plato to the highest ranks of influence. Writing roughly between the years 399 and 349 BCE, Plato leaves us a body of work that systematically examines issues ranging from politics to ethics and metaphysics to epistemology.[1] MacIntyre does us a service by identifying the books of Plato most significant to his ethical thinking, which include his dialogues *Gorgias*, *The Republic*, *The Symposium*, and *The Laws*. Socrates is the main character in each of these dialogues with the exception of *The Laws*. *Gorgias* is the earliest of these writings and likely has the most direct contact with the thinking of Socrates, with the later three demonstrating the development of Plato's own thought on ethics and politics. In examining the transition between Socrates and Plato and then looking at the further development of Plato's thought, we will see three important themes emerge: the relationship between reason and ethics, the nature of justice, and the relation between desire and what is good.

What is striking about the insights offered by Socrates and Plato is how they can be at once primitive and remote while still being quite

---

1. Plato, *Dialogues of Plato*, 1:7.

relevant to our moral thinking today. There is also a clarity in some of these insights that modern thinking has made ambiguous and confused, which will make our effort to examine the thought of these ancient authors all the more fruitful. As MacIntyre points out, Plato does not always succeed in convincing us of his position—indeed he seems to lose faith in some of his most fundamental conclusions toward the end of his life—but there is no doubt that Plato moves the ethical football down the field in really important ways.[2] So, let's start with the debate offered to us in *Gorgias*, and then we can move on to the manner in which Plato develops these insights in his later writings.

Gorgias Part I: The Importance of Reason to Ethics

Gorgias, one of Plato's earlier dialogues, is named after a Sophist featured in the book's debate about *areté* and the supreme good. In his debate with Socrates Gorgias asserts that rhetoric is the *techné* (the skill or ability) by which *areté*/virtue is taught, which in turn is the means to achieving a person's supreme good.[3] Gorgias, along with his successors in the dialogue, Polus and Callicles, agree and proclaim with increasing passion, that a person's supreme good is to have the freedom to have one's own way in everything.[4] Callicles, as the last to voice the Sophist position, asserts that the supreme good is the power to satisfy all desires.[5] Socrates has both arguments and questions that disrupt the Sophist line of thought, although the questions seem to be more disturbing to their position than the arguments posed by Socrates.

Socrates raises a series of concerns about the assertion that rhetoric is the skill that produces virtue. First, he asks the Sophists what they mean by rhetoric or what is the nature of rhetoric since the art of persuasion can come in different forms. Socrates names two of those forms: persuasion by means of rational argument whose method is to provide reasons based on knowledge for coming to a conclusion, and persuasion by means of subjecting a listener to psychological pressure, which produces an ungrounded conviction or belief. Gorgias recognizes the

---

2. Cf. *SHE* 46 and 49 for MacIntyre's comments on the problems regarding Plato's arguments and the doubts Plato harbored about his own arguments.
3. Plato, *Gorgias*, 452d–e.
4. Plato, *Gorgias*, 452d–e, 473d, 492c.
5. Plato, *Gorgias*, 492a.

distinction and says rhetoric is the second form of arguing: to convince others not on the basis of reason but on the basis of psychological pressure.[6] Gorgias provides an example of what he means through his experience of visiting patients with his brother Herodotus who was a physician. It was often the case that Herodotus was unable to convince his patients to undergo a painful remedy for some ailment, but Gorgias would be able to convince them on the basis of his skill with words rather than his medical expertise. Gorgias likewise asserts that if a physician or a skilled orator were applying to the assembly for the position of state physician, the orator would win every time because the orator would far exceed the physician's ability to convince the assembly despite the fact that the physician had the skill to actually do the job.[7] This, Gorgias says, was why credit for building the walls and harbors of Athens was not given to the builders or the architects, but to the politicians Themistocles and Pericles, who convinced the populace to undertake those projects.[8] Skill in argumentation was the greatest power available to the fourth-century Greek. The Sophists also maintained that rhetoric was in itself neutral. It could be put to good or bad use because it was not restricted by reason or knowledge.[9]

Given Gorgias's assertion that rhetoric is neutral and independent of reason and knowledge, Socrates follows with another question. If the Sophists purport to teach *areté*, which takes into account what is just in a specific place, does the Sophist need knowledge of what is right or wrong? Gorgias is unclear in his response but does seem to admit that the orator will need some level of knowledge concerning local views on right and wrong to teach *areté* in a specific city.[10] MacIntyre at this point provides some helpful observations to understand the implications of the argument. He says that the idea that techniques of persuasion are morally neutral is recurrent throughout history.[11] The Sophists hold this position, as do contemporary politicians and advertising executives, and no doubt their position is accurate to a certain extent. The problem with this position is it does not capture the entire relationship between reason and rhetoric. Rhetoric can be employed absent reason, but that does not

---

6. Plato, *Gorgias*, 454e–455a.
7. Plato, *Gorgias*, 456b.
8. Plato, *Gorgias*, 455e.
9. Plato, *Gorgias*, 456c–457c. *SHE*, 27.
10. Plato, *Gorgias*, 460a–c.
11. *SHE*, 27.

mean reason has no relationship or impact on rhetoric. MacIntyre asserts that if rhetoric is entirely nonrational then reason and knowledge become irrelevant to moral phenomena because reason is irrelevant to rhetoric as the skill that builds virtue, the most important aspect of ethics for the Greeks.[12] This is a problem highlighted by Socrates's next point, which states that without knowledge of right and wrong, a person will defeat her or his effort to pursue what is good. Even when rhetoric achieves its goal of the power to do whatever one wants, if a person is mistaken about what is actually in his or her own interest, that person will be self-defeating. In his discussion with Polus (the successor of Gorgias in the debate), Socrates points out that an all-powerful tyrant can do things that are not in her or his interest without the right knowledge.[13] This is true of obvious mistakes, like killing an adversary whose allies have the ability to overcome the tyrant, and it is true of subtle moral concerns such as the one manifest in the question, "Is it better to inflict injustice or suffer injustice?" It is in the debate about suffering or committing injustice that the ambiguity of Greek moral terms (which include good, bad, pleasure, and pain) again rears its head. Socrates clears away some of this ambiguity, which is helpful not only to his contemporaries, but to us as well because they are ideas we are still trying to work out in contemporary morality. So, let's take a look at this discussion and its implications before we move on to Plato's more developed thought in *The Republic*.

Gorgias Part II: Moral Terminology and the Common Good

Socrates asserts to Polus that inflicting injustice is the greatest evil, so much so that a person who commits injustice should be an object of our pity. Polus responds incredulously asking, "Is not suffering injustice a greater evil?"[14] The question that pops up in their exchange is what does Socrates, Polus, and all of us mean by the term evil? In broad terms, you can break evil into two different types of experiences: the evil of physical pain and the evil of moral pain. MacIntyre points out that this ambiguity is represented by the Greek words being used in the debate: *agathos* or good (which we've seen before) is opposed to *kakos* or bad. Another important aspect of the debate is the opposition between the Greek words

---

12. *SHE*, 27.
13. Plato, *Gorgias*, 466d–467b; *SHE*, 28.
14. Plato, *Gorgias*, 469a–b.

kalos, which means honorable, and *aischros*, which means disgraceful. Having defined those terms we can look at the question more clearly and ask which is worse: experiencing *kakos*, such as suffering the pain of an injury, or *aischros*, which is dishonor? We can make arguments on either side of that equation, but in the context of this distinction, Socrates is able to get the Sophists to admit that inflicting injustice is worse than suffering injustice due to the Sophist understanding of the greatest good.[15] For the Sophists, the greatest good is to convince the people to give you the power to do whatever you want, which is done by means of rhetoric and argumentative persuasion. A person who suffers injustice still has the ability to gain such power, but one that suffers dishonor is disempowered. The citizens of the city-state will never be convinced to give power to a disgraced person.

In his analysis of this exchange, MacIntyre provides some further observations that are helpful in seeing implications that go beyond the fact that Socrates has once again outwitted his rivals. First, MacIntyre points out another terminological distinction in the discussion that has bearing on our thinking today. A baseline principle of utilitarianism, a highly influential ethical theory in our day, is the idea that what is morally good can be equated to whatever supports pleasure and what is morally bad is anything that produces suffering. Socrates offers a significant critique to this position when he asserts that although pleasure and pain are closely related to good and bad, they are not the same.[16] This is true because good and bad are ideas that evaluate pleasure and pain.[17] Although pleasure is often good and pain is often bad, one can still have good pains and bad pleasures. A philosophy that simply equates good/bad with pleasure/pain is missing the difference between the terms, which causes problems for moral decision making. Sometimes pursuing what is truly good requires voluntarily taking on suffering, the intense physical training of elite athletes being a primary example. In a moral calculus where pain is simply equated with evil (or what should be avoided) the productive aspects of suffering pain become obscure.

A second observation offered by MacIntyre (which re-presents one of his recurring themes) is the importance of society's role in defining moral values in the arguments of both the Sophists and Socrates. For the Sophists, the goal of rhetoric has two aspects, which are the acquisition

15. Plato, *Gorgias*, 474c, 475e.
16. Plato, *Gorgias*, 500d.
17. *SHE*, 30.

of power and the subsequent ability to do what one wants. The paradox of such an approach is the fact that the person who seeks to master the people through persuasion ends up being mastered by the people because the power seeker must accept the terminology and moral conceptions of the community in order to convince the people to hand over power. The successful orator can get his or her way, but only on the community's terms and through the approval of the community.[18] In the end, the community retains the most power because the community defines the terms of the debate and is the ultimate judge that determines who will be able to wield power.

MacIntyre makes the further point that the role of the community is even more subtle and more important in the argument of Socrates. During his engagement with Callicles, the last of the Sophist lineup, Socrates asserts that the satisfaction of all desires is not a good description of the supreme good because it is impossible to satisfy all human desire. For Socrates, the formula of satisfying all desire is a path to unhappiness because regulating our desires and developing discipline to satisfy them in the right way produces more happiness than merely fulfilling all of our desires.[19] MacIntyre argues that the person of boundless desires is like a leaky sieve, never filled and never satisfied, so to have endless desire (which is the dynamic set up by the Sophist view of the greatest good) is to ensure that you will never get what you want. Desires need a limit if they are to be satisfied.[20] Reading *Gorgias*, it seems like this argument falls on deaf ears because Callicles doesn't even take the time to address it. MacIntyre does us the service of pointing out its fundamental importance in two ways. The first is the fact that the desires of an individual, like the moral ideas of a community, are not static.[21] They change, and this is a fact that we will come back to when we examine modern moral philosophy, which for the most part treats desires as if they are static. Desire is becoming important to the Greek discussion of ethics and will be central to the moral thought of both Plato and Aristotle. A crucial question, which is largely omitted in modern morality due to its static approach to desire, is the question of which desires should be encouraged and which should be discouraged.[22] For Plato and Aristotle, desire

18. SHE, 29.
19. Plato, *Gorgias*, 503c.
20. SHE, 30.
21. SHE, 32.
22. SHE, 32.

is important not only because of its influence on our moral choices, but also because of the impact habits have on desire. The Greek approach to morality takes place in the context of habits (the Greek word for habit is *ethiké*),[23] and that context ensures that the dynamic aspects of desires will be incorporated into moral philosophy.

The second point, which is more important to Plato's project in *The Republic*, is the idea that the concept of a good must include a limit, and the limits are provided by the rules of a community. MacIntyre asserts, "Any good we desire can only be specified by specifying the rules which would govern the behavior which would be or procure that particular good."[24] That's a tough sentence to decipher, so let me offer an example to illustrate MacIntyre's point. Using the sport of baseball, we all know that hitting a home run is good in light of the rules of the game. Home runs help a team beat its opponents, so behavior that supports the hitting of home runs is considered good behavior. Working with a coach, examining the components of your swing, hitting practice, and exercise to make you strong are all considered good actions. They are considered good actions because of the rules that have been established by the community of baseball. The rules of baseball set the context to determine what actions are good and what actions are not. This is true of society in general, as well. Individual actions are determined to be good or bad on the basis of how they contribute to the common good. This is one of the reasons ethics can be so complicated. Often the decisions that are important to the health of the community can be very harmful to the person making the decision. Yet that does not mean that the community will not approve of some decisions that are in the interest of the individual that come at a cost to society. Many would agree that minority rights are crucially important to a flourishing society, even if that requires the majority in that society to alter their behavior in order to respect those rights. We cannot do justice to these complexities at this point in our analysis, however. The point that Socrates, Plato, and MacIntyre are making is that we know what is good as individuals by means of the rules established by a specific community. To know what is good one must examine, understand, and identify the common life that makes the pursuit of a rich and rewarding life possible. This is the subject of Plato's famous work, *The Republic*, which is up next in our historical discussion.

---

23. Aristotle, *Nicomachean Ethics*, 1103a17.
24. *SHE*, 31.

Leadership Reflection: *Agathos* and Leaders Like Agamemnon

It seems like the influence of the Sophists is alive and well today in leadership literature. The Sophist idea that the power to get what one wants is the greatest good leads quickly to an approach to ethics where moral considerations are sidelined and even seen as impediments to the pursuit of power. This influence can be seen in the fact that many leadership writers claim that leadership is a morally neutral concept; a tool to wield power, whether for good or for ill. Leadership in this view can only be judged on the basis of a leader's effective power, understood as an ability to get followers to accomplish some mission.[25] Given the history of thoroughly corrupt leaders—names such as Hitler, Stalin, and Pol Pot come to mind—it would seem that there is plenty of reason to say that leadership can be an amoral crusade, even a crusade better done without any moral scruples at all. In this approach to the relationship between ethics and leadership, applying the idea of *agathos* to Agamemnon, where Agamemnon is seen as a great and powerful leader despite kidnapping and using a young girl as a slave, is merely an early example of the recognition that influential leaders are often awful human beings.

Yet there does seem to be another side to this story, one chronicled by authors Dean Ludwig and Clinton Longenecker in their influential analysis of the ethical failures of leaders.[26] The moral corruption of leaders is such an enduring phenomenon that they describe it as a disorder that goes all the way back to the Old Testament when they name it the Bathsheba Syndrome. The story of Bathsheba is another ancient story of leadership corruption, this time by a supposedly virtuous leader, King David, who not only takes the married woman Bathsheba to bed, but arranges to have her husband killed in battle in an attempt to evade responsibility for his sin. Ludwig and Longenecker offer a penetrating analysis as to why people like King David and so many leaders after him succumb to the moral challenges and temptations posed by successful leadership. Their analysis challenges the idea that leadership is morally neutral in the fact that the adultery of David significantly diminished his ability to lead Israel. They link that immoral act to what they call a "downward spiral of unethical decisions that had grave consequences for both his personal life and the organization that he was called upon to lead

---

25. Cf. Stavridis, *Sailing True North*, xv for a recent example of a long line of leadership authors asserting leadership as a morally neutral tool.

26. Ludwig and Longenecker, "Bathsheba Syndrome," 265–73.

and protect."[27] It would seem that David's lack of ethics had a significant impact on his leadership; his ability to influence others to follow him. Ludwig and Longenecker also point out that the leadership influence of contemporary King Davids also suffers. When their deeds are found out, almost all of those leaders are relieved of their leadership responsibilities. If leadership is a morally neutral phenomenon, why should they be fired? Did they merely have the misfortune of leading an intolerant, judgmental group or is there another way to understand the relationship between ethics and leadership?

I would offer that there is another way to understand that relationship, and despite the fact that there are many immoral leaders in history, there is a link, a very important link, between morally good behavior and leader effectiveness. This link is obscured by the complexity of leadership and the many, many motivations that might entice a person to follow a leader. Despite the ambiguity and complexity of leadership and the motives of individual people, the language we use about leaders gives us a glimpse into the relationship between the ethics of a leader and the ability of a leader to influence followers. I want to argue that the term leadership has an implicit moral content that is important to leader effectiveness. To put it simply, the difference between tyranny and leadership lies in the moral character of the leader. The following analysis of the relationship between unethical behavior and leadership serves as only a brief introduction to a topic that has both depth and an exceedingly long history.

Although the unethical behavior of leaders can manifest in many ways, there are two broad types of immoral or false leadership whose practitioners can be called either tyrants or manipulators. Tyrants lead or influence through coercion, and manipulators influence through lies and deceit. Both sets of tactics are recognized as immoral, but I would also assert that those tactics are ineffective and inferior to morally good methods to influence followers. Looking at the method of a tyrant first, we see that the primary motivator in the tyrant's tool kit is fear. While some, including Niccolò Machiavelli (one of our later authors to be examined), assert that fear is the strongest motivator of followers, even a superficial analysis demonstrates that fearful followers will not out-produce inspired followers. Fear as a motivator is limited by the tyrant's reach. As soon as the threat a tyrant holds for a follower subsides, so will their work and performance. Followers positively inspired by a leader (as opposed

---

27. Ludwig and Longenecker, "Bathsheba Syndrome," 265.

to being intimidated or coerced) will work to fulfill their aspirations and those of their organization long after the leader leaves the scene. Fear only motivates while the danger is present. Once the danger recedes, the follower will look to his or her own interests. Likewise, a manipulator can inspire performance, even high performance, over the short term, but that influence is inevitably short-lived. Given the proximity of most leader/follower relationships and the human phenomenon of habit or moral character, the dishonest leader will eventually be found out. It is only a matter of time. And once their dishonesty is discovered, deceitful leaders lose all power of influence. They have proven themselves untrustworthy, which results in a radical reduction of their authority.

Perhaps the most obvious historical example of such a leader is Adolf Hitler. Hitler is often (almost always?) included on lists of the greatest leaders in history despite the fact that many would be quite comfortable describing him as the perfect tyrant. Maybe a more precise description of him is an opportunistic despot whose talents and aggression were perfectly aligned to seize power at that junction in history. "Great leader" seems a strange title to bestow upon him given the fact that the way he led produced horror and catastrophe. Few people would follow Hitler if they knew what he was truly about. Thus, he needed to lead by treachery and coercion. Such leadership cannot endure, and despite the uniqueness of the times and his skill set to match those circumstances, the leadership failures of Hitler produced incredibly short-lived results and long-lived, almost incomprehensible suffering. He led by force, cruelty, and deception. As a result, he could not compete with the better-resourced and better-led Allied forces. Had he fostered a better team, he might have been able to see his looming failure and stave off the catastrophe of his own making. Instead, his leadership produced the profound humiliation of his once proud homeland and even led to his own death in the depths of despair deserted by all others, save his wife.

These are not the results of great leadership. Indeed, they are the result of catastrophically bad leadership, which points to the idea that the concept of leadership does indeed imply morally good conduct. The immorality of a leader alienates the very followers the leader is trying to attract. People are repulsed by immoral behavior, and rational followers will only entrust themselves to immoral leaders if they have no other choice. On the other hand, humans are drawn to people who are morally good. A leader whose behavior exhibits a morally good character inspires the trust and admiration of others, which fosters the leader's ability to attract and influence followers. Artificial externals may obscure this reality at times and even for long periods, but as circumstances shift, people can recognize the moral features of their leaders. They can and will commit to the good leaders. Morally bad leaders, on the other hand, will be distrusted by their followers, kept at arm's length, and rejected as soon as circumstances allow. The Roman poet Ovid once said, "If you want to be loved, be lovable." Morally reprehensible people are not terribly lovable, and reprehensible leaders will be deserted by their followers as soon as it is practical.

Getting back to Agamemnon, it's not that his corruption does not matter to his leadership—it does. A leader who leads a morally upright life will attract followers and generate trust in his or her relationship with followers. This is why corrupt leaders in the corporate and political world of today will be dismissed when their misdeeds come to light. Those misdeeds inhibit their ability to do their jobs as leaders. Corrupt leaders do not always get dismissed when caught, however. This is not because leadership is morally neutral. It is because there are other factors at play when it comes to pushing a leader out of power. In the case of Agamemnon, at the dawn of history when morality is just beginning to be understood, it is likely that followers did not fully understand the implications of immoral behavior for leader effectiveness (although in all likelihood the intuition of distrust of corrupt leaders was already present), nor was it likely that followers at that point in history would have the power to affect a situation. The circumstances in contemporary times are different, and I think you can make the case that the difference does not lie in a superior understanding of the relationship between ethics and leadership. Our leadership experts often still separate ethics from leadership effectiveness, a position reflected in the fact that many people still point to Hitler as a great leader. What makes leader immorality more likely to end in a fired CEO or a politician resigning in disgrace is advances in political and organizational theory that originate in the social contract theories of the sixteenth and seventeenth centuries. In organizing political systems based on the consent of the governed, Enlightenment thinkers fostered organizational structures that enabled followers to act on their intuition that it was not in their interest to follow corrupt leaders. There is a long history between Agamemnon and the advances of Enlightenment organizational thinking, so let's get back to the history and evolution of thinking that produced those advances.

5

Politics and the Moral Psychology of Plato's *Republic*

MACINTYRE MOVES FROM *GORGIAS* to *The Republic* because of the close relation between ethics and politics in Plato's thought, and in *The Republic* we see Plato attempt to tackle issues in both areas. He does so through the concept of justice, a subject of debate he inherits from his predecessors that is a bridge between ethics and politics. It is a bridge because it is an idea that is applied to both individuals and communities. *The Republic* tries to capture justice on both the level of ethics and as a form of political life. In addition to ethics and politics, Plato also brings in elements from the fields of psychology and metaphysics (the field of philosophy that examines first causes or unchanging ideas). This is a lot to cover in one book, and MacIntyre points out a number of areas where Plato struggles to measure up to the task.[1] MacIntyre also sees a more accurate presentation of morality and politics in Plato's later works, *The Symposium* and *The Laws*. Given that background, MacIntyre discusses the moral and psychological ideas laid out in *The Republic*, and then addresses how Plato refines them in his later dialogues.

---

1. Cf., *SHE*, 46 for one critique MacIntyre offers concerning Plato's thought in *The Republic*.

The Question of Justice in *The Republic*

Central to Plato's analysis in *The Republic* is the idea of justice. He asks what it means to call something just. MacIntyre tells us that this is not just a search for synonyms because saying that justice is good only raises the further question of what we mean by good. To grasp the meaning of justice, we must understand the function it serves in our language. We have to be able to describe what the idea of justice conveys when we speak the word. If we were to compile a list of just actions, justice is the idea—the criterion—that would enable us to judge whether something belonged on the list or not.[2]

Plato raises the question of justice in the context of the Greek debate about justice that precedes him. Recalling the Theognid literature from the 500s (Plato is writing around 370 BCE), we remember that *areté* is equated to justice. Unlike Homer's time where virtue concerns the attributes necessary to play a role well, virtue is now tied to the general idea of what makes a person excellent, what makes a person just. So, in pursuing a definition of justice Plato is continuing the previous ethical discussion regarding what it means to be an excellent person.

In this context, it would seem that to be an excellent person or to live an excellent life would be in everyone's self-interest. Yet that is not the common understanding of justice in Greek culture at the time. The speakers in *The Republic* make this point clear. The character Thrasymachus argues that justice should not be described as what is needful, beneficial, or advantageous,[3] yet that is exactly how justice was understood by the Greeks at that time. And the people most able to define what was needful and beneficial were the powerful. The powerful in their society had the ability to define what was just and did so in a way that supported their own interests.[4] Another character in the dialogue, Glaucon, further asserts that everyone knows that injustice pays better than justice. It may be just to observe the rules governing private property, but a person who is able to steal without being held accountable ends up richer than someone who abides by the rules of justice. According to Glaucon, everyone would be unjust if they were powerful enough because people pursue their natural desire, which is self-interest (the Sophist concept of the

---

2. SHE, 33, 34.
3. Plato, *Republic*, 336d1–336d2; SHE, 33.
4. Plato, *Republic*, 339a1–339a2; SHE, 34.

natural person is again at work in Glaucon's argument).[5] Plato pushes back on the argument that self-interest is the realm of the natural person alone, observing that conventional people, the people who abide by the rules of justice, also pursue their own self-interest.[6] He doesn't stop there, however, taking on the broader and more difficult question of how justice can be more profitable than injustice.[7]

The Greek discussion of the desires of the natural person paints a picture with no direct link in the relationship between justice and happiness. Justice, as a compromise among people where aggression and wrongdoing are punished, is a convention that enables people to be left to their own devices without fear of being attacked or terrorized. In this context, justice is good in the sense that it is better than being brutalized, but it does not actually produce happiness. A result of this view of justice, however, is the relationship between justice and the happiness of an individual person becomes arbitrary. The two have no intrinsic relationship. One of Plato's goals in *The Republic* is to correct this context and provide one in which justice as the foundation of *areté* is seen as a specific virtue that enables a person to be happy and even achieve their greatest happiness.[8]

To accomplish this goal Plato must get at the nature of justice itself and cannot be content with providing synonyms for justice or even lists of actions that are just. A list of acts traditionally thought to embody justice, such as telling the truth, repaying debts, or doing good to friends and harm to enemies, cannot rise to the challenge because these acts, depending on the circumstances, are not always just; they are not always the right thing to do. What is needed is a criterion that enables us to form the list in the first place. What is it that enables us to describe an action as just? To answer that question, Plato turns to an examination of justice as a trait not only of an individual but as a characteristic of a community. Individual actions can be described as just, as can a person, as can a state. Since the state provides the largest context in which to study justice, Plato proposes to examine justice on a state or communal level. Having done that, he can then apply those insights to justice on the level of the individual person to see how justice functions in that context.[9]

5. Plato, *Republic*, 359b1–359c4.
6. Plato, *Republic*, 362e1–363e3; *SHE*, 36.
7. Plato, *Republic*, 368b7–368c1.
8. *SHE*, 35.
9. Plato, *Republic*, 368e–369a.

Justice in the Community

Plato begins his analysis of the ideal state by observing that humans are not self-sufficient and have many needs. Cities come into being to provide for those needs on the basis of human collaboration. What cannot be achieved by a solitary person can be achieved through the cooperation of many people. The labor necessary to provide for the many needs of individual people must be divided into different types of tasks that are then executed by the people with the skills required for each task. People who know how to farm will grow the food. People who know how to rule will govern. People who know how to fight will defend the community. Plato spends much time covering all the necessary functions of a community (which we will not) and concludes that justice in the state is a form of harmony. The healthy state, the just state, is the state where the division of labor is respected and the individual people are content to execute the role for which they have the skill to contribute.[10] Justice in the state is everyone knowing their place and performing their role. In addition, such harmony includes not only the fulfillment of one's role but accepting the correct relationship between that role and the functions of the other classes of people. The rulers will be in charge of the other classes of people. Followers in a harmonious community accept the authority of those rulers.[11] Having arrived at a view of justice as a harmony between various parts of a whole, Plato applies his analysis to his concept of a person's soul to see what it means to be a just person.

MacIntyre tells us that Plato's understanding of the human soul is a function of his psychology, which in addition to politics, is crucial for an understanding of Plato's ethics. Initially the Greek word for soul, *psychi*, referred merely to the principle of life or animation. *Psychi* pointed to the difference between a live human and a dead corpse.[12] Greek notions of the soul became more complex over time, and in *The Republic* Plato asserts a threefold division of the soul. As a matter of fact, the primary divisions of labor Plato attributes to a city (rulers, soldiers, and producers/laborers) are based in part on his psychology and the three parts of the soul, which he sees as reason, spirit or emotion, and appetite.[13] The fact that the soul has parts in Plato's understanding is a product of his

---

10. Plato, *Republic*, 433a–433b.
11. Plato, *Republic*, 434a6–434c1.
12. *SHE*, 39.
13. *SHE*, 36.

application of logic to psychology. Plato asserts that "one thing cannot act in opposite ways or be in opposite states at the same time and in the same part of itself in relation to the same other thing; so if we find this happening we shall know that we are not dealing with one thing but with several."[14] To put it simply, a person cannot be going up and going down at the same time. A person cannot be awake or asleep at the same time. But a person can be hungry and refuse to eat at the same time. Given the fact that conflicts can arise within a person—we can both want and not want something at the same time—Plato asserts that the soul must have different parts to account for this conflict. Using the example of a thirsty person who refuses a drink (perhaps the person thinks there is poison in the drink), Plato identifies reason (one aspect or part of the soul) that restrains the appetite (another aspect of the soul) for thirst.[15] The third part of the soul for Plato is spirit or emotion, which can also conflict with reason or appetite. An angry person might refuse food from a person with whom he or she is angry despite hunger for the food.[16] Having identified these different parts of the soul, Plato asserts that the just soul is the one in which each part of the soul plays its proper function, and those functions have a hierarchy of authority, just like the community. The just person is ruled by reason, which finds support in spirit or emotion. The appetites, like the laborers in a city, must be content to be ruled by reason. The unjust person is the person in whom either emotion or appetite is in charge. If appetites or emotions become strengthened or enlarged, they attempt to enslave and rule over reason, which will entail a life of misery for the individual.[17]

Before returning to Plato's concern over what pays better, justice or injustice, let's take a look at two observations MacIntyre makes that help us to understand the strengths and weaknesses of Plato's arguments. First, he notes that the problem Plato is tackling by pursuing the nature of justice is how to understand an idea with a single meaning that can be applied in many different ways to many different subjects. Plato uses logic, the science of formal principles of reason, to answer the challenge. MacIntyre tells us that Plato has done something very significant by that use of logic asserting,

14. Plato, *Republic*, 436b.
15. *SHE*, 37.
16. Plato, *Republic*, 439d–440b.
17. Plato, *Republic*, 442a–442b.

> What is important is that the theory of meaning has been decisively brought on the scene. The logician has entered moral philosophy for good. But even though, from now on, the systematic and self-conscious logical analysis of moral concepts will be at the heart of moral philosophy, it can nonetheless never be the whole of moral philosophy. For we have to understand not only the logical interrelation of moral concepts, rules, and the like but also the point and purpose such rules serve.[18]

MacIntyre is pointing out something we often take for granted. Humans have not always sought to understand ethical ideas by means of rigorous logical analysis, and we are in debt to Plato for his introduction of logic into our attempt to understand ethics. MacIntyre is also giving us a preview of later criticism he will level at modern philosophers who tend to reduce morality to reason alone, the preeminent attempt of this being Immanuel Kant's pursuit of a purely rational morality. Unfortunately, ethics is not that simple. As MacIntyre points out, to have a good understanding of ethics we cannot remain merely at the level of the logical interactions of moral concepts. We also have to see how they relate to the goals and values that those concepts serve. It is not enough to have a clear definition of an idea such as justice. We must also see how justice relates to goals we are pursuing as individuals and as communities. Plato gives us a tool in logical analysis that helps us to understand ethics. Ethics cannot be reduced to the tool, but it can be seen through the lens of logic in its relation to our understanding of the human person. Ethics concerns logical relationships between the purposes and motives that drive people to do what they do, and even to theories of societies (politics) because different motives and purposes will arise for individuals on the basis of different social orders. If I am a young man in the twenty-first-century United States, I may grow up with dreams of being a football player. If I am a young man in twenty-first-century Germany, I would more likely dream of being a soccer (football of another type) player. Those dreams are similar but different, and set the dreamers to pursue different paths in life. Logical analysis resides in the middle of such a context. It is logic that helps the athlete pursue the behaviors and habits that will lead to success in a chosen sport. Plato's introduction of logic to the understanding of ethics enables and requires us to relate the ideas of ethics to these different fields of human knowledge (e.g., politics and psychology) that enable a person to pursue a fulfilling life. It is an enormous contribution.

18. *SHE*, 43.

MacIntyre's second observation is the importance of Plato's psychology not only to succeeding generations of ethicists, but to the problems of Plato's analysis regarding the nature of justice. Plato's threefold division of the soul is enormously influential for subsequent schools of Greek philosophers and their view of ethics.[19] It is a construct that informs the moral thinking not only of Plato's followers, but that of Aristotle and his followers, and other classical moral schools such as Stoicism and Epicureanism. In addition, MacIntyre describes Plato's view of the soul in *The Republic* as problematic in a number of ways. The most important problem for Plato's ethics is the way he understands the relationship between reason and the appetites, or desire. Plato maintains a rigid division between reason and the appetites in which reason is always in the right. MacIntyre observes that "reason, in the Platonic scheme, can only dominate, not inform or guide appetite, and appetite of itself is essentially irrational."[20] One problem with this approach is that it is not always true. MacIntyre points out that a reasonable desire for a drink may be able to correct an irrational fear of being poisoned.[21] Second, this misdescription limits Plato's options as he attempts to make the case that justice pays better than injustice. Given the complete divorce of reason from desire in Plato's thought, Plato can only offer explanations of the relationship between justice and injustice where appetite is a senseless and uncontrolled force that must be corralled by reason. Plato's psychology forces him to play on the terrain of the Sophist approach to the supreme good, getting whatever one wants.[22] Playing on that terrain and only offering the pleasure of reason as superior to all other pleasures (a description of which we will see in a moment) makes Plato's argument narrow and less effective. There are other ways bodily desires can be integrated into notions of justice, but they are unavailable to Plato, and without them he offers an intellectual view of happiness that often fails to resonate with the average person.

Turning to Plato's explanation of why justice pays better than injustice, we see him combine his division of the soul and his analysis of the best and worst forms of political structures to provide an answer. According to Plato, the worst political structure is the tyranny of the despot. Despotism is the worst political arrangement because the despot,

19. *SHE*, 37.
20. *SHE*, 47.
21. *SHE*, 38.
22. *SHE*, 47.

in Plato's view, is ruled by the lowest bodily appetites. Rather than being governed by reason, the despot is dominated by bodily desires that have absolute control over the despot and are completely irrational. Absolute irrationality then becomes the rule for the state over which the despot holds sway. Plato links the psychology of the despot to that of the unjust person. The despotic ruler as the model of injustice is opposed to the just person, and it is in this context that Plato describes how the just person is happier than the unjust person.[23] His rationale for the conclusion is threefold. First, as Socrates argued in *Gorgias*, unjust people have no limit or curb on their desires and thus will never be satisfied. Second, an unjust person does not have the perspective to know what pleasures are the greatest and therefore lead to happiness. Only the philosopher who knows the pleasures of the body and the pleasure of the intellect can know that the pleasure of intellect is superior. Third, pleasures of the intellect are genuine pleasures, while pleasures of the body are often merely the cessation of discomfort (the pleasure of a drink subsides once thirst is satisfied) and are therefore not genuine pleasures.[24]

Macintyre doesn't pull any punches in his assessment of Plato's conclusion. "These are bad arguments," he says.[25] While that appraisal may be a little harsh, I would agree that Plato's arguments are not terribly convincing, and MacIntyre offers good reasons as to why. According to MacIntyre, the type of person that undermines Plato's analysis most is *l'homme moyen sensuel*, or the person of average appetites. Not everyone who is unjust fits Plato's caricature of the despot who is a "senseless sensualist or an unchecked tyrant" recklessly pursuing pleasure.[26] Plato's depiction of the unjust person who is not a ruler of a state appears as a miniature version of the tyrant: a watered-down neurotic who weakly pursues bodily pleasure. Another possibility, however, is simply an ordinary person: the person who is moderate in all things, including immoral acts and vicious character traits. MacIntyre points out that Plato's description cannot account for the person whose reason can restrain the person's vice today for the purpose of enjoying greater vice tomorrow.[27]

MacIntyre goes on to say that Plato's argument does have merit, however, because it places the relation of desire and reason at the center

23. *SHE*, 46.
24. *SHE*, 46.
25. *SHE*, 46.
26. *SHE*, 47.
27. *SHE*, 47.

of understanding justice, at the center of understanding ethics. This is a strength Plato refines further in his dialogue *The Symposium*. The weakness of presentation in *The Republic* lies in Plato's rigid division between reason and appetite, where reason can only dominate appetite. That weakness is modified and improved in Plato's later book, *The Laws*. We will turn to the insights of these last two works to wrap up MacIntyre's analysis regarding Plato's contribution to the history of ethics.

Leadership Reflection: The Importance of Leadership to Diversity and Collaboration

Plato describes the justice of a community in terms of every member contributing to the community in the way that fits his or her position in society. In his view, the just society is a harmonious community where everyone is willing to play their part to the best of their ability. It is a description of justice quite different from contemporary notions of a just society. Twenty-first-century Americans more likely view a just society in terms of fairness, where each member of a society is granted rights and opportunities commensurate with the rights and opportunities of all the other members of society.[28] Plato's conception would likely be condemned in the contemporary context as the roles that people were assigned in the Greek city-state were decided on the basis of their birth, a capricious and arbitrary standard at best. While such a critique of Plato's notion of justice is fair, especially in our modern context, Plato's observations regarding harmony and the importance of people contributing to a society in different ways recognizes the crucial importance of diversity in a community and the leadership challenges associated with managing diversity. An organization of any complexity needs different people with different skill sets to accomplish different tasks. What is a leader to do when the differences necessary for the effective functioning of the organization give rise to different levels of reward and prestige? How does a leader keep a team together, keep each member of the team performing his or her allotted role, even when that role is entirely unpleasant or unpopular?

A historical example of this challenge can be seen in Winston Churchill's interactions with Welsh coal miners in the fall of 1942 at the height of the Second World War. Coal mining was a tough job. It was

---

28. Cf. Rawls, *Theory of Justice* for one of the most influential descriptions of justice as fairness in twentieth-century political theory.

physically demanding and dangerous, and as members of one of the lowest social classes in British society, coal miners were not highly regarded. Coal mining was one of the few jobs that struggled to compete with the lifestyle of a soldier. Being a coal miner was often as dangerous and taxing as service in the military and was certainly less appreciated by British society. Despite the negative aspects of the job for individual workers, coal mining was absolutely crucial to the British war effort. Coal provided much of the energy necessary for the British military to operate, not to mention supplying the energy needs for Great Britain's civilian population.[29] England needed those workers to do a difficult and unglamorous job for Britain to prevail.

So how did Churchill address the situation in his role as prime minister? He spoke to them directly, describing the purpose of their work and why it was so important. It was urgent that each coal miner understood the importance of his role and how that role contributed to the mission of protecting Great Britain. Churchill was able to show the miners that their work was equal in importance to the work of the soldier in achieving the military victory their nation so desperately needed. And he made the point in his typically eloquent fashion stating,

> We must not cast away our great deliverance; we must carry our work to its final conclusion. We shall not fail, and then some day, when children ask "What did you do to win this inheritance for us, and to make our name so respected among men?" one will say: "I was a fighter pilot"; another will say: "I was in the Submarine Service"; another: "I marched with the Eighth Army"; a fourth will say: "None of you could have lived without the convoys and the Merchant seamen"; and you, in your turn, will say, with equal pride and with equal right: "We cut the coal."[30]

Here we see Churchill playing a crucial leadership function. He gets his followers to play their unattractive role not by fear or coercion. Rather, he seeks to inspire them. Churchill recognizes the truth that every leader must understand, which is humans are creatures of purpose. Above all, we desire for our lives to have meaning and significance. Churchill was able to demonstrate to the miners the purpose and the critical importance

---

29. Cf. Woodson, "We Cut the Coal," for a brief description of the history and circumstances of Churchill's interaction with the miners.
30. Churchill, *War Speeches of Winston Churchill*, 339–40.

of their work to Great Britain through his powerful words, and England was better able to defend itself as a result.

An organization must be able to get its members to do the different tasks necessary not only to sustain its existence, but also for its ability to flourish. As Plato correctly observes, communities are collaborative enterprises that exist so that the many needs of the people who populate those communities can be met. This can only be done through a division of labor, teamwork, and cooperation. And leadership is crucial not only to seeing what must be done for the good of the whole, but it is also instrumental in sharing that vision with the members of the community so each person can play her or his part in making the community the best it can be.

6

Plato's Description of Desire and Habit in Relation to Morality

MacIntyre asserts that by introducing logic into the study of ethics, Plato links morality to psychology, politics, and a theory of human knowledge. We have raised the issues of Plato's psychology and politics in his analysis of justice. Now we need to take a brief look at his theory of human knowledge (this is the philosophical field of epistemology) and its relationship to unchanging realities (the field of metaphysics) to get a good view of Plato's improvement on the Sophist conception of the supreme good. Introducing Plato's metaphysics will also help us to understand how Aristotle recognizes weaknesses in Plato's moral thought and how Aristotle is able to move beyond those weaknesses in the development of his own approach to ethics.

Plato and Aristotle, like many other ancient Greek thinkers, had a significant focus on the phenomena of change and permanence. The contrast between things that change and things that do not change was a constant field of enquiry for the ancient Greeks. In Plato's thought, permanent things are considered to be "more real" than objects that are subject to change. In comparing an object such as an actual tree with the idea of what a tree is, Plato concluded that the idea was more substantive because it was permanent and unchanging. An actual tree would grow and develop over time, but it would also decay and eventually die. This is in contrast to the idea of a tree, which Plato thought to be not only permanent, but also the reality that made the tree a tree in the first place. It is the idea of what a tree is, what Plato called a form, that describes the essence and characteristics of trees and enables an actual tree to be considered a tree. This analysis applied not only to trees, but to any objects that existed and to any of the character traits that could be attributed to an object. So, the ideas or forms of whiteness, or skinniness, or shyness, or hardness are the realities that do not change and enable objects to be white, skinny, shy, or hard. The greatest forms in the thought of Plato are the beautiful and the good, which for Plato are almost interchangeable and the source for all that is beautiful and good in the world. Plato's famous allegory of the cave is told in *The Republic* to explain how the forms are more real than actual material objects.[1] For Plato, only the educated philosopher can accurately understand the nature of the universe and the forms that make the universe what it is. It is within this theory of knowledge and existence that Plato explains the nature of human desire and its relation to ethics in *The Symposium*. MacIntyre points out that in his later works, including *The Laws*, Plato seems to doubt the independent existence of the forms,[2] and his student Aristotle explicitly rejects that description of the forms, which enables significant development in Aristotle's moral theory. Nevertheless, the forms are crucial to understanding the argument Plato makes regarding the relationship between desire and moral choice.

The Symposium is one of Plato's most rich and influential dialogues. It depicts a drinking party where various participants of the party sing the praises of love. Love, represented by the Greek word *eros*, is the highest form of desire for the Greeks. Eros in English implies sexual desire, but for the Greeks *eros* indicates desire held with passion. *Eros* for the Greeks thus includes sexual desire, but is more general, referring to strong desire for any object. The dialogue starts with praise for the sexual love between men and adolescent boys that was common in Greek society at the time. The various speeches praising love culminate in the description offered by Socrates, who has been educated about the topic of love by the female sage Diotema. The object of love in Diotema's telling, the object of desire, is not just beauty, but to give birth in beauty. The human person desires beauty and wants to possess it forever.[3] Although the nature of an individual person is mortal and subject to death, beauty can be possessed forever from the perspective of the form of beauty because as a form,

---

1. Cf. Plato, *Republic*, 514a–520a which presents Plato's Allegory of the Cave, which is his most well-known description of the Forms and the intelligible world.
2. *SHE*, 49.
3. Plato, *Symposium*, 206a–206b.

beauty is an unchanging and eternal principle. When a person makes the principle of beauty a part of his or her character, which is another way of saying that a person develops virtues or beautiful character traits, the person will become immortal in the memory of the community, which unlike the individual, does not die.[4]

What's important about Plato's analysis regarding love or desire is its relation to ethics. The love of desire is the dynamic driving morality. In his famous *Confessions*, St. Augustine says simply that love is the weight that moves us.[5] We pursue what we desire. The problem this raises for moral choices is not everything we desire is good for us. Again, this is the distinction missed by the Sophists. Desiring the wrong things can literally destroy a person (e.g., drug addiction). In more routine cases, however, it is disordered desire that leads to a diminished life. The person of vice puts lesser goods before more important goods on a continual and habitual basis yielding a life that focuses on base pleasures to the neglect of greater goods. The dialogue of *The Symposium* highlights the reality that what is good cannot simply be reduced to what a person desires. Good refers to things that will actually satisfy a person. What provides the greatest satisfaction in Plato's view is contemplation of the form of beauty. This is the case because the form is the height of beauty. The form of beauty is the principle that enables any object that is beautiful to be beautiful. It is the wellspring that enables all other objects of love to be desirable in the first place. And as a form, beauty is the most permanent of all beautiful things.[6] In addition, the happiness offered by contemplating the form of beauty can only be appreciated by the few people who have the wherewithal and education to know and appreciate the forms. It is a height that can only be attained by philosophers.

MacIntyre, under the influence of Aristotle's later critiques, says that Plato is wrong to define happiness in terms of possessing an out-of-this-world transcendental property.[7] That being said, MacIntyre again points out a really important insight Plato is providing to the historical understanding of moral concepts. Good, in Plato's (and MacIntyre's) view, cannot simply mean what a person desires. Good as a moral concept enables us to evaluate possible objects of desire. The idea of good helps us to

---

4. Plato, *Symposium*, 212a.
5. Augustine, *Confessions*, 13.9.
6. Cf. Plato, *Symposium*, 210a–211c for Plato's description of the process that enables a person to scale the height of beauty and the description of beauty itself.
7. *SHE*, 53.

figure out what is truly fulfilling and is thus worthy of desire. When we determine something to be good, we are saying that it is something that is actually desirable and therefore worth pursuing through our moral choices.[8] We can be mistaken in what we think is good, but that does not change the fact that when properly applied, the idea of good will direct our desires to the things that are truly beneficial to us, the things that should be the objects of our moral choices.

MacIntyre then turns to *The Laws* and presents a later version of Plato's political thought than what is seen in *The Republic*, and it is in this updated political context that Plato refines his psychology concerning the relationship between reason and desire. MacIntyre asserts that Plato seems less sure of his doctrine of the forms at this point in his thinking.[9] This doubt likely serves as a foundation for the difference in approach between *The Republic* and *The Laws*. In *The Republic*, the focus is on the leaders of the ideal state, the philosopher-kings, who must be educated or given knowledge concerning the form of justice in order to govern well. The idea of an educated elite who must understand justice in order to rule is not abandoned by Plato in *The Laws*, but his focus is now on the people, the followers, rather than the leaders.[10] If it is doubtful that many can be educated concerning the abstract nature of the forms, the form of justice being the crucial form, how does the population tend toward justice? MacIntyre tells us that Plato was pessimistic regarding the possibility of establishing a just state at all given his experience as a political consultant of sorts in the kingdom of Syracuse.[11] Plato's work there, which involved guiding the would-be ruler Dion, ended in the very form of government Plato thought worst: the tyranny of a despot. The probability of a state being just on the basis of a just ruler likely seemed remote to Plato at that point. This context raised the question, "How can a city aspire to being a just community if the very idea of justice is in doubt and the leaders are often unable to bring about justice through their own action?"

Given Plato's pessimism, his analysis in *The Laws* is probably not an attempt to provide a comprehensive answer to this question. Yet even if an actually just state is impossible in Plato's view, thinking about what a just state would be like is still important to him because it enables people to judge real cities and to work toward more just societies on the basis of

---

8. *SHE*, 53.
9. *SHE*, 53–54.
10. *SHE*, 54–55.
11. *SHE*, 45.

those judgments.[12] In addition, the analysis of *The Laws* yields another insight important to both his psychology and to the later moral thought of Aristotle. Earlier we described MacIntyre's criticism of Plato's rigid division between reason and appetite in the human soul found in *The Republic*, where reason could only dominate the appetites. The appetites were understood as purely irrational and needed to be dominated by reason to be directed at justice. Plato's psychology was linked to his politics. Reason was exercised in the state by the rulers who coerced the laborers by means of law to do what was just. The relation between reason and appetite in *The Republic* is completely negative.[13] Appetite is always wayward and must be corrected by reason.

In *The Laws*, Plato comes to recognize that the populace need not be coerced into justice. They could also be educated and habituated towards justice. Plato replaces reason as constraint for raucous and unruly appetites with a conception of the human soul in which desirable habits and character traits can replace the restraint of reason. The people can be encouraged to live in accordance with justice through education and the virtues that the laws of society promoted. The people can be conditioned and habituated into just ways of life.[14] The implications this change has for the relationship between morality and psychology are significant. If desires can be informed by reason or even rationalized, a more accurate view of human behavior, of ethics, can be proposed. And not only is accuracy concerning moral thought improved; the relevance of ethics to the average person is enhanced as well. In the context of a psychology where bodily desires are integrated with and joined to reason, the greatest good no longer has to be associated with an intellectual view of happiness that does not resonate with most people. The normal daily desires, which include bodily desires, can now be further incorporated into moral analysis. We see further progress along these lines in the thought of Aristotle, who is up next in MacIntyre's history.

---

12. *SHE*, 45.
13. *SHE*, 55.
14. *SHE*, 55.

Leadership Reflection: Plato, Habits, and the National Football League

Plato's insight that people can be trained and educated to have excellent habits was not only significant for his time but is still applicable in today's world. Plato's view of virtue, articulated in *The Republic* and further developed in *The Laws*, influenced the entire classical approach to ethics and was particularly important to the manner in which Aristotle approached the ideas of habit and virtue. Recognizing that education and the development of morally excellent habits was superior to coercing people to obey laws, both Plato and Aristotle saw the task of government to be the formulation of laws that would lead to a virtuous citizenry. In their view, the purpose of a legislature was to write laws that would lead citizens to develop morally excellent habits.[15]

Such an approach to the relationship between politics and ethics would likely win few supporters today. Paternalism, understood as government interference in a person's autonomy for that person's own good, has been criticized by many contemporary thinkers. A recent example of the unpopularity of an overly paternalistic government was the attempt by New York City to ban large sugary soft drinks in an effort to curb the obesity crisis among its citizens. The regulations proposed by the mayor's health department were struck down by the courts because they were intrusive of citizens' freedom, and the city council never attempted to legislate the ban because it was simply too unpopular among the residents of New York.[16]

While the political regulation of habits seems difficult to achieve in the context of contemporary democracy, that does not mean Plato's insights regarding the development of habits lies wholly outside the realm of leadership. It may not be appropriate or effective for governments to manage the development of habits, but that does not mean smaller and more intimate settings do not offer an opportunity for leaders to help develop the habits that lead to success in life. The family is an obvious setting in which leaders (parents) not only have the ability but also have a real responsibility to teach their followers (children) to develop the habits that lead to a flourishing life.

---

15. Cf. Aristotle, *Nicomachean Ethics*, 1099b30–1099b31 for his assertion that the goal of politics is the formation of moral character among the citizens of a community.

16. Cf. Grynbaum, "New York's Ban on Big Sodas is Rejected by Final Court."

A modern example of a leader focusing on habits in order to achieve success in a highly competitive context is the work of head coach Tony Dungy in the National Football League. In his book *The Power of Habit*, author Charles Duhigg describes Dungy's theory of coaching which included a focus on habit formation, of all things. His theory didn't seem to sit well with the owners who interviewed him for head coaching jobs. It took him four tries to finally land a head coaching position in 1996 with the Tampa Bay Buccaneers, one of the worst teams in the league at the time. Dungy recognized that speed of execution was a key competitive advantage for his players and teams. His goal as a leader and coach was to enable his players to recognize cues and react to those cues in an effective manner in particular situations on the football field and to then habituate those reactions.[17] Once those reactions became learned as habits through repetition in practice, the speed of executing the correct reaction was maximized because the player did not have to "think" about the correct action to take. That thought process was now memorized in the physical habits that the players had been taught and trained to accomplish. Daniel Kahneman in his influential book *Thinking Fast and Slow* distinguishes two general types of thinking, which he labels system one and system two thinking. System one thinking is described as human thinking that is fast, automatic, and even unconscious, while system two thinking refers to the thinking that is slow, intensive, and deliberate.[18] Dungy's leadership transitioned the reactions of his players from the slow and deliberate process of system two thinking to the fast and unconscious process of system one thinking. Interestingly, it is not that the players were no longer thinking. They were still thinking, but in a different manner than the deliberative thinking that typically accompanies complex situations. They were observing cues and making judgments on the basis of those observations, but the habituation of this process enabled them to make those judgments more quickly than their opponents. As the leader producing this change in behavior, Dungy had to make sure he was habituating his players correctly to the cues that started their habitual reactions, and that those reactions were also the correct ones to perform. Having committed those cues and reactions to their habitual memory, to their muscle memory, his teams were able to compete at the top levels of the

---

17. Cf. Duhigg, *Power of Habit*, 60–66 for a description of Dungy's work with the Buccaneers.

18. Cf. Kahneman, *Thinking Fast and Slow* for Kahneman's psychological description of system one and system two thinking.

NFL for the greater part of the next decade. The Buccaneers won the Super Bowl one year after Dungy got fired, and he subsequently led the Indianapolis Colts to the Superbowl title in 2006. As the leader of his teams, Dungy was able to teach the habits of excellence, and the performance of those teams took off. In our next chapter, we will see Aristotle assert that moral habits are developed in the same ways that athletes train for competition.[19] It is an observation that can be applied by every leader in any leadership setting and leads to the high-level organizational performance that every leader hopes to achieve.

---

19. Aristotle, *Nicomachean Ethics*, 1114a6–1114a9.

7

Aristotle's Impact on Greek Ethics

IT COMES AS NO surprise that MacIntyre addresses the ethical thought of Aristotle following that of Plato. What might be more surprising is the fact that arguably the two most influential moral thinkers in the 2,500-year history of European ethics knew one another and worked together. At the age of seventeen, Aristotle (384–322 BCE) moved from northern Greece to Athens to study at Plato's Academy, where he spent the next twenty years of his life. Following Plato's death and after six years of empirical studies outside of Athens, Aristotle moved to Pella in Macedon at the request of King Phillip to tutor the king's son, Alexander the Great. After two years as Alexander's tutor, Aristotle returned to Athens and established his own school, the Lyceum, where he wrote many of his books. Although Aristotle was a prolific writer, authoring 150 books (according to one biographer), only about thirty of his writings come down to us from antiquity, and many of those are compilations of his lecture notes put together by later editors rather than actual books. The work we will examine, *Nicomachean Ethics* (named for Aristotle's son Nicomachus),[1] is one of those compilations and represents some of his most mature thinking on ethics.

The moral thinking of Aristotle is not an easy nut to crack compared to that of Plato. His writings are not easy-to-read dialogues, but are treatises that were likely written for a small audience of students familiar with the language and concepts Aristotle frequently used. The ideas Aristotle articulates in these treatises are both dense and broad and can

---

1. *SHE*, 57. Cf. Natali and Hutchison, *Aristotle*, 19–55 for a thorough recounting of Aristotle's career.

therefore be difficult to encapsulate succinctly. That being said, examining his thought is well worth the effort. MacIntyre notes in his later book *After Virtue* that Aristotle is influential in the history of ethics because he served to consolidate the important moral insights that had developed in Greek culture over the previous centuries while adding his own significant insights to that tradition.[2] His analysis is noteworthy not just for his time, but for ours as well. And Aristotle, like Plato, does not get everything right. Despite his conceptual ability, Aristotle struggles (like all of us) to step outside of his own culture to see things more broadly. So, in studying Aristotle we will see astute moral insights alongside conclusions that some find preposterous and even immoral. Following MacIntyre, our plan to get at the good and bad of Aristotle's moral thought will be to follow Aristotle's example of beginning with the end in mind. We will begin with Aristotle's definition of the term "good" and examine how his notion of the highest or supreme good drives his entire approach to moral analysis. In that context, we can then examine the constitutive elements of Aristotle's approach to morality, which will help us appreciate his contribution to the understanding of ethics. The end of that analysis will bring us back to his consideration of the supreme good. In returning to the end—which for Aristotle is the ultimate goal of moral striving—we will examine MacIntyre's appraisal of Aristotle's strengths and weaknesses, which raises the questions addressed by Aristotle's successors, as well as subsequent medieval and modern philosophers. Indeed, Aristotle's moral thought is of such significance his thinking is still central to twenty-first-century ethical discussions.

Aristotle's View of Good as a Concept

Every craft and every inquiry, and similarly every action and project seem to aim at some good; hence the good has been well defined as that at which everything aims.[3]

MacIntyre begins his chapter on Aristotle describing the above quotation as trenchant, and it certainly is one of the high points we will see when examining Aristotle's ethics. In MacIntyre's view, Aristotle's formulation

---

2. MacIntyre, *After Virtue*, 146.
3. Aristotle, *Nicomachean Ethics*, 1094a1–1094a3, as noted in *SHE*, 57.

accurately describes the way humans use good as a word and concept, and he gives two ways of seeing how defining "good" in terms of goals helps us to understand what it means to say something is "good." First, he says that if we call the objects of our desire, the things we are aiming at, "good," we are saying that the things we are seeking are the things desired by people who want what we want.[4] This abstract statement is not the easiest to understand. MacIntyre uses an example of a cricket bat to explain. As an American I will illustrate with the example of a baseball bat. By calling a baseball bat good, I am applying attributes to the bat that people who know and want baseball bats would desire in a bat. A baseball bat is good if it is the right length, if it is light, if it is strong, if it is made of the right material (wood or aluminum), and if it looks cool. MacIntyre asserts that calling something good and not indicating that the object is in some way desirable is to speak unintelligibly.[5] It would make no sense. To say a baseball bat is good when it is short, heavy, made of stone, and ugly is to say something absurd to the people who know how to use and like using good baseball bats. People want good things because there is a relationship between the concept of good and being an object of desire. Simply put, the idea of good is applied to things that are sought after or desired. Here we have an example of the helpful manner in which Aristotle's thought communicated to us through MacIntyre's analysis sheds light on basic, yet crucial ethical concepts. MacIntyre provides a nice summary of how this notion of good is related to moral thinking. "If I choose between two alternatives, then I must envisage something beyond these alternatives in light of which I make my choice, that for the sake of which I shall choose one rather than another, that which provides me a criterion in my deliberation. This will in fact be what in that particular case I am treating as an end."[6] That end, that goal, that which is worthy of being desired, defines what it means for something to be good. So, if the goal is to hit a baseball effectively, effective hitting becomes the criteria that directs the making of a baseball bat. Looking cool is still important, but not as important as the actual hitting. It is good for hitters to look cool, but if the hitter is ineffective, he will not be playing much, no matter how cool he looks. What this example implies is an ordering of goods—that is, some goods are more important than others. And when it comes to the moral life, the supreme good—what Latin authors called

4. *SHE*, 58.
5. *SHE*, 58.
6. *SHE*, 71.

the *summum bonum*—is the criteria that trumps all others. For Aristotle's approach to ethics, defining the supreme good is crucial because it becomes the standard that guides all moral choices. So, what is the answer that Aristotle provides for the greatest good a person can pursue? This is definitely a question for moral philosophy. So, let's take a look at what he has to say.

Aristotle on the Supreme Good

What is the greatest good, the supreme good to be achieved by the human person? For Aristotle, such a good must be chosen for its own sake and must not be a component of some other state of affairs, nor is it one good among others. The final or ultimate good in his view will be chosen over all other goods.[7] And that good is represented by the Greek word *eudaimonia*, which MacIntyre tells us is badly translated into English as happiness.[8] Happiness in English focuses primarily on the emotions associated with the state of happiness. *Eudaimonea* covers the emotional aspect of happiness, but implies more than that. *Eudaimonea* refers to the living of a flourishing and productive life over a significant period of time.[9] It represents the strong intuition in Greek thought that *areté* and happiness have an intrinsic relationship.[10] For Aristotle, it means both behaving well and faring well, which is yet another of Aristotle's formulations identified by MacIntyre as important to understanding ethics. MacIntyre tells us that this formulation helps us to see a significant contrast between Aristotle's thought on the one hand, and the thinking of Plato and Socrates on the other. Aristotle has a different starting point in his analysis of ethics than his predecessors. Socrates and Plato start from the perspective that it is better to suffer torture on the rack than to have a soul burdened with the guilt of doing evil. MacIntyre observes that Aristotle does not confront this position directly, but asserts that it is better to be free from having done evil and free from torture on the rack. Plato's question examines how we can account for goodness in a way that is compatible with the fact that good people often suffer torture

---

7. Cf. Aristotle, *Nicomachean Ethics*, 1097a26–1097b21 for Aristotle's description of the highest good as happiness.

8. *SHE*, 59.

9. Aristotle, *Nicomachean Ethics*, 1098b20–1098b21.

10. *SHE*, 59.

or injustice. Aristotle, on the other hand, first asks about the form of life in which doing well and faring well can be found together. MacIntyre helps us to see that Plato's approach concerns how to survive in a society where the just person is tortured and even executed, while Aristotle's is concerned with building a society where the just person is not subjected to torture and death.[11] Despite the differences, both sets of questions are still clearly relevant to us today.

Aristotle concludes that the supreme good, the happy life, is the life of virtue.[12] *Areté* ends in *eudaimonia*. In Aristotle's calculus, every moral choice is measured by the supreme good because good as a concept is the thing aimed at, and the thing aimed at provides the criteria for the aiming. The goal is the bullseye a person aims at by making a moral choice.[13] If a moral decision moves a person toward the supreme good, which is the cultivation of virtue, it should be chosen. This is the case because virtues not only make a person good, they enable a person to live a fulfilling, productive, and happy life. Virtue is the answer to Aristotle's question of how a person is to live well and to fare well. If a decision promotes vice rather than virtue, it should be avoided because that choice serves to prevent a person from achieving his or her ultimate good.

This is not the end of the story for Aristotle's ethics, however. Critics raise many questions regarding Aristotle's virtue-based approach to morality, with the following three questions being among the most significant. First, often the choice that will lead to virtue in the long run will produce horrible results in the short term. For example, the decision not to cheat on a test will prevent a person from becoming a cheater, but it may also produce a failing grade on the test. Which is more important, the long-term character concern about cheating or the short-term consequence of a failing grade? And this example implies a second question. What is it about virtues that make them such great happiness producers? Put another way, how do we know that making choices that produce virtues will lead to the greatest happiness? Lying is often seen as a vice, but what if a person's lies enable the person to get a lot of money? The person might not be honest, but is an honest person really happier than a rich person? A third question that criticizes a virtue-based approach to

---

11. *SHE*, 60.

12. Aristotle, *Nicomachean Ethics*, 1098a16–1098a17.

13. Cf. Aristotle, *Nicomachean Ethics*, 1106b20–1106b35 for Aristotle's description of the relationship between virtue and the mean and how virtue enables choices that hit the target of moral excellence.

ethics asserts that concern for one's moral character can be entirely self-serving. If your desire to be honest leads to the suffering of someone else, would not your desire to tell the truth be a selfish and therefore immoral act? How does Aristotle's account of pursuing virtue above all else answer these questions? To get at his answers, we will need to look at further elements of his moral thought to include his view of deliberation, its relation to habit, and what I would describe as Aristotle's threefold criteria for making moral decisions. Having examined these elements, we can return to our three questions to see if Aristotle's answers satisfy.

Moral Deliberation: The Integration of Reason and Desire That Produces Habits

For Aristotle, deliberation is the human thought process that underlies all moral decisions. Unlike Aristotle's view of theoretical thinking, which concerns unchanging principles, and his view of productive science, which is the thinking associated with making things, deliberation is the thinking associated with making choices that have an impact on the situations humans find themselves in on a daily basis. There are two distinctive aspects of Aristotle's view of deliberation that are worthy of our examination. First, deliberation is concerned with choosing the means to achieve a particular goal. Goal determination is a function of theoretical thinking for Aristotle, while the focus of deliberative thinking is determining the means by which to achieve the goal.[14] So moral deliberation is the thinking that concerns the practical decisions necessary for a person to successfully achieve his or her goals in life.

The second distinctive aspect of Aristotle's conception of deliberation is the integration of desire and reason that results from deliberation.[15] Aristotle describes deliberation in the context of his moral psychology, which takes up where Plato's psychology leaves off. He affirms Plato's threefold distinction in the human soul between reason, emotion, and appetites/desires.[16] Building on Plato, Aristotle provides further clarity

---

14. Aristotle, *Nicomachean Ethics*, 1112b11–1112b15.

15. Aristotle, *Nicomachean Ethics*, 1113a10–1113a13.

16. Cf. Aristotle, *Nicomachean Ethics*, 1102b13–1103a4, 1105b19–1105b29 for Aristotle's description of the human soul in relation to ethics and virtue. He notes that he is only providing enough detail in his description of the soul that is necessary to understand ethics. He goes into further depth regarding the nature of the soul in his book *De Anima*, which commentators point out is not entirely consistent with the

in regard to how the psychological aspects of human nature relate to one another and how those relations affect our understanding of ethics. We ended our discussion of Plato's psychology in his work *The Laws*, where Plato makes the transition from a view of human nature in which reason can only dominate emotion and desire to a view in which desire and emotion can be rationalized or trained by reason through habituation. Aristotle likewise describes a dynamic relationship between reason and desire in the soul, as deliberation and choice integrate reason and desire to form a person's habits/moral character. Following Plato, Aristotle asserts that the person of *areté* will deliberate and choose rationally.[17] For a person to be morally excellent, that person must use reason to guide appetites and emotions in making moral decisions. As we all know, however, reason is not always up to the task of directing appetites and emotions. Aristotle makes a key observation of why this is the case when he says in the context of our desires, "If appetite and desire do not obey the ruling element (reason) . . . they will go far astray. The active gratification of appetite will increase the appetite with which we were born, and if the appetites are great and intense, they push aside the power of reasoning."[18] As we deliberate and make choices, those choices accumulate into habits that enlist our desires. We want to do the things that we are in the habit of doing, which is one of the reasons habits are so hard to change. If a person deliberates and only has in mind the satisfaction of bodily appetites, those appetites will become the dominant consideration in making choices because the person will habituate himself or herself to making choices based on those desires.

The good news is appetites need not dominate reason in this way. As MacIntyre helpfully points out, Aristotle's thought recognizes that reason and desire can conflict, but it is not necessary that they do.[19] Desire for pleasure can corrupt a person, but that desire can also help a person choose what reason points out as good. Aristotle asserts that reason in the form of deliberation can guide desire.[20] In his view, the virtuous person is

---

description of the soul provided in *Nicomachean Ethics*. Throughout my description of Aristotle's moral thought I will use the terms appetite and desire interchangeably. Both terms indicate the sensations humans experience in association with the biologically based needs and wants that humans feel throughout the broad range of their activity.

17. Aristotle, *Nicomachean Ethics*, 1103b31.
18. Aristotle, *Nicomachean Ethics*, 1119b6–1119b10.
19. *SHE*, 62.
20. Aristotle, *Nicomachean Ethics*, 1113a12.

the person who has trained himself or herself through the application of right reason to be in the habit of doing what is good. Once habituated, a virtuous person's desires are integrated with reason. The person of *areté* desires "all the pleasant things that contribute to his health and well-being ... moderately and in the way he should, and also other pleasures as long as they are neither detrimental to health and well-being, nor incompatible with what is noble nor beyond his means."[21] A simple example is a comparison between my wife and I when we eat fast food. My wife is habituated to eat healthy food, and I am not. She always regrets eating fast food because she feels horrible after the meal. Me, not so much. Her intellect has guided the formation of her eating habits, which yields the desire for healthy food. She is therefore much less likely to order fast food than someone like me. Once trained by reason, desire can reinforce the choices that reason determines are good to pursue. MacIntyre emphasizes that in Aristotle's account, the sign of a virtuous person is a person who derives pleasure from doing what is good and is able to choose well between pleasure and pain.[22] In the context of *areté*, the power of desire is now integrated with reason by means of the deliberation process.[23] This integration enables the virtuous person to be quite good, even excellent at making good choices because both reason and desire are united in the deliberation that produces a person's practical choices, which in turn further forms that person's habits or moral character. It is on this foundation that MacIntyre emphasizes an aspect of ethics that is ignored by many other ethicists, which is that our desires can be criticized and even reformed. A key aspect of the moral life for both Aristotle and MacIntyre is the idea that if a person is to be morally excellent, that person must examine his or her desires and encourage the good ones and discourage the bad ones. It is a theme we will see again in MacIntyre's critique of modern ethics.[24]

Given Aristotle's view of the supreme good and the relation he posits between deliberation and habits, we can assert (without controversy) that Aristotle's study of ethics is the study of habit. We do not have habits

21. Aristotle, *Nicomachean Ethics,* 1119a16–1119a18.

22. *SHE,* 64–65. Aristotle, *Nicomachean Ethics,* 1104b3–1104b7.

23. Such integration provides a context for the idea of integrity as a moral concept. A person of integrity is a person of *aret.* Such a person is a well-integrated whole who knows how to make good moral choices and wants (desires) to make good choices.

24. The idea that desires can be criticized and reformed is one that MacIntyre repeats a number of different times throughout *Short History of Ethics.* Cf. *SHE,* 87 and 149 for two examples of this assertion.

by nature, but human nature provides the capacity to develop habits.[25] These habits can either be good or bad, depending on the nature of the choices a person makes over time. Aristotle asserts that it is not possible for us to be different from what our choices have made us to be.[26] In his view, choices have consequences for our character that are inescapable. *Areté*/virtue in Aristotle's view is nothing other than the excellent habits that are produced through deliberation that enable excellent moral decisions. Here is his brief description of the habit formation process:

> For a given kind of activity produces a corresponding character. This is shown by the way in which people train themselves for any kind of contest or performance: they keep on practicing for it. Thus, only a person who is utterly insensitive can be ignorant of the fact that moral characteristics are formed by actively engaging in particular actions.[27]

As MacIntyre observes, the practice of making brave choices will eventually result in the habit of courage, habitual excellence in facing danger or fear. Brave acts repeated over time produce a brave person.[28] Moral excellence is therefore a function of practice. To put it positively, through the human capacity to learn, the ability to develop wisdom, people are able to get better and better at making good moral decisions by putting into practice the noble moral ideals to which they are exposed. This is not an easy process, however. It often entails confronting past mistakes and overcoming bad or unhealthy habits that have developed previously. Yet despite the difficulty of the process, we see examples of people learning from their mistakes and overcoming their bad habits on a daily basis. Whether it is a recovering addict or simply a person who has the humility to apologize for the hurt he or she has caused a loved one, we know that such moral improvements can be accomplished over time through practice. And we can also see that this difficult route is the way we can live an admirable and fulfilling life. We all know the easy paths of pursuing addiction and nursing grudges has a pleasure that is as short-lived as it is destructive. Humans can improve their moral character over time if they commit to practicing the choices necessary to produce that improvement.

---

25. Aristotle, *Nicomachean Ethics*, 1103a23–1103a24.
26. Aristotle, *Nicomachean Ethics*, 1114a21.
27. Aristotle, *Nicomachean Ethics*, 1114a6–1114a10.
28. *SHE*, 64.

This hints at the way Aristotle answers the question of why he sees developing virtue as the key to happiness. Before addressing that question more fully, however, it is important to examine the threefold criteria for making moral judgments posited by Aristotle.

Aristotle's Threefold Criteria for Moral Choice

We have spoken about deliberation, how it integrates reason and desire, and how it relates to habit formation. What we have not spoken about yet is how human deliberation is guided in making good moral decisions. What are the ideas, the criteria that enable the faculty of deliberation to produce good results? To risk being redundant in answering the question, we can say it is by knowing what is good that deliberation can achieve a good result. We can untie this "good" knot by going back to Aristotle's description of good as a concept. According to Aristotle, good things, good goals are the things that we aim at through decisions that are truly fulfilling.[29] For example, I decide to take tennis lessons so that I can be a good tennis player. Lessons enable me to appreciate tennis more because it is enjoyable to engage in an activity with the skill necessary to do that activity well, not to mention the happiness that comes from beating other good tennis players that the lessons will also support. So, the first level of criteria guiding choices in an Aristotelian approach to ethics is making decisions that will achieve what can be described as a short-term goal. In the prior example, taking tennis lessons serves the truly fulfilling goal of becoming a better tennis player.

What makes the process of deliberation complicated is the fact that we have multiple goals that we may be pursuing simultaneously, and those goals have complex relationships. Short-term goals are not the only way to evaluate moral choices, and Aristotle helps us identify other criteria that are more important than just achieving a short-term goal. A good example to describe the relation between the different types of moral criteria posited by Aristotle is a student enduring the rigors of medical school in order to become a physician. In the first two years of medical school, students have to take and pass a battery of difficult exams. The only way to gain the coveted MD letters after one's name is to pass all of these tests. There are different ways to go about passing the tests, however. One can study hard in order to accrue the knowledge

---

29. Aristotle, *Nicomachean Ethics*, 1094a2.

necessary to pass the test, or a student can let other people do this and simply cheat off someone who has done the hard work necessary to pass the test. Most people would say that cheating is not the right or a good way to pass those tests, and Aristotle's further criteria for making moral choices makes clear why that intuition is correct.

Deliberation and its relation to habits make the choice to study rather than cheat the clearly better practical/moral choice. We can see this in the habits associated with both cheating and studying and the long-term results those habits produce. The habits of a cheater are problematic on multiple levels. They include a poor work ethic, the tendency to use the skill of another during an actual test, and the lack of knowledge the absence of studying yields. Studying, on the other hand, enables a person to develop good work/study habits, supports performing independently and well when being tested (either on paper or in real life), and provides a student the knowledge necessary to be a good physician. In the context of Aristotle's ethics, the habits associated with cheating are impractical; they are unhelpful to living a flourishing life (both as a physician and in general), and are therefore blameworthy. In the context of morally excellent habits, in the context of virtue and the Greek concept of *areté*, passing a test by means of study creates habits beneficial to living a fruitful life, and the choices that produce those habits are therefore praiseworthy. Returning our analysis to deliberation, we can say that deliberation will enable a person to figure out what is the best way to pass a test not just by looking at passing the test itself, but by taking into account what habits will be built by means of those moral choices and choosing the actions that produce good moral character.

So, what is one to do if the short-term outcome is in conflict with the longer-term goal of developing excellent moral habits? In Aristotle's system, the answer is easy. One should always choose the decision that enables excellent moral habits. This conclusion is not based on an idealist desire to seize the moral high ground, either. Aristotle sees ethics as the science of practical reasoning. Cheating might seem to be the practical decision when a student feels the pressure to get a good grade on a test. Aristotle's system makes it clear (and confirms our intuitions) that the decision to cheat is a horrible one from a practical perspective, especially when the cheater is successful at not getting caught. Cheating and its associated habits may achieve a good grade on a test, a good short-term result, but they are habits that will not and cannot produce success over a long period of time. The grade is a short-lived and temporary good compared to the habits and knowledge developed in passing the test on one's own merit. Praiseworthy habits are praiseworthy and worth more than the short-term good because they make a flourishing and well-lived life possible.

In Aristotle's context, deliberation is difficult, not only because different types of goals can conflict, but also because the correct choice, the good choice, often is harder to make. Becoming a good person can seem much less urgent than failing a test, and that is not the only difficulty involved. Aristotle has further criteria for moral choice than just making a praiseworthy choice that produces good habits. He also brings in the social contexts in which people make their choices. Ethics is not just about the choice a person makes for himself or herself. It also brings in communal concerns. And this is the case because the greatest happiness is not just the flourishing of individuals, it is the flourishing of communities. He explains his view in the context of the relationship between politics and ethics by asserting,

> Thus, it follows that the end (goal) of politics is the good for humans. For even if the good is the same for the individual and the state, the good of the state clearly is the greater and more perfect thing to attain and to safeguard. The attainment of the good for one person alone is, to be sure, a source of satisfaction; yet to secure it for a nation and for states is nobler and more divine.[30]

An example that supports Aristotle's assertion is the nobility associated with service in the military. Many societies see the willingness of individuals to serve and even sacrifice their lives for the defense of their country as crucially important and noble. The assumption behind the nobility of sacrificing oneself for the good of the community is the fact that the good of the community is more important than that of the individual.[31] If that were not the case, sacrificing one's life to defend the community would simply be foolish and certainly not noble.

The concerns of the community add the last and highest consideration to moral choice for Aristotle. Going back to our earlier chapters, we can remember that *areté* for the Greek is defined by the roles necessary

---

30. Aristotle, *Nicomachean Ethics*, 1094b6–1094b10.

31. This is not to say that a community can be good without valuing an individual. The goodness of a community is defined by its ability to enable its individual members to flourish in freedom. Thus, the decision to sacrifice one's life for the good of the community must be a free decision on the part of the individual. A community that coerces the individual to make that choice is not worthy of the sacrifice.

for the harmonious operations of the *polis*, which has two implications for the ethical deliberations of each person. First, the standards of moral choice can vary. The virtues of a soldier, a physician, and a mother are different, so effective deliberation has to account for the role a person inhabits within the community. Second, the virtues that support playing that role are the ultimate criteria for making a decision because the actions of that role are important due to the way they support the greatest of all goods, the flourishing of the community. We can see this play out in the case of our medical student aspiring to fill the role of physician within society. In this context, cheating is wrong not only because it leads to blameworthy habits; it is also wrong because medical students who cheat their way to their credentials will literally be a menace to their communities. Developing virtues will often be the same in the context of the individual and his or her role in society, but it is an important distinction to make because it helps us answer the question raised earlier about the possible selfishness of virtues. And having covered Aristotle's notions of deliberation, habit, and his three criteria that guide deliberation, we can now provide Aristotelian answers to the three criticisms of a virtue-based approach to ethics.

Answers to Aristotle's Critics

Our discussion of Aristotle's ethics provides significant resources to answer the questions we raised earlier. First, in Aristotle's view, short-term consequences are not as important as the long-term impact of the habits we develop in pursuit of those short-term goals. If a choice supporting a short-term goal means developing a vice (defined as a bad habit), one should not make that choice. There are very few short-term outcomes worth the risk of becoming a bad person. And again, this is not because of a superficial desire to claim the moral high ground. Rather, it is a function of the recognition that virtues lead to rich and flourishing lives and vices do not. This points to another benefit of Aristotle's view that habits are the most important consideration when making a moral choice. If habits are the primary concern and the most enduring outcome of a moral choice, then the various criteria of excellence in making moral choices quickly become the principles that guide a person's deliberation. When humans recognize that excellent moral habits are crucial to living a rich and flourishing life, they are provided a powerful motivation to choose excellence. Most people desire rich and flourishing lives and are thus willing to make the excellent, albeit often difficult choices that produce virtues.

How about the question of the relation of virtue to the happy life? Does the life of virtue really constitute the happy life? Unsurprisingly, Aristotle answers yes to this question and provides a rationale for that yes.[32] In Aristotle's view, the good things that constitute a happy life can be placed into three general categories: external goods, goods of the body, and goods of the soul. External goods are things such as money, shelter, good schools, and friends. Goods of the body are things like health, strength, and even good looks. Goods of the soul are the virtues. Aristotle asserts that each category of good is important to human happiness. The different types of goods intertwine and are mutually dependent. It is very difficult for a person to develop morally excellent habits without the goods of food, shelter, the love of parents, and an excellent education. In Aristotle's analysis, happiness is made possible by goods of the body and is enhanced by external goods. He reserves pride of place to goods of the soul, however, asserting that the excellence of virtue constitutes happiness by making the other goods possible to attain.[33] Aristotle also maintains that virtues lead to an additional happiness, which is the gratification associated with performing morally excellent actions and the satisfaction of knowing that one has excellent moral character.[34] Twentieth-century psychologist Viktor Frankl, a survivor of the Auschwitz concentration camp, points to the depth of the satisfaction virtue itself provides when he describes the virtues he and others needed and developed to overcome the suffering meted out by the Nazis. The survivors were lucky to be sure, but they were also virtuous in the face of unimaginable suffering and could take solace in the satisfaction of the character they developed in enduring the crucible of Nazi horror.[35]

Our third question concerns the possible selfishness of virtues. A concern for virtue could come at the cost of the interests of others. If telling the truth in a specific situation leads to the harm of another, it seems selfish to tell the truth because of a desire to promote one's own honesty. We would need more detail to see if lying in such a situation can be

---

32. Cf. Aristotle, *Nicomachean Ethics*, 1098b8–1099b8 for Aristotle's full discussion of the goods that constitute human happiness.

33. Aristotle, *Nicomachean Ethics*, 1098b29–1098b30.

34. Aristotle, *Nicomachean Ethics*, 1099a13–1099a16.

35. Cf. Frankl, *Man's Search for Meaning*, for Frankl's remarkable discussion of survivor interpretations of their experience in the death camps.

justified. One might say that if a lie literally saved a person's life, it might be justified from a moral perspective.[36] Generally speaking, however, Aristotle would assert that developing morally excellent habits does not only serve the interest of the individual, it serves the interest of the community, and it is the interests of the community that gives the ultimate justification for the importance of virtues. As we said earlier, in Aristotle's moral system, virtues are important because they enable the individual to play his or her role well in society. The greatest good is the good of the society, and morally praiseworthy habits are defined as praiseworthy by the society or community because the community needs people to have them so the community and its members can flourish. Developing virtue is not self-serving because it does not merely serve the interests of the individual; it is crucial to the proper functioning of the community as well.

MacIntyre on the Inescapable Role of Reason and the Failure of Reason

Turning to MacIntyre's appraisal of Aristotle's ethics, we see an interesting observation he makes in the simple assertion that human actions embody principles.[37] Reason and rationality are so fundamental to ethics and human behavior in Aristotle's thought that a bodily movement not guided or inspired by some rational purpose cannot even be described as an action. Unlike most animals whose behavior is driven by instinct, every action pursued by humans is shaped by reason. It is a broad and even a controversial claim, but the distinction MacIntyre is making can be seen in the example of the difference between dancing and a seizure. The seizure, similar to a reflex, is a movement of the body, but it is not purposeful and therefore is not a human action as defined by Aristotle or MacIntyre.[38] Dancing, which is probably not the first thing that comes to my mind when thinking about reason and human behavior, is purposeful and is therefore an action. And the purposefulness of dancing can be attributed to rationality or reason in multiple ways. People dance for

---

36. This is a complex moral discussion that I cannot describe fully in this context. In short, one can make the argument that lying to save another person's life can be justified in the context of the natural law principle of forfeiture, where an unjust aggressor could forfeit the right to the truth due to the injustice of his or her aggression. Few would say an SS soldier should be told the truth when he asks for the location of Jewish people.

37. *SHE*, 73.

38. *SHE*, 72–73.

many reasons. It is enjoyable. It can serve as a mode of expression. It is a social activity that is enjoyed with other people. It can be rationally observed and even criticized from the perspective of aesthetics and beauty. Dancing is also an activity that matches the movement of the body to the rhythm of the music. Reason envelops a phenomenon as "un-rational" as dancing in a myriad of wonderful ways. In Aristotle's approach to moral philosophy, we cannot escape the crucial role of reason, and that role is more fundamental to human activity than we typically realize.

The idea of ethical failure brings us to another interesting observation on the part of MacIntyre, which is the idea that human failure is central to moral reasoning. We cannot come to a good understanding of ethics, either philosophically or in our own moral decisions, without coming to grips with our failure to reason well regarding ethical decisions. To put it in MacIntyre's words,

> For human desires are not straightforward drives to unambiguous goals in the way that biological instincts and drives are. Desires have to be given goals, and people have to be trained to reach them, and the point of having principles is in part to detect and diagnose failure in the attempt to reach them. Thus, fallibility is central to human nature and not peripheral to it. Hence the portrait of a being not liable to error could not be the portrait of a human being.[39]

If we want to improve our ethical behavior and our moral character, we must examine the mistakes we make. Often those mistakes are big and embarrassing, and that's the good news. That might sound strange, but it is through the pain and humiliation of failure that we learn most thoroughly. I wish I could learn through my successes or the mistakes of others as well as I can learn through my own mistakes. We all know, however, that it is through the pain of our own failures that we learn the most powerful and often the most important lessons in life. It is through the rational analysis of failure that we can understand where our true good lies.

MacIntyre's Criticism of Aristotle

The supreme good, the happy life for the Greeks, is the life of virtue. *Areté* ends in *eudaimonia*. It is a rather broad formulation, however. There are many virtues, and there are many forms of life in which virtue can play

---

39. *SHE*, 76.

the dominant role. Is there one form that outranks all the others? Aristotle says there is, and it is in this ultimate formulation of the greatest good that we finally hear MacIntyre criticize Aristotle's thought. MacIntyre notes that despite Aristotle's conceptual brilliance, he struggles to step outside the values of his own culture when examining specific virtues.[40] Some of the virtues examined by Aristotle are universal and some are culturally bound. Honesty, courage, and justice are virtues necessary for any society to function well. Yet some of the virtues proposed by Aristotle clearly demonstrate his bias for the Greek nobleman of his time. The height of moral virtue reaches its climax for Aristotle in the great-souled or magnanimous person, who is the moral agent that recognizes his or her virtue and claims great honors based on those great qualities. In MacIntyre's view, the great-souled person described by Aristotle is an appalling, narcissistic, and self-serving picture for the apex of virtue.[41]

MacIntyre is similarly critical of Aristotle's description of the highest *telos*, end, or goal of an individual human life, which is the contemplation of truth. Aristotle distinguished between moral and intellectual virtues. Since reason is the aspect of human nature that distinguishes the human person from all other things and provides humans a greater dignity than all other things, Aristotle sees the highest goal for an individual as contemplation and the intellectual habits associated with thinking. Despite Aristotle's differences with Plato, his views of the happiest and most fulfilling form of human life closely resembles the greatest good of contemplating the form of beauty that Plato describes in *The Symposium*. Aristotle says the happiest life belongs to one who engages in the metaphysical contemplation of the truth.[42] MacIntyre does not hesitate to criticize Aristotle's assertion stating, "The whole of human life reaches its highest point in the activity of a speculative philosopher with a reasonable income."[43] One would expect him to follow with a modern-day sarcastic "really?" MacIntyre may be a little harsh in his criticism, but it does seem odd that a thinker who is so perceptive regarding the richness of a life well lived that satisfies the human desires for knowledge, friendship, beauty, and even bodily pleasure can present such a narrow view of happiness at the height of his moral analysis. It is a view that excludes

40. SHE, 68.
41. SHE, 79.
42. Aristotle, *Nicomachean Ethics*, 1117a5–1117a7.
43. SHE, 83.

many people and yields the question, why would Aristotle reach such a conclusion?

The answer to this question is what we will consider next as we see MacIntyre pause in his analysis of history to capture the impact of Greek thought on ethics. MacIntyre will next provide a brief discussion on key differences between classical Greek morality and modern morality, as well as some of the cultural limitations of Greek ethics in which we will be able to see how the conclusions of Aristotle are both supported and limited by the Greek communities of his time. Following that discussion, we will transition out of the ethical history of ancient Greece and enter that of Rome and the coming epoch of Christian moral thought.

Leadership Reflection: Humility, Human Error, and Leadership

A chapter on Aristotle's moral thought is an odd place to focus on the importance of humility to leadership. Magnanimity, Aristotle's most exalted moral virtue, seems to be the antithesis of humility. Yet one of the greatest leaders in American history was President Abraham Lincoln, a leader who not only had a self-deprecating style, but seemed to be genuinely humble. A quick story about Lincoln demonstrates that humility. On November 13, 1861, seven months after the beginning of the US Civil War, Lincoln made a visit to the commanding officer of the Union forces, General George McClellan, at McClellan's quarters. Lincoln was there with Secretary of State William Seward and John Hay, Lincoln's private secretary. The general was still out for the day, so the three men waited an hour until he returned. Upon his return, the general's porter informed the general that the president was waiting in the quarters to meet with him. McClellan went straight to his bedroom, and a half hour later, the president was told that the general had gone to bed for the evening and was unavailable. Hay was indignant, but Lincoln told Hay it was "better at this time not to be making points of etiquette and personal dignity."[44] A remarkable reaction on the part of a leader, no less the president of the United States, to a rude subordinate. It is an illustration of Lincoln's remarkable humility. What the story does not show, however, is how humility makes a leader more effective. It did not seem to produce any positive results in that situation. Examining one of MacIntyre's key insights regarding Aristotle's thought

---

44. History.Com Editors, "This Day in History."

will help us see the importance of humility to leadership, and how it was one of the virtues that made Lincoln a truly great leader.

Earlier we noted MacIntyre's observation that human error and ethical failure are intrinsic to moral striving. His assertion that human desires are not straight forward drives aimed at unambiguous goals recognizes the complexity not only of ethics, but also of life in general. To be successful in life, we have to give our desires direction toward worthy goals and then train ourselves to achieve those goals in the right manner. Given the fact that we do fail (sometimes in spectacular fashion), fallibility and the lessons we gain from it are intrinsic to human wisdom. If this is the case in the context of individual people, how much more does it apply to leading organizations whose complexities are much greater than the concerns of a single individual? Not only do leaders need to navigate the multiple individual desires that are present in any group of people—desires that may be in direct competition with one another—leaders also need to make organizational goals clear so the different members of their team can understand and aim for those goals together. Given the fact that leaders will make mistakes pursuing organizational goals just as individuals make mistakes pursuing their own individual goals, developing the character traits to deal with human error effectively is crucial to successful leadership.

Chief among the character traits necessary to deal with human error and failure effectively is the virtue of humility. Humility is a complex virtue that has multiple benefits not only to leadership, but to living a flourishing life in general. To be brief, I will define humility simply as the ability to recognize one's own limitations, mistakes, and weaknesses. Even with that simple definition—and there are many other ways to describe humility—we can discern a number of benefits humility can offer leaders that will enhance their ability to lead.[45] First, leaders who are aware of their limitations are more willing to consult with followers and even seek out the ideas and advice of followers regarding the best way to complete the tasks of the organization. As technology continues its never-ending development, there are few fields where a leader can have

---

45. The writings of philosophers, theologians, and psychologists regarding the nature of humility and its value is broad and quite controversial. Although humility is generally neglected in Greek moral thought, it is treated with great depth and in a positive light by the Jewish and Christian ethical traditions. Modern and feminist philosophy have taken a more negative/critical view of humility, while contemporary psychology has generally described humility as a positive character trait. Cf. Owens et al., "Expressed Humility in Organizations," 1517–138 for a recent psychological evaluation of the relationship between humility and leadership.

all the technical knowledge and all the ideas necessary to accomplish an organization's mission effectively. No doubt leaders must be technically competent in their field, but if they do not have the humility to recognize that the sum of their followers' knowledge far outstrips that of the leader alone, they will limit their organization to their own ideas and put their team at a disadvantage relative to teams that have leaders who actively seek solutions and innovations from the members of their teams.

Second, mistakes will be made on the part of both leaders and followers. Leaders who have the humility not only to examine their own mistakes, but to do so in front of their team provide two advantages to an organization. The first advantage is the actual process in which a leader examines and corrects his or her mistakes and the organizational deficiencies that arise from those mistakes. Such an examination is necessary for any organization to operate effectively and overcome the weaknesses produced by leadership error. In addition, and even more important, by having the humility to admit mistakes and then correct those mistakes, the leader is authorizing subordinates to do the same. The leader is creating an environment where followers do not have to fear the imperfections of their human nature. In that context, followers are encouraged to examine their own errors without fear of punishment for making a mistake and are therefore empowered to correct those mistakes when they are identified.

Third, humility is a trait that will strengthen the relationship between leaders and their followers. There are risks in this aspect of humility. It must be displayed with other virtues of leadership to play the positive role of improving leader/follower relations. Humility cannot be mistaken for weakness or incompetence on the part of the leader. This is one of the problems history has shown us about General McClellan's disrespect and impertinence toward President Lincoln. McClellan had no respect for Lincoln's virtues as a leader. McClellan often referred to the president in his personal correspondence as the "gorilla."[46] This was not a failure on Lincoln's part. McClellan had a long-documented history of arrogance (his behavior toward Lincoln was only one manifestation of that arrogance) that prevented McClellan from seeing Lincoln's strengths as a leader. McClellan's mistake, however, can be made by others who are not arrogant, but mistake humility for weakness. The humility of a leader must be demonstrated on the foundation of strength, courage, and a baseline of technical competence if followers are to respect the humble leader.

---

46. Cf. Lehrman Institute, "War Effort."

Once that baseline is established, however, humility can play a key role in fostering the relationship between an accomplished leader and his or her followers. One of the pitfalls of accomplished leaders that can quickly lead to alienation from their followers is the arrogance that often results from repeated success that enables a person to achieve leadership responsibility in the first place (likely one of McClellan's downfalls). Unfortunately, it can be rare that successful people maintain their humility as they take on greater leadership responsibilities. The leaders who are able to maintain their humility despite their success have a distinct advantage over competent but arrogant leaders. Competent, humble leaders attract followers for two reasons. The first is they are able to relate to their followers. Followers are often impressed and even intimidated by remarkable and successful leaders. Humble leaders can reduce the distance between them and their followers by acknowledging their own imperfections. Humility humanizes larger than life leaders, thus making them people to whom their followers can relate and to whom their followers can become loyal. The second way humility links leaders to their followers is by making the strengths of leaders observable in a counterintuitive manner. Humble leaders are attractive to their followers because leadership humility enables followers to focus on the excellence of the leader's personal character. A humble leader will be less likely to cause envy and enmity among his or her followers, thus enabling those followers to appreciate the leader's positive qualities outside a lens of jealousy. A person who has humility despite the talent and achievements that typically lead to arrogance will likely be viewed with admiration and affection by his or her followers. A humble greatness is an extraordinary moral combination that will attract followers in any organizational environment. When one reads of the reaction of Lincoln's followers to the news of his assassination, we see the historical evidence concerning the power of humility to link a leader to his or her followers. At Lincoln's deathbed, the president's secretary of war and former political adversary, Edward Stanton, mourns his beloved leader with the grieving and long remembered sentiment, "Now he belongs to the ages."[47] It is a sentiment recognizing Lincoln's greatness, but made possible by the love and loyalty engendered by Lincoln's humility.

---

47. Goodwin, *Team of Rivals*, 743.

8

Classical Ethics, Modern Contrasts, Stoics, and Epicureans

BEFORE TURNING TO THE Greek and Roman schools of philosophy that follow Plato and Aristotle, MacIntyre takes a break from history and the thought of individual philosophers to highlight some of the most important aspects of Greek ethics up to this point. To do so, he offers a brief comparison of ancient ethics to modern moral thought. In some ways, the modern categories are more familiar to our way of thinking about ethics, so it is helpful to look at the ancients through the lens of modern philosophers. We also get a brief introduction to Immanuel Kant, a German philosopher and ethicist from the 1700s who is considered by many to be the most influential moral thinker of the modern period. Once MacIntyre makes that comparison, he dives back into the state of Greek ethics after Aristotle's writing and the impact of the changing political context on the moral concepts of the time. Huge empires, Greek and then Roman, displace the small city states in the Mediterranean basin, which has a significant impact on the way people see an ethical concept such as *areté*. It is in this setting that MacIntyre describes the thinking and contributions of the Stoics and Epicureans to the history of ethics. In following MacIntyre's description, we will cross the final historical territory between ancient classical thinking and the coming dominance of Christian thought that will stretch from its introduction into Roman society, through the empire's fall, and all the way up to the high middles ages in the thirteenth and fourteenth centuries.

Contrasts Between Ancient Greek and Modern Ethics

One of the questions that becomes central to Greek moral thinking as the result of Aristotle's ethics is "What am I to do if I am to fare well?" As we roll along with Aristotle's thought, it seems like a perfectly natural question to ask. Yet, as MacIntyre observes, that formulation differs significantly from the dominant schools of modern morality. Unlike Aristotle, modern ethics asks, "What should I do if I am to do what is right?"[1] Doing right and faring well, which go together in Aristotle's view of morality, are independent in the thought of modern authors such as H. A. Prichard and Immanuel Kant. Modern moral thinkers defend a view of ethics in which morality cannot have justifications external to itself. MacIntyre points out Prichard's assertion that Plato makes a fatal error in trying to show that it is in a person's interest to pursue justice. If we do justice because it is in our interest, according to Prichard and others, we do not have the correct motivation to do justice and are therefore not acting in a morally correct manner.[2] If a person does not do what is right for its own sake and is pursuing self-interest, then the person's intent is not right, the right intent being to choose justice for its own sake whether it benefits the person or not. MacIntyre observes that what is implied by Prichard in making this distinction is as follows: what is in our interest is logically independent of what is just and right for us to do.[3] This is in contrast to the Greeks (including Plato and Aristotle) where Greek moral considerations are framed by linking objects of desire with moral goals. Although Plato and Aristotle struggle to make clear the relationship between doing well and faring well, they presume an interdependence between those two things.[4] For them, the happy life is bound up with moral concerns, with moral excellence. A virtuous life is desirable because it produces a happy life. Given that difference MacIntyre stops at this point and asks "whether it is modern ethics which is clarifying a valid distinction that the Greek moral vocabulary fails to observe or Greek ethics which is refusing to make a false and confusing distinction?"[5] It is in the context of this distinction that MacIntyre makes two points. The first is the fact that we can see the

---

1. *SHE*, 84.
2. *SHE*, 84–85. Cf. Prichard, "Does Moral Philosophy Rest on a Mistake," 21–37, as cited by MacIntyre.
3. *SHE*, 85.
4. *SHE*, 85.
5. *SHE*, 85.

historical transition of moral concepts in this difference. MacIntyre uses the idea of duty to illustrate the point. Second, despite being a product of schools whose thinking was dominated by the likes of Kant and Prichard, MacIntyre sides with the Greek way of thinking as a better way to approach ethics. Let's take a look at both aspects of his argument.

Contrasting Views of Duty as a Concept

There are two salient differences between the Greeks and modern thinkers in MacIntyre's comparison. The first, as I've already noted, is the role that the idea of desire plays in both schools of thought. The second is the social context (another of MacIntyre's consistent themes) in which ethics is viewed by the ancient and modern schools of thought. For the Greeks, ethical thinking and evaluation happens in the context of a person's role within society. Whether a person is a farmer, a soldier, a doctor, or a police officer has great significance for the evaluation of that person's choices and character. A modern thinker like Immanuel Kant (b. 1724) posits a different societal context for the evaluation of morality. Kant posits a context of any and all human societies (which we will see is similar to the Stoic and Epicurean approaches to ethics) because Kant is trying to establish an objective system of morality in which it is our role as a person, our role as a member of the human race, that provides the context in which moral evaluations can be made. MacIntyre then turns to the moral category of duty to see how these two differences impact the understanding of that term. When philosophers detach a person from her or his role but still leave the person with a concept of duty, the concept inevitably changes from what it was when it was viewed in the context of a role such as a mother or a fireman.[6] The difference in the approach to desire also has an impact on duty as a concept. Recalling Prichard's point, modern notions of duty are not based on what the Greeks call desire and Kant calls inclination. Inclination or desire is often opposed to what is the morally correct action to take in the ancient and modern schools. For the moderns, however, even when inclination aligns with the right moral action, it is merely a coincidence because desire and morality are independent of one another in modern ethics. For Kant, it is only when an action is motivated by duty—that is, when it is motivated by the adherence to

---

6. *SHE*, 93.

moral law—is it considered a moral decision at all.[7] Kant and his followers assert that choices based on inclination have no moral value and are therefore not moral choices.

MacIntyre contends that this new context in which to evaluate moral duty has an impact on how a duty is understood. We cannot make sense of duty in modern ethics by attaching it to other ordinary human actions because other ordinary actions are linked to our desire and purpose for choosing, considerations excluded from moral evaluation by Kantian philosophers.[8] The pursuit of duty becomes a realm unconnected to other human behavior, and thus we have a strong distinction between practical choices and moral choices.[9] Moral choices in the modern sense are often seen as very impractical, while morality in the ancient Greek sense is literally the science of practical thinking. A practical choice *is* a moral choice for a thinker like Aristotle. As a result, MacIntyre asserts that the concept of duty disconnected from other aspects of human behavior is weakened because it is less clear.[10] For example, actions that are clear to a person due to her skill and role as a doctor are less clear to an individual as a person. The doctor has a duty to stop and help an accident victim on a highway if first responders have yet to arrive; that duty is less clear to a person who has neither the skill nor the responsibility of the doctor. Why should I stop to help if I do not have the skill to help and society does not expect me to help? Society may have some expectation for a person to assist in this circumstance, but it has less force and clarity than the duty understood based on a doctor's role in the community. MacIntyre traces the transformation of duty as a moral concept starting from the Greek context in which it is understood as fulfilling a role that can be evaluated in terms of normal human desires. Next, duty becomes something to be done no matter what you may privately desire. Finally, there is a Kantian duty in which the idea of duty is divorced from desire altogether. In this last stage, the motivation for duty becomes unintelligible compared to other desires, aims, and purposes. Kant provides an abstract reason for why one should do her or his duty, which is out of reverence for moral principles.[11] Others simply say that a person should do one's duty for no

---

7. Kant, *Groundwork of the Metaphysics of Morals*, 44.

8. *SHE*, 86.

9. Cf. Kant, *Metaphysics of Morals*, 3 for his assertion that a practical rule can never be considered a moral law.

10. *SHE*, 86, 94.

11. Kant, *Metaphysics of Morals*, 11.

other reason than they should or they ought to do it.[12] For example, in contemporary military culture, which has a strong focus on duty, the reason to do one's duty is because it is the right thing to do. And it is here where MacIntyre sides with the ancient Greeks, saying that duty in the context of a specific role and linked to desire is much clearer than the modern version because duty in this sense is still connected to the behavior expected in the person's societal role.[13] To do something because it is the right thing to do fails to provide a compelling reason for fulfilling a duty. The duty of a man as a father is clear and often compelling to the person playing the role of a father. The duty of a person, on the other hand, is rather opaque in comparison and will lack force when pitted against other human desires. I may have a duty to tell the truth because it's the right thing to do, but am I really going to do that when telling the truth hurts a loved one or prevents me from attaining something I really want? Most of us know the answer to that question.

Questions of Relativism and Moral Principles Guiding Human Societies

This discrepancy between ancient and modern ethics is not all bad in MacIntyre's view, and even if the modern thinkers end up muddying the waters regarding duty, we can see the roots of that struggle arise from problems within the thought of Plato and Aristotle. MacIntyre notes that linking duty to the human person outside the context of a single society rather than linking it to the role a person plays in one society clarifies both risks and opportunities for the understanding of ethics.[14] One risk in the ancient approach lies in the close connection of societal roles to moral evaluations. If the evaluations we make about our choices depend upon the rules for evaluating those roles in a specific society, does that mean we are doomed to the kind of relativism that thinkers like Socrates, Plato, Aristotle, and later modern thinkers like Kant were anxious to overcome?[15] Does tying moral evaluation to a specific social structure force us back into the position of the Sophists, where we can make no claim that is true about all people, but only people in specific times and places?

12. *SHE*, 86.
13. *SHE*, 94.
14. *SHE*, 95.
15. *SHE*, 95.

MacIntyre's response to the question is worrisome given his penchant for taking on complex issues. He says it is complicated. Part of the answer can be seen in the implications of Aristotle's thought. Some features of human behavior are the same in all societies, and on this basis, one can claim that there are moral principles that will be operative in any human community. Friendliness, truthfulness, courage, and justice are always valued.[16] They are attributes necessary for a community of individuals to function well together. Yet despite the fact that these attributes are always present, they can be understood and practiced in extraordinarily different manners depending on the culture and history of specific communities. Ideals can look different in different communities and can be applied in a wide variety of ways. For example, the manner in which parents educate and train their children varies to an extraordinary extent across cultures, but the idea that it is the responsibility of a parent to prepare a child for adulthood is also extraordinary in its consistency across the same broad range of cultures and practices.[17] The diversity of moral practices does not preclude the existence of moral principles that transcend individual societies. So, the answer to the question is more of a both/and answer, rather than an either/or answer. The application of moral principles differs vastly across time and location. The principles themselves, however, can be quite consistent.

As MacIntyre notes, some moral principles transcend individual communities and societies because they are essential for human cooperation. MacIntyre also asserts that these principles are valuable because they enable more purposes and goals than would otherwise be possible if the principles are not valued. For example, lying makes clear the importance of truth telling as a norm for any community. This is the case because lying presupposes most people tell the truth. A liar cannot achieve the goal of misleading the audience if the audience does not presume the liar is telling the truth.[18] The norm of truth telling enables people to both lie and tell the truth successfully, where the absence of truth telling would cripple a community due to the absence of trust produced by incessant deception. And the fact that truth telling is valued by all societies does

---

16. *SHE*, 95.

17. Cf. Bernstein, "Parenting Around the World," for a discussion on the differences in child-rearing between collectivist and individualist cultures.

18. *SHE*, 96.

not preclude diversity in the way honesty is understood and practiced in a particular community.[19]

Further, a norm for truth telling does not guide a person in the decision to tell the truth or to lie in a specific situation. Telling the truth is generally encouraged, but there are situations, such as being a spy in Nazi Germany, where lying is not only permissible but is a moral imperative. MacIntyre asserts that both Plato and Aristotle make a mistake in this context that has an impact on later ethicists. Plato and Aristotle assume that people draw practical guidance from the necessary framework of norms that structure the morality of a society. In making this assumption, they mistake the Greek social structures of their time to be the universal social structure for humans in general. This leads later philosophers to address moral concerns as if they are independent of social structures. Ethics becomes a field separated from and unrelated to other aspects of human life, such as politics.[20] The modern notion of the person outside a social context is related to the failure of classical thinkers to recognize the limitations of their own cultural context.[21]

Good as an Idea at the Intersection of Desire and Society

Before moving back to MacIntyre's historical account, it is important to address one more insight he has with regard to Greek ethics, which concerns the familiar themes of good as an object of desire and the further role that a society can take in shaping that idea. Greek moral terms can be understood in relation to the idea of desire. MacIntyre asserts that Greek moral evaluations grade our actions in the context of desire. The goal desired by a person is the criteria that determines the choices a person should make. Combining that idea with the fact that not all desires are good, one can then ask the further question of which desires should serve as the criteria for judgment? To answer this question, we need not only to know what we should desire now, but what in the long run we should want to desire.[22] The attempt to figure out what we ought to desire seems out of step with modern moral thought where desires are not a topic for ethical examination. Since they are not examined, they are presumed to

---

19. *SHE*, 96.
20. *SHE*, 97.
21. *SHE*, 97.
22. *SHE*, 87.

be static. Yet Aristotle's thought on the nature of desire in relationship to choice and habit seems to be hitting on something important and accurate. The reality is humans can shape their desires through choice and habit. If that is the case, then a crucial moral question becomes, what desires should a person encourage and what desires should be discouraged?

The answer to such a question seems to be based on more than just personal preference. Both Plato and Aristotle assert that some objects of desire are objectively better than others, and the use of the term objectively implies an impersonal criterion that originates from a source other than the tastes of an individual person. This goes back to the question of what we mean by the term "good." Good can express my personal approval of an object or an action, but it typically means something more than just my own preference. It expresses what should be chosen on the basis of criteria that govern behavior in a specific situation. MacIntyre describes how such criteria are provided by the social practices usually expressed through the rules of a community.[23] We can again turn to sports to illustrate his point.[24] The rules of a sport provide the context in which we can say a player or a piece of equipment is good. For example, a good wrestler is strong, fit, quick, has great endurance, and can execute wrestling moves with power and precision. All of these features enable an athlete to successfully complete the tasks of wrestling within the rules that govern the sport. Thus, if I say that a wrestler is good, I am saying more than I approve of his wrestling. I am saying that the wrestler can perform the functions of the sport well or better than others. I am using objective criteria, criteria that apply to more than one person or more than the tastes of one individual. They are criteria that other people have agreed upon to determine what makes a good wrestler. And that evaluation is based on the rules and practices of the sport of wrestling established by a community of wrestlers. The Greek approach to ethics makes the same argument with regard to being a good person in the context of the Greek city-state.[25] The rules and practices of the *polis* determine what it means to be a good human person in that community. This is not to say that communities can define ethics completely and are infallible in their definitions. It is to say, however, that there are criteria to determine what

---

23. Cf. *SHE*, 88–90 for MacIntyre's description of how criteria for understanding the term good often derive from the rules and practices of a community.

24. Cf. *SHE*, where MacIntyre uses cricket and football to illustrate his point. I use the American form of wrestling to convey the point.

25. *SHE*, 89–91.

is good that are offered to the individual members of a community that are impersonal and not chosen by the individual.[26] The criteria are given to the members of the community who can understand them, apply them, and even adapt them to unanticipated situations. The word good, then, implies individual preference, and it implies criteria for judgment provided to the individual by her or his community. In addition, even though these impersonal norms are objective—that is, they transcend the judgment of the individual—that does not mean the societal criteria governing the concept of what is good is unchanging. As societies change, so will the understanding of what is good. In making that observation we return us to a fundamental premise of MacIntyre's analysis, which is the idea that moral concepts, such as the understanding of what is good, change over time. Such ideas have a history, and that history is important to understanding these ideas.

Back to History: Stoic and Epicurean Thought in the Impersonal Empire

At this point, we can return to MacIntyre's historical analysis. In doing so we see that change is afoot in the Greek world after Aristotle, and the thinking of Aristotle may have played a role in some of those changes.[27] With the rise of Aristotle's pupil, Alexander the Great, the political structures of Greek antiquity begin to shift from the *polis*, the small city-states that comprised the Greek world of Plato and Aristotle's time, to the great empires that would succeed them. Within this movement from the self-government of small communities to the distant governments of powerful empires, Aristotle's view of the contemplative life can be seen as having some impact. In making the contemplative life the kind of life to which the elite should aspire, Aristotle provides a rationale for removing them from governing the *polis*. The empire of Macedon, established by Phillip and expanded by Alexander, has no need for a governing elite. Governing is for the king, and the king is quite content to let the elite play the role of contemplative, private citizens.

MacIntyre asserts that the decline of the Greek city-state and the rise of empires had an enormous impact on the moral thought of the time. The new political order limited the moral possibilities of the elite.

26. *SHE*, 88.
27. *SHE*, 99.

Gone were the days when moral and political calculations were a daily experience for the aristocracy governing the city-states. In their place was a much-diminished context for moral and political striving. Rather than governing themselves, the elite were reduced to being private citizens bereft of political power, their fortunes determined by a distant powerful government.[28] The elite have meager responsibilities and therefore have meager opportunity for moral development. The central human experience in this context of powerlessness is anxiety, insecurity, and lack of hope. This is true not just of slaves and the lower classes, but the upper classes as well.[29] Little stands between the individual and outside forces that can cause profound suffering and even death.

The new political environment has an impact on the moral thinking of citizens affected by these changes. MacIntyre asserts that the conceptual relationship between happiness as acquiring objects of desire that are truly good for the person through the virtues that make that acquisition possible has changed in this new environment. Plato and Aristotle presumed that *areté* and *eudaimonia*, virtue and happiness, were connected. Their understanding of that connection was always under development; they continually examined it and tried to articulate the nature of that relationship. They did not, however, question that the connection existed, for in their way of thinking, if virtue did not promote happiness, there was no reason to be virtuous. In their view there would be no point to being morally excellent, to having morally excellent habits, if that excellence did not lead you to achieving your goals.[30] Happiness for them is the achievement of desires that are truly good for the person, and virtue or *areté* is the means to achieving that end. The generation of thinkers living in the individual powerlessness and anxiety of the great empires, however, did not see it that way. For them happiness cannot consist in the achievement of desire, and therefore virtue is detached from goal achievement. This is the case because the achievement of desires in the context of powerlessness may literally become impossible. You may desire to be married, but if your spouse is enslaved or killed, two possibilities a married person in an empire would have little control over, that desire would turn to grief rather than happiness. Virtue for these thinkers ends up consisting of the absence of desire, and virtue itself becomes sufficient to make someone happy. The person who is virtuous in

28. *SHE*, 99–100.
29. *SHE*, 102.
30. *SHE*, 102.

the sense of desiring nothing has nothing to worry about because there is nothing for the person to lose that is of value to him or her. The person without desire is able to bear even slavery without injury. Virtue in this context is seen as self-sufficiency. The virtuous person has detached himself or herself from desire, which enables the person to avoid disappointment over desire left unsatisfied and promotes independence from circumstance when life deals you a very bad hand.[31] These are precisely the concerns and dynamics that shape two of the more influential schools of ethics from this time period: Stoicism and Epicureanism. Before looking at those two schools, however, MacIntyre provides further analysis regarding virtue and happiness that helps us to see how the changing political environment changed the understanding of those ideas. It is an analysis that can enrich our contemporary views on the relationship between virtue and happiness as well.

The Impact of Good and Bad Societies on Virtue and Happiness

Building on the thought of Plato and Aristotle, MacIntyre provides a more precise account concerning the relationship between virtue, happiness, and desire. He does this by describing how different types of societies—that is, good and bad societies—impact the understanding of morality. A good society is one where it is relatively easy to follow the rules and achieve the goals people in that society want to achieve. The opposite of this is a society where there is a set of traditional rules, but rule following and the virtues that enable rule following do not lead to success.[32] In the words of a modern theorist, John Rawls (b. 1921), a just society will provide the rewards promised for living up to its values and rules.[33] For example, in contemporary America, many think that diligence, conscientiousness, and perseverance should eventually pay off in achieving a decent standard of living no matter a person's gender or race. If those attributes did not lead to success, it would reflect poorly upon the justice of the society. MacIntyre asserts that life in a bad society will alter the conceptual relationship between happiness as the satisfaction of

---

31. *SHE*, 102.
32. *SHE*, 103.
33. Rawls, *Theory of Justice*, 121.

desire and virtue. To understand how this is the case, we must look at the relationship between rules and goals.[34]

MacIntyre asserts that human communal life cannot really exist without certain rules. Those rules concern truth telling, promise-keeping, and basic fairness or justice.[35] These rules tell us what not to do to be a good member of society, but they do not tell us what to do in a positive sense. Rules provide norms that dictate how our actions should conform, but they do not tell us which actions to perform.[36] Rules are crucial, however, in providing an environment where goals can be effectively pursued. Goals, on the other hand, do tell us what actions to perform. It is the end, our goal, that provides the target at which we aim with our actions. Our actions will be determined by the goal we are trying to achieve. In this context, we can see that our virtues empower us to choose actions that fall within society's rules.[37] Virtues enable us to perform our actions in a particular way. Virtue-based rule following enables us to achieve our goals for two reasons. Good habits will guide our actions to conform to the rules of our community, and the community will then approve of and sanction our success. Virtues also enable us to see what choices need to be made to actually pursue our goals successfully. Virtues, then, are fundamental to happiness because they support our ability to achieve our goals in those two ways. Virtue and happiness are not identical, but in the context of the Greek approach to ethics, they are clearly related to one another.

This is the background to the changes in the understanding of virtue and desires in the centuries ruled by the great empires, both Greek and Roman. The empires were not societies in which following the rules enabled the successful achievement of goals. Satisfaction of desire was often prevented by external circumstances over which the individual person had no control. Since goal achievement is impossible for many in this situation, happiness is located solely in what the individual can control, which are his or her virtues. And in one sense, such a move is in line with the thought of Plato and Aristotle, who recognized that once a person becomes habituated to good action, that person can desire to do that action and derive significant satisfaction from simply exercising excellent

---

34. *SHE*, 103.
35. *SHE*, 103.
36. *SHE*, 103.
37. *SHE*, 104.

habits and being a virtuous person.³⁸ The satisfaction provided by virtue is the one remaining satisfaction available to the citizen of the empire, and it becomes the sole focus of desire during this time period. To desire anything outside of virtue is to court extreme unhappiness because cultivating desire for things that can be taken away from you will inevitably bring unhappiness. In the big empires, unless you are the emperor, you will eventually be deprived of the things you hold dear.

The Ethics of Apathy and Tranquility: Stoics and Epicureans

The founders of the Stoic and Epicurean schools of thought, Zeno and Epicurus, were contemporaries, being young men when Aristotle died in 322 BCE. Zeno (b. 334 BCE) was from the Greek island of Cyprus, and Epicurus (b. 341 BCE) was born on the Greek island of Samos. Both made their way to Athens to study and teach later in their careers, but there is no indication that they ever met one another. Typically, their two schools of philosophy are viewed as having little in common. Where the Stoics discouraged people from fostering desire for any external good, Epicureanism is known as a type of hedonism where pleasure is to be desired since it is considered the highest good. Despite their differences, both schools flourished after the deaths of their founders up to and through the time of the Roman Empire. MacIntyre notes that despite significantly different approaches to the world and ethics, the two schools produce practical decisions that are quite similar and foster attitudes that help people endure the difficulties of living as subjects in an empire.³⁹ In the following discussion we will first look at Stoic thought, examine the thought of Epicurus and his followers, and then make a comparison between the two schools.

MacIntyre tells us that Stoic ethics cannot be separated from the Stoic understanding of the universe. The Stoics see the universe as both material and divine. The *logos* (the Greek word for reason) is the divine law that governs the cosmos. For the Stoics, all the operations of the things that populate the universe manifest reason in their operations. Reason is the divine principle ruling all activity, including the moral activity of humans. The Stoics, like later Christian thinkers, believe that the

---

38. Cf. Aristotle, *Nicomachean Ethics*, 1099a7–1099a20, for Aristotle's description of how the exercise of the virtues is in itself pleasurable and therefore desirable to people who desire to be noble.

39. *SHE*, 107.

physical universe and morality come from the same divine source.[40] The growth of an acorn into an oak tree, the hunting techniques of a lion, and even the motions of the stars are all governed by reason or the *logos*. The same is true of humans and human choices, which makes the Stoics strict determinists. They believe everything must happen the way it does happen, including human actions and choices. The only thing that escapes the all-encompassing power of the *logos* is internal human attitudes. Despite their determinism, Stoics still consider the human person to be free, and that freedom consists in the human ability to intellectually assent or dissent from the *logos*.[41] Assent to the logos enables a person to order his or her moral character according to reason and thus become a virtuous person, a person of *areté*. It is this aspect of Stoic thinking that joins the Stoics to the classical thinkers that precede them. The virtuous person is the person whose choices are guided by reason. If one agrees with the *logos*, one will be virtuous and happy. If one disagrees, if one does not choose in accordance with reason or the *logos*, that person will not be virtuous and will relegate himself or herself to unhappiness.

In the context of their cosmology, MacIntyre asserts that the Stoics focus on the importance of virtue to the pursuit of a good life, like Plato and Aristotle before them. They also observe the traditional cardinal virtues of practical wisdom, justice, courage, and temperance (or self-control) expounded by their predecessors. Where the Stoics differ from Plato and Aristotle is their approach to desire. For the Stoic, the person of virtue should and is able to cultivate a passionless absence of desire and disregard of pleasure and pain because such desires or aversions are contrary to reason. Desires and aversions stoke a person's emotions when making decisions, which the Stoics see as the antithesis of rational or virtuous decision making. The Stoic disregards the attraction of external goods and is thus protected from their loss.[42] The sage, the name Stoics give to a person who reaches the height of virtue, cultivates apathy for all external goods. By liberating himself or herself from the desire for any external or material good, the sage becomes truly independent or free. It is through freedom from desire of all types that the sage achieves peace of mind. Here we see the impact of the societal context MacIntyre described earlier. The Stoics assert that one should not desire or become

40. *SHE*, 106.
41. *SHE*, 105.
42. *SHE*, 106–7.

inordinately attached to anything else, even a spouse, because you will of necessity lose it. And when you do lose the thing you are attached to, you will be unhappy. Without attachments you are not in danger of losing anything. As a result, you achieve peace of mind.[43] There is nothing to be anxious about if you have nothing to lose.

MacIntyre tells us that the Epicureans, unlike the Stoics, have no theological commitments regarding the nature of the universe. The cosmos and natural phenomena have a material origin rather than a divine one. For Epicureans, morality is concerned with the pursuit of pleasure.[44] Virtue for them is the art of pleasure. Epicurus argues, however, that many pleasures bring pain, and thus the avoidance of pain is a greater good than enjoying pleasure. In addition, Epicurus sees moderation in external goods as the only way to prevent pain at their loss. He also asserts that freedom from intense desire is a condition for the ability to appreciate pleasure.[45] While the Epicurean focus on pleasure as the greatest good is certainly a departure from a thinker like Aristotle, there is much that keeps Epicureanism within the main traditions of Greek moral thought. The Epicurean caution against growth in desire harkens back to Socrates's argument against the Sophists where he maintains that pursuit of desires will lead to their increase and subsequent unhappiness because limitless desire cannot be satisfied. In addition, the moderation of the Epicureans has echoes of Aristotle's assertion that moderation is a key aspect of morally excellent habits. Aristotle affirms that excellence lies at a mean between extremes (for example, courage is a mean between cowardliness and recklessness), and that current of thought flows into the Epicurean concern for moderation. In addition, the Epicureans assert the same cardinal virtues as the rest of the Greek moral tradition.[46] As a result, the hedonism or pursuit of pleasure advocated by Epicurus holds much more in common with the Greek moral tradition than the excesses associated with contemporary hedonism.

Given the significant differences between the two schools, we might question the commonalities MacIntyre sees in them. MacIntyre claims that although Stoics and Epicureans espouse different moral paths, the goal of the moral life in each school is remarkably similar. The Stoics advocate developing apathy so as to achieve peace of mind in a world

---

43. *SHE*, 107.
44. *SHE*, 107.
45. *SHE*, 107.
46. *SHE*, 107.

where desires are unlikely to be satisfied. The goal of the moral life for the Epicureans is achieving tranquility through the development of virtue and the avoidance of pain. Thus, a key goal for both schools is the avoidance of pain.[47] The concern for the avoidance of pain can be seen in the emphasis both philosophies place on the pain of loss. The Stoics assert that you must detach yourself from desire for things so that you are not unhappy when you lose them. The Epicureans similarly contend that you should not have immoderate desire for things lest you feel the pain of their loss. Fear of loss driven by a societal context where the individual is powerless shapes both approaches to morality, and the schools end up thriving because they offer a way to console a person who has no other way to confront the cruelties of life.[48]

Leadership Reflection: Leadership and the Opportunity for Moral Development

MacIntyre observes that the establishment of the great empires had a significant effect on the moral development of the aristocrats and elites of that time period. Gone were the days when it was their responsibility to order and govern their communities in their role as members of the *polis*. The retreat of their civic responsibilities affected not only their moral thinking, as MacIntyre explains, it also affected the development of their moral character. Without the responsibility to do the morally challenging activities necessary to govern well, the citizens who could have and would have led the Greek city-states no longer had the ability to develop the morally excellent habits that result from pursuing those challenging actions. The requirement for citizens to have the courage to speak publicly in the legislature no longer existed. The development of integrity for leaders faced with temptation offered by the laurels of their office was no longer a possibility. The citizen statesmen no longer needed the will and fortitude to confront foreign adversaries because that role had been taken by the emperor.

MacIntyre's observation that the development of moral excellence is based on shouldering great responsibility can be seen in the thinking of ancient authors such as Aristotle and Cicero (b. 106 BCE). Aristotle described magnanimity, or greatness of soul, as the height of the moral

47. *SHE*, 108.
48. *SHE*, 108.

virtues.[49] Magnanimity was the virtue that crowned all the other virtues and made them better. The magnanimous person, in Aristotle's view, was a truly virtuous person who was able to recognize his or her virtue, and on the basis of that self-knowledge, undertook great tasks in service to the *polis*.[50] Magnanimity, as the source of ambition to take on great tasks, becomes the driver of developing further virtues because great tasks serve to challenge and develop those who undertake those challenges. Cicero furthered Aristotle's analysis as Roman democracy was failing in the first century BCE in his description of glory. Cicero believed that great people concerned themselves with the political community.[51] Leaders who aspired to great service in politics were honored because public service was the best venue to display greatness of spirit. Such service provided both the stage and the opportunity to display the character traits most worthy of honor. Public debates, whether in court or the Roman Senate, were the forums where a civic official could demonstrate the eloquence and intellect necessary to win the admiration of fellow citizens.[52] The challenge of public leadership also offered risk of sacrifice, which further contributed to the glory of the Roman Statesmen. It was in risking one's own welfare for the benefit of other citizens that the statesman could win the most renown.[53] The greatest glory in the Roman Republic was reserved for leaders who sacrificed for their country and therefore served that country well.

The insights of MacIntyre and our ancient authors are directly applicable to leadership. As anyone who has experienced the responsibilities of leadership can tell you, living up to those responsibilities is demanding. Leadership is often exercised in complex and dynamic environments that demand an array of excellent moral characteristics. Excellent leaders must be courageous in taking risks and prudent when a situation calls for caution. They must be demanding of their subordinates and compassionate with them at the same time. Leaders need to have a native confidence in their own talents and the humility to recognize their weaknesses and limitations. They must be able to inspire large groups while simultaneously developing authentic relationships with individual followers. And

---

49. Cf. Aristotle, *Nicomachean Ethics*, Book IV, chapter 3 for Aristotle's description of the magnanimous person.
50. Aristotle, *Nicomachean Ethics*, 1124b24–25.
51. Cicero, *On Duties*, 2.46.
52. Cicero, *On Duties*, 2.49.
53. Cicero, *On Duties*, 1.83.

the list of significant and often competing character traits can go on and on. How can one hope to have all the qualities necessary to exercise the authority of leadership well?

The good news is that in a virtue-based approach to ethics and leadership excellence is based on practice. One can develop the virtues necessary to excellent leadership through practice and the development of excellent moral habits. In that context, the path to becoming a capable leader is to get in a leadership position as soon as you can. With the practice made possible by the actual responsibilities of leadership, you can develop the traits necessary to be an excellent leader. The bad news is you will likely fail as an inexperienced leader. And not only will you fail, that failure will likely be public. To be a leader is to work on stage in front of your followers. There is no avoiding the fact that a leader will make mistakes, and those mistakes will be known by others. The one silver lining is that few environments are better for learning and learning quickly. We learn best from our mistakes, especially when we are embarrassed by them. Unfortunately, the risk of public failure discourages many from pursuing leadership responsibility in the first place. Yet, as Aristotle's notion of magnanimity makes clear, by taking on these responsibilities, leaders will improve and benefit from the moral development offered by leadership responsibility.

A last observation about the power of leadership to shape moral character is that character formation is not necessarily positive. In making moral choices and learning under pressure from those choices, leaders will create moral habits. They will create their moral character, and that character can be good or bad. The challenge is to make sure leaders are building truly good character traits, and it is a significant challenge. All too many leaders fail to make the choices that will yield morally good character. This is the case because leadership, and life in general, does not always reward morally good actions with good results for the leader. Immediate consequences, important as they may be, can distract leaders from their focus on developing the virtues necessary to serve and lead their communities well in the long run. Too often doing the right thing is the most difficult option available to a leader. For example, by telling the truth in difficult situations, leaders might cause great harm to themselves or to the people they care about. Yet the leader who does not adhere to high moral standards, whether the motivations are self-serving or altruistic, over time will develop a corrupt moral character. We all know the saying, "The road to hell is paved with good intentions." Hell, in this case, is becoming a leader with bad moral habits, becoming a person of vice, becoming a leader with a vicious moral character.

Withstanding temptation and the pressure to make the bad moral choices that lead to corrupt character is therefore crucial, and not only to the leader but also to the community the leader serves. Bad habits such as dishonesty or a lack of integrity will not always catch up with a leader, but given the repeated nature of habits and our long lives, they are likely to harm a leader over any significant period of time. And the ramifications for the community can be even more serious. Not only will organizations or communities be unlikely to escape the problems of corrupt leaders, corruption on the part of one leader can spread to the corruption of both peers and followers. Organizations and societies with bad moral cultures yield horrible environments for their individual members and far too often end in catastrophes that hurt the vulnerable members of a community the most. One of life's great injustices is the fact that corrupt leaders often escape the worst effects of their corruption, while people wholly innocent of that corruption can be devastated by it. The importance of leaders developing the right moral habits as a result of their leadership experience cannot be overstated. Those habits are crucial not only to their own happiness and success, but they are of even greater importance to the life of the communities for which leaders are responsible.

9

Christian Morality as the Bridge Between Ancient and Medieval Ethics

MacIntyre's study of the historical period dominated by Christian moral thought, which is a period of nine hundred years beginning with the end of the Roman Empire (roughly 400 CE) and going through to the thinking of William of Ockham (b. 1287), seems quite brief (to put it mildly) compared to his treatment of single authors such as Plato and Aristotle. MacIntyre explains at the end of his chapter on Christian morality that he was faced with the choice of being overwhelmed by the encyclopedic breadth of Christian medieval ethics or treating Christian ethics in a marginal fashion. He chose to keep it at the margins, not because this was a better approach, but rather it was more manageable for the goal he was pursuing with his book.[1] An interesting point to consider as well is the fact that MacIntyre was writing as an atheist when he authored his history of ethics, although he did become a Christian convert some fifteen years after writing the book. Given that background and reading his history, there is no doubt that MacIntyre was familiar with the contours of Christian moral thought, but Christianity was likely not the significant concern that it would become for his later philosophy.

As something of an outsider commenting on Christian moral thought, MacIntyre begins his account by making observations about Christianity in general and about Christian moral thought in particular that seem to be at odds with the dogmatism and rigidity sometimes

1. *SHE*, 120.

associated with Christian morality. MacIntyre observes that religions capable of outliving and transcending individual societies often exhibit sets of belief and behaviors that are relatively independent of specific cultures. As a result, such religions exhibit a significant degree of flexibility regarding the behavior built into the practices of their community. Those religions have an ability to adapt to the wide diversity of moral standards that have existed throughout the world and throughout history.[2] The long history of Christianity and the many societies within which Christian moral thought has played a significant role indicates such an adaptability. Given this adaptability, MacIntyre sees a primary challenge in approaching Christian moral thought as actually discovering what it is and what ideas constitute Christian ethics.[3] Since moral practice can vary widely, even across cultures or societies that are considered Christian, MacIntyre looks to identify general themes in Christian moral thought that can be found in all Christian moral outlooks. Following his identification of these themes, he evaluates the moral thought of three Christian thinkers, two of whom are well known, St. Augustine and St. Thomas Aquinas, and one who is relatively obscure, William of Ockham. By examining the ethics of these three men, he describes some of the most important turning points for Christian ethics across this nine-hundred-year period.

The Unity of Christian Thought That Sets the Stage for Christian Ethics

In approaching the themes that provide a consistent context for Christian moral thought, MacIntyre begins by noting that it is easy to miss the unity of the Bible given the diversity of authors, culture, types of literature, style, language, and purposes of its many books. The one thing that unites this extreme variety in the Bible in MacIntyre's view is God. Without God, the Bible has little unity, but with the idea of God, it is quite united.[4] This unity flows into the themes MacIntyre identifies as central to Christian moral thought. He summarizes those themes succinctly. For Christians, God is the father of all men and women. God (like many fathers) commands obedience. Humans should obey God because God knows what is best for them, and obeying him is best. If humans disobey

---

2. *SHE*, 110–11.
3. *SHE*, 111.
4. *SHE*, 110.

God, they become estranged from him. Having become estranged from God, they need to know how to reconcile themselves to God so that they can return to an authentic relationship with God.[5]

The ethical construct that emerges out of these themes and the Jewish law of the Old Testament is a morality based on obedience to God's commands. In that context, an immediate question to be asked is why should a person obey God? MacIntyre provides three different rationales to answer the question: a person should obey God either due to his holiness, his goodness, or his power.[6] Let's take a look at each of these motivations.

Christian Motivations for Obeying God

MacIntyre states that using the holiness of God as the motivation to obey God's commandments keeps a person within the confines of religious concepts. In the context of God's holiness, a person should follow God's commands because God is worthy of worship. The relationship between the worshiper and the object of worship is one of abasement on the part of the worshiper. The finite and fragile human stands in awe before the omnipotence and infinity of God, which leads a person to obey God due to his superiority. Obedience on the part of the inferior human to the superior God is a natural corollary to or a natural result of this relationship. MacIntyre points out that the key to this approach is having a conception of God in which God is truly transcendent, truly worthy of worship. As infinite, God cannot have a body because to have a body is to be limited, to be finite. God in this context must be infinite, for if God were to be finite, something else might become more worthy of worship than God.[7] The downside of infinity's grandeur, however, is God becomes abstract and his existence becomes questionable. In our experience, existence and particularity go hand in hand, so by making God infinite, the human ability to relate to God is diminished. With the backdrop of the abstraction of the infinite monotheistic God, MacIntyre sees in the transition from theism to monotheism the dynamic that prefigures a future jump from monotheism to atheism.[8]

---

5. *SHE*, 111.
6. *SHE*, 112.
7. *SHE*, 112.
8. *SHE*, 112.

Another option MacIntyre identifies as motivation to obey God's commandments is the goodness of God. Goodness in this case cannot be defined as obedience to God because that would lead to a vacuous circle. To say that it is good to obey God's command because God is good does not provide any evidence that God is actually good; it merely asserts God's goodness in the context of his commandments. To say that God is good without the assertion being meaningless requires having a standard for goodness that is intellectually independent from the idea of God. Without that, good becomes just another word for God and does not shed any light on why it might be good to obey God's commandments. If, however, there is a standard for goodness independent of God, then each person can become her or his own judge of what is good. So, if each person is her or his own judge, why should a person listen to God rather than relying on one's own judgments? A quick answer to this question is God is omniscient and humans are not, so it is wise to rely on God's infinite intelligence rather than on one's own intellect when it comes to making moral decisions.[9] God's goodness makes his commands sound rational and reasonable. God becomes the consultant to our moral decision-making business. In this context, it ends up being smart to follow God's advice, but taking God's advice is different than the biblical call to obey God as the sovereign ruler of the universe. The good, understood as rationality and reason, does not inspire obedience.[10] God's power, on the other hand, does.

MacIntyre contends that God's power as the motivation for obeying his commands is both effective and risky. The possibility of eternal damnation for wrongdoing is a great motivator to make morally good choices. The risk, however, is such motivation can turn the primary motivation in ethics to self-interest. I will choose good because I do not want to be punished. Yet one of the primary thrusts of ethics is the need to overcome self-serving actions and habits. So, if obedience to God's command results in selfish habits due to selfish motivation, such obedience may end up being counterproductive in the long run.[11] Despite this risk, MacIntyre does see a benefit of moral motivation based on God's power due to the impact it has on the relationship between virtue and happiness. As we pointed out in the last chapter, in bad societies where the development of virtues in order to follow rules does not produce success,

9. *SHE*, 113.
10. *SHE*, 113.
11. *SHE*, 113.

Christian Morality as the Bridge Between Ancient and Medieval Ethics

the relationship between virtue and happiness is changed. A bad society short-circuits the process in which virtues are developed to achieve the goals that produce happiness because the virtues no longer produce goal achievement due to factors outside the person's control. For the Stoics, virtue itself becomes the grist of happiness. For many people living in this context, however, being virtuous has no point. And the reality is many people throughout history have lived in societies where the relationship between being a good, moral person and living a happy life is nonexistent. In desperately poor or horribly unjust societies, living a morally excellent life reaps meager material benefit and can actually lead to further suffering. It is here that belief in the power of God can maintain the connection between virtue and happiness. The two may not be related in this world, but a just and omnipotent God will bring them together in the next world.[12] The power of this motivation is undeniable. To see the impact in having faith that God will reward being a good person in the next life, just look at the extraordinary sacrifices people have undergone for the sake of righteousness and for the sake of their God, up to and including martyrdom. There is a further risk, though, in the fact that such belief will foster the idea that justice can only be achieved in the next life, which can lead to passivity and despair in the present life.

According to MacIntyre these motivations are woven throughout the ethical thinking of individual Christians and the most influential Christian ethicists. In addition, in the context of the historical engagement between Christian thinkers and non-Christian moralists, we see the Christians able and willing to absorb the parts of pagan moral philosophy they see as compatible and even enhancing to Christian moral thought. MacIntyre notes that for medieval thinkers, the understanding of the Christian God and the moral implications of that understanding ends up being a mix between the commanding presence of Yahweh in the Old Testament and the god of the Greek philosophers, which were usually conceptions of the divine based on the thought of Plato or Aristotle.[13] Yet this adaptation of nonreligious philosophy to Christian thinking does not prevent significant innovations in Jewish and Christian ethics from being emphasized within religious circles and even provides avenues for religious thought to influence thinkers outside of Christianity. A primary

---

12. *SHE*, 113–14.

13. *SHE*, 117. It is important to note that this assertion marginalizes the texts of the New Testament for the understanding of Christian ethics, a position many Christians would see as unconvincing.

example of this cited by MacIntyre is the idea of the equal dignity of every human being.[14] Such equality is a glaring omission in a thinker such as Aristotle. We see that principle, one of the most important moral ideas in the history of ethics, first articulated in the opening chapter of the book of Genesis, which tells us that all people, both men and women, are created in the image and likeness of God (Gen 1:26–27). It is an idea asserting the intrinsic dignity of each and every individual person. Such dignity has a long tradition of being transgressed, but it is a moral principle that has become more and more influential and more and more prevalent over time. The reason for its growing strength is similar to the reason that all societies have a bias for truth telling. The expectation of truth telling leads to better outcomes than a society based on deceit. Likewise, a society that respects the dignity of each person produces an environment more conducive to the happiness of its members. So, in Christian moral thought we see a combination of biblical themes and innovations integrated with the thinking of the classical approach to ethics. We will now turn to a few historical examples of that integration.

The Contribution of St. Augustine to Christian Ethics

St. Augustine of Hippo (b. 354 CE) is one of the most influential Christian thinkers of what is called the patristic intellectual period of Christianity, which stretches from the early one hundreds (just after Christians completed writing the books of the New Testament) to around the year 700 CE. Patristic authors often stood at the intersection between the ideas communicated through the Bible and the philosophical ideas of Hellenism, the name of the Greek intellectual culture of the time. Patristic authors wrote in Greek in the east of the Mediterranean basin and in Latin in the west of the Mediterranean and were responsible for formulating many of the teachings about Christ that come down to Christians today. Doctrines such as the Trinity, the relationship between the members of the Trinity, and Christ's nature as divine and human all stem from the intellectual ferment of this period.

St. Augustine of Hippo was born to a devout Christian woman and a Roman administrator in North Africa in what is now the country of Tunisia. An ambitious and upwardly mobile member of Roman society, Augustine was named the official rhetorician or spokesperson for the

14. *SHE*, 115.

Roman emperor as a young man before his conversion to Christianity. After that conversion, Augustine left the service of the empire, becoming a priest and eventually a bishop in the city of Hippo in North Africa. One contemporary author describes St. Augustine's thought as "Ancient Philosophy Baptized"[15] because Augustine had a deep understanding of both the Bible and classical philosophy. Indeed, it was in part due to his study of Greek philosophy that Augustine left Manichaeism (a popular and controversial religion of his time) to become a Christian.

While there's no doubt that the primary influence on Augustine's moral thought was Christian Scripture, MacIntyre observes that his views also exhibited a significant dependence on the thought of Plato. In Plato's philosophy, the form of the *Good*, that is the *summum bonum* or the highest good, plays what can be described as a divine role. In the *Republic*, Plato asserts, "Not only do the objects of knowledge owe their being known to the *Good*, but their *being* (*ousia* in the Greek) is also due to it, although the *Good* is not being, but superior to it (that is to being) in rank and power."[16] In Plato's view, the Good not only illuminates all things, enabling humans to comprehend things as objects of their thinking (he invokes the light of the sun to serve as a metaphor for this illumination), the Good also causes the existence of those things. Plato's view on the Good supporting the existence of all things has much in common with the Jewish and Christian view of creation in the book of Genesis. Given this common ground, Augustine provides a Christianized version of Plato's metaphysical thought where God rather than the form of the Good is the source of all things that exist and God likewise illuminates the human mind to be able to understand the nature of that existence.[17] Applying the Greek moral concepts to Christian ethics, Augustine agrees that getting what one desires, as long as it is truly good, is the foundation of happiness.[18] In the moral sphere, the illumination provided by God to human reason enables a person to move from transitory and ultimately unfulfilling worldly desires to the heavenly desire of God himself. Moral excellence for Augustine consists in developing the habits to love God above all other things and make practical choices that are consistent with that love.[19] MacIntyre observes that Augustine's view of happiness as the

15. Cf. Rist, *Augustine* for a description of Augustine's thought in these terms.
16. Plato, *Republic*, 509b.
17. *SHE*, 117.
18. Augustine, *Trinity*, 13.8.
19. Cf. Augustine, *Morals of the Catholic Church*.

contemplation of God (based on the writing of St. Paul and Plato) bears close resemblance to the happiness achieved in contemplating beauty that Diotema described in Plato's *Symposium*.[20]

The Contribution of St. Thomas Aquinas to Christian Ethics

St. Thomas Aquinas (b. 1225) was deeply influenced by Augustine's theology and moral thought. The primary Greek philosopher influencing the thought of Thomas, however, was not Plato, but Aristotle. Aristotle had so much influence on St. Thomas that he eventually referred to Aristotle simply as "The Philosopher." What may be surprising, however, is St. Thomas's dependence on and support for the thought of Aristotle was quite controversial at the time of his writing. A little historical background is helpful to understand that the work of St. Thomas, which is considered utterly traditional in Catholic circles today, was considered scandalously innovative during his own time and led to the initial condemnation of his writings.

As a writer during the high Middle Ages, St. Thomas was working during the vibrant time of cultural renewal and thinking in Europe that preceded the Renaissance. Just before the birth of St. Thomas, two of Christianity's most influential and dynamic personalities had emerged on the European scene in the persons of St. Dominic Guzman (b. 1170) and St. Francis of Assisi (b. 1181). Both Dominic and Francis established what were called mendicant religious orders. These groups of men took vows of poverty and wandered the European countryside preaching the Christian gospel. Their wandering was quite different from the other religious orders of the time established in monasteries that were enclosed communities. Members of religious orders traveling the European highways in the poverty-stricken rags of paupers was both new and controversial. The radical call to the gospel offered by Francis and Dominic was also immensely popular, attracting many followers to these orders, among them St. Thomas Aquinas. St. Thomas joined the order of St. Dominic, known as the Order of Preachers, and became one of the most influential thinkers of his time, teaching and writing at the University of Paris, the leading intellectual center in thirteenth-century Europe.

Although the Franciscans and Dominicans were initially looked upon with skepticism and suspicion due to their novelty, the source of

---

20. *SHE*, 117.

Christian Morality as the Bridge Between Ancient and Medieval Ethics   119

the controversy regarding the thinking of St. Thomas lay primarily in his focus on Aristotle's philosophy. Up until the twelfth century, Plato had been the dominant philosopher of Christian culture largely due to the long shadow of St. Augustine's influence and his focus on Plato's thought. Augustine was not influenced significantly by Aristotle because much of Aristotle's work was lost to Western Europe after the second century. Augustine read virtually none of Aristotle's work; he only mentions reading Aristotle's *Categories* in his own writing.[21] It was only with the increased contact in the eleventh and twelfth centuries between Christians and Muslims, who still had access to Aristotle's thought in the Middle East, that the body of Aristotle's writings were reintroduced to the Christian thinkers of Western Europe. As a student of St. Albert the Great, Thomas was exposed to the thinking of Aristotle and recognized Aristotle's philosophy as a source of thought that the Christian tradition had to address. This was controversial for two reasons. First, the source of this new thinking was Islam, a foreign religion that was in continual conflict with Christianity. Second, although Aristotle had much in common with Plato, he departs from Plato in significant ways and even criticizes Plato, who was considered by Christians like Augustine to be the greatest non-Christian thinker in history. As a result, much of Thomas's teaching was condemned shortly after his death by the bishop of Paris. Over time, however, the quality of Thomas's thinking overcame its early condemnations, and he is now considered one of the greatest philosophers in the Christian tradition and in European history.

Given the breadth and depth of St. Thomas's writing, it is difficult to provide a concise summary that does it justice. So, this brief overview will hopefully serve as a guide and inspiration for further study on his thinking, his ethical thinking in particular. MacIntyre asserts that unlike Augustine's approach where the Christian believer is trying to escape desire for the world, St. Thomas proposes an approach to ethics where desire is transformed so that it is oriented toward morally good goals.[22] Although Aristotle and St. Thomas have different intellectual contexts for their understanding of morality (the *polis* or city-state sets the stage for Aristotle, while God and obedience to divine law is the setting for St. Thomas), St. Thomas is able to adapt Aristotle's moral concepts to his remarkably different framework. MacIntyre points out that in doing so,

---

21. Augustine reports his reading of *The Categories* in *Confessions*, 4.16.28.
22. *SHE*, 117.

St. Thomas demonstrates that the conceptual links Aristotle establishes between virtue and happiness not only have the flexibility to be applied in different intellectual and political environments, but they are also a permanent part of any discussion of ethics that describes reason and desire as important to moral choice.[23] MacIntyre observes that St. Thomas makes the thinking of Aristotle more useful to succeeding generations of thinkers because he provides an example for applying the enduring aspects of Aristotle's ethics while putting to the side some of the mistaken views of Aristotle and his ideas that are relevant only to the culture of ancient Greece.[24]

A further contribution St. Thomas makes is his application of Aristotle's concept of good to the Christian notion of God. By using Aristotle's notion of the good, St. Thomas establishes the goodness of God as the motivation for doing what is morally good. As we mentioned earlier, for God's goodness to be the motivation for ethics, the idea of what is good must be conceptually independent from the idea of God. St. Thomas is able to establish this independence by applying Aristotle's notion of good—that which should be desired—to God.[25] The Christian God is presented in the pages of the Bible as the fulfillment of all desire. A person's relationship with God is therefore the highest good; in Aristotle's terms, that relationship offers the greatest happiness to which a human can aspire. Since the idea of good is independent from the idea of God, St. Thomas concludes that even the non-Christian can recognize what is good independently of the Bible, a point that is affirmed by the Bible itself when St. Paul recognizes the ability of Gentiles to determine what is morally good in his *Letter to the Romans* (Rom 2:14). The Aristotelian point of moral rules is to enable a person to achieve good things, to achieve the things that actually satisfy human desires, and St. Thomas is able to apply this insight in the context of Christianity.[26] In abiding by God's commandments, the person develops the virtues necessary to acquire what is good, the highest good being a relationship with God himself. The Aristotelian morality of St. Thomas provides a particularly clear case for making the goodness of God the motivation for following God's commandments.

23. *SHE*, 118.
24. *SHE*, 118.
25. *SHE*, 118–19.
26. *SHE*, 118.

William of Ockham on the Power of God in Relation to Ethics

Despite this clarity regarding God's goodness as the basis to follow his commandments, changes in history were underway that made the moral thinking of St. Thomas less accessible to succeeding generations of Christian ethicists. In the next chapter, we will see a shift away from the importance of the community to the understanding of ethics and the rise of the individual as the primary focus for morality.[27] This change in focus is the result of rapid changes in the forms of social life that Europe was undergoing with the approach of the Renaissance and the religious controversies of the Reformation. The idea that humans achieve their happiness and goals in the context of a community begins to take a back seat to an approach where happiness or (in Christian theological terms) salvation is achieved through the individual soul and its relation to God. In this individualistic context, obeying the commandments of God is inspired by God's power rather than his goodness.[28]

William of Ockham becomes one of the most important philosophers to make God's power the motivation for obeying the commandments rather than God's goodness as a reason to obey them. Despite being relatively unknown today, William was an influential thinker in his time and made intellectual contributions that continue to impact contemporary thought. His most famous formulation, Ockham's Razor, bears his name and refers to the idea that the correct answer to difficult philosophical questions usually resides in the simplest answer. William (b. 1287) was born in the southwest of England and was educated by the Franciscan friars in London and Oxford. He spent his early life in England but was brought to Avignon France (the seat of the papacy at the time) when some of his teachings were examined for heresy. While in Avignon, William studied the thought of the pope of the time, Pope John XXII, and concluded that the pope himself was a heretic. Unsurprisingly, that conclusion did not sit well with the pope and other church authorities. William fled to Germany under the protection of the Holy Roman Emperor, a political rival of the pope, where he spent the remainder of his days.[29]

---

27. *SHE*, 119.

28. *SHE*, 119.

29. Cf. Spade, *Cambridge Companion to Ockham*, 17–27, for a brief summary of William's life.

MacIntyre observes that William's approach to philosophy is quite dramatic in its assertion that God's commands are arbitrary and require obedience not on the basis of them being reasonable, but on the basis of the sovereign power of God.[30] A quote from William himself demonstrates his position quite well:

> I reply that hatred, theft, adultery, and the like may involve evil according to the common law, in so far as they are done by someone who is obligated by a divine command to perform the opposite act. As far as everything absolute in these actions is concerned, however, God can perform them without involving any evil. And they can even be performed meritoriously by someone on earth if they should fall under a divine command, just as now the opposite of these, in fact, fall under a divine command.[31]

For William, the formulation of God's commandments is guided by the absolute freedom and sovereignty of God. For example, in William's approach God has the power to say that murder is good, and if God so decrees that murder is good, humans would do good in committing murder. A contemporary commentator provides a succinct explanation of the advantages of William's thinking, as well as a brief rationale behind William's method:

> One advantage of this approach is that it enables Ockham to make sense of some instances in the Old Testament where it looks as though God is commanding such things as murder (as in the case of Abraham sacrificing Isaac) and deception (as in the case of the Israelites despoiling the Egyptians). But biblical exegesis is not Ockham's motive. His motive is to cast God as a paradigm of metaphysical freedom, so that he can make sense of human nature as made in his image.[32]

God's sovereignty and power over the human person is perfectly complete in William's approach to morality. The only concern of each person in the ethics of thinkers like William is to understand God's commandments and obey those commandments, no matter what. William's thought is the forerunner of the individualism that will come to

---

30. *SHE*, 119.

31. William of Ockham, *Opera Theologica* 5:352 as cited in the Internet Encyclopedia of Philosophy, "William of Ockham (Occam, c. 1280—c. 1349)" on the thought of William of Ockham.

32. Cf. Internet Encyclopedia of Philosophy, "William of Ockham (Occam, c. 1280—c. 1349)."

dominate the thinking of ethicists from the Renaissance and the Reformation through to the modern individualist approaches to morality we see today. Our next task will be to examine the turns taken by those Renaissance and Reformation thinkers.

Leadership Reflection: Sophists, Thomists, and Modern Schools of Leadership

Going back to the debates between the Sophists and Socrates, we remember that the Sophists argued that the greatest good is for people to get whatever it is that they want. Simply put, people are happiest when they get what they want. While the Rolling Stones lamented that you can't always get what you want, Socrates criticized the Sophists because getting what one wants will not make a person happy if what the person wants is not good. Tragically, people often do want things that are horrible for them and reap the rewards of getting those bad things by living profoundly unhappy lives (any perusal of recent mafia movies drives that point home in a powerful way). Aristotle's thinking is similar to the Sophists in that he sees happiness in terms of satisfying desire, but he sides with Socrates and Plato when he makes the crucial distinction that satisfying a desire will achieve happiness only if the thing a person wants is actually good for that person. Satisfying the desire for wine will not yield happiness if a person is an alcoholic. On the basis of this observation, Aristotle asserts that the idea of what is good includes a judgment of whether the thing desired is actually good or not, and not just the fact that the thing is desirable. Something is good only if it should be desired.

MacIntyre observes that St. Thomas helped succeeding generations of thinkers by identifying the good ideas of Aristotle and using them in a different context. Aristotle did not operate in the intellectual context of the Jewish and Christian understanding of God, so when St. Thomas applies Aristotle's notion of good to the desire for God, he is offering an innovation that sheds new light on why Christian believers should desire to be morally good people. St. Thomas is also applying a concept from classical Greek morality to Christian thinking that stands in contrast to the ethics of the present-day leadership industry and even the ethics of the most prestigious leadership schools in the United States. One can see the Sophist notion of good as getting what one wants without examining the moral worth of that desire at play in modern schools of leadership. A recent article in *Vanity*

Fair magazine highlights the moral failings of executive leadership at Enron and Facebook and notes that some of the executives embroiled in those failures were prominent graduates from Harvard Business School (HBS), likely the most influential business school in the United States today.[33] The author, Duff McDonald, asserts that the unethical conduct of the two executives under the spotlight of his analysis cannot only be traced to ideas they espoused while studying at HBS, but they are also reinforced by the school's much acclaimed case study teaching method. McDonald provides a description of the method as,

> A discussion-based pedagogy that asks students to put themselves in the role of corporate Übermensch. At the start of each class, one unlucky soul is put in the hot seat, presented with a "what would you do" scenario, and then subjected to the ruthless interrogation of their peers. Graded on a curve, the intramural competition can be intense—MBAs are super-competitive, after all ... To help students overcome the fear of sounding stupid and being remorselessly critiqued, they are reminded, in case after case—and with emphasis—that there are *no* right answers.[34]

Although no moral criteria are offered to guide the deliberations of students on the hot seat, McDonald notes that the moral culture of HBS provides two powerful moral principles by which students, some of whom will be future titans of industry, should guide their choices. In the cultural context of HBS, actions are considered good if they lead to career enhancement or corporate profits (there is a strong relationship between the two principles, too).[35]

Few would be surprised that a business school might emphasize these two principles because they are fundamental to the mission of any business school, which is to educate people on how to run successful businesses. It is difficult to have a successful business without maximizing its income and making decisions that are in the interest of its personnel, especially its leaders. Yet few would also have difficulty in seeing the problems and shortcomings of such a narrow approach to business ethics. It is often the case that a decision that is good for a person's career or the corporate bottom line could have horrible effects on other important considerations (the environment, health, liberal democracy—the list of

---

33. Cf. McDonald, "When You Get That Wealthy."
34. McDonald, "When You Get That Wealthy."
35. McDonald, "When You Get That Wealthy."

other considerations is likely infinite) and should therefore be considered immoral and rejected. The approach to ethics and leadership executed in the HBS teaching method and by other leadership writers that assert leadership is an amoral enterprise is in fact a return to the Sophists. Without an approach to moral choice that attempts to account for what is truly good, the moral thinking of humans is inevitably reduced to doing what one wants, and corporate profits and career enhancement are the primary objects of desire in the case of business executives. The Sophists might be pleased with that kind of approach to leadership and ethics, but is it any wonder that present day leaders are so often faulted for moral failure and the failure to serve their followers or customers? The amoral approach to leadership is not amoral at all. It defaults to a self-centered approach to leadership, which anyone can tell you is a road every leader should shun. Following St. Thomas and employing Aristotle's definition of what is truly desirable and therefore truly good would greatly enhance the moral education of business students compared to the Sophistic approach currently used by business schools. Without such a change, the education of America's future business leaders will likely continue to alienate the general population through the narrow, self-centered leadership ethics so prevalent today.

10

Re-Thinking Ethics in the Post-Medieval Era

THE RISE OF THE mendicant religious orders, the establishment of European universities, and the conflict with the Islamic world led to a period of cultural and intellectual dynamism in the twelfth, thirteenth, and fourteenth centuries that Western Europe had not experienced since the fall of the Roman Empire. That dynamism was the precursor to the tumultuous changes that would later take place during the Protestant Reformation, the Renaissance, and the beginning of modern philosophy, which was heavily influenced by the Scientific Revolution. MacIntyre provides a focus on four thinkers that span this timeframe: Martin Luther, Niccolò Machiavelli, Thomas Hobbes, and Baruch Spinoza who all had significant influence on the changes in ethical concepts during these historical movements. We will first examine the moral thinking of Martin Luther, whose ethics are clearly influenced by William of Ockham's thinking regarding the absolute nature of God's commands,[1] before turning to Machiavelli, Hobbes, and Spinoza.

Martin Luther: Individualism, the Corruption of Desire, and the Commands of God

For MacIntyre, the thought of both Luther and Machiavelli mark the break from the community and systematic approaches to ethics in the

---

1. *SHE*, 121.

Middle Ages, introducing the distinctive context that would dominate later modern ethics, which is the focus of ethics on the individual person. The views of both thinkers move away from the community as the setting in which to understand moral concepts.[2] Although the Reformation and Renaissance have distinct sources from which they spring and significant differences in their focus, they are also movements that overlap in European history, and we will see some of that overlap in the focus on the individual for each movement's moral thought. Martin Luther (b. 1483) was initially an Augustinian monk who lived in Wittenberg, Germany. In 1517, he authored his famous *Ninety-Five Theses* that originated in his criticism of the Roman Catholic practice of selling indulgences and is the document that is seen by many as the spark that lit the fire of the Protestant Reformation.[3] Luther's eventual excommunication by the pope and his other revisions of Christian teachings led to his establishment of a new Christian Church, which was followed by other religious reformers working independently of him in various parts of Europe (initially Switzerland and England). Luther had many theological interests and offered many innovations from the prevailing Catholic practices of the time, not least of which was his view of the individual in relation to morality. MacIntyre observes that Luther provides powerful categories to his followers through which they can interpret their religious experience, the most important being the experience of the individual who is alone before God. Death, in Luther's approach, provides the background for understanding an individual's relationship with God. When you die, it is you who dies alone. The dead person, the person stripped of all social connections standing before the judgment seat of God, is the paradigm for Luther's understanding of the individual.[4]

Another emphasis provided by Luther that makes the confrontation between the individual person and God fraught with anxiety is his view that human nature is totally corrupt. Building on notions of sin found in the writings of St. Augustine and his view that it is only through faith in Jesus Christ that a person is saved, Luther asserts that human desires are totally corrupt and are thus the source of antagonism between what humans want and what God commands. In his calculus, human will (the seat of desire) and even reason are completely enslaved to sin so humans must act against their will and reason. The human person is not saved

2. *SHE*, 121.
3. Cf. Beutel, "Luther's Life," 3–19 for a brief overview of Luther's life and career.
4. *SHE*, 126.

by works because works are the product of sinful desire.⁵ In MacIntyre's telling, we can describe Luther as the anti-Aristotle. Indeed, Luther sees Aristotle as the buffoon who misled the church in regard to ethics.⁶ In Aristotle's approach, human wants and needs provide the criteria for judging human actions. Wants and needs are also the starting point for practical reasoning in the thought of a Catholic thinker like St. Thomas Aquinas. In Luther's approach, which is supported by John Calvin, another influential Protestant reformer, human needs and wants cannot provide good guidance to moral behavior because all such needs and desires are symptoms of sinful human nature.⁷

The ethical question that follows upon Luther's backdrop in which desires and needs provide no guidance to human choice, is how should a human judge what to do? For Luther, that guidance can come from the commands of God alone. Here we can see the influence of William of Ockham and his approach to obeying the commandments on the basis of God's power.⁸ Like Ockham, Luther sees God as arbitrarily omnipotent. Good and right in this view are solely determined on the basis of what God demands of the individual person.⁹ The only true and morally good rules are divine commandments that have no further rationale or justification outside of the fact that they are the demands of God.¹⁰

Another important aspect of Luther's ethics highlighted by MacIntyre as Luther's most significant contribution to moral philosophy is his support for the absolute rights of secular authority.¹¹ Luther is supported by Calvin in his stark division of morality between the religious sphere on the one hand, and that of the political and economic spheres on the other. Ethics in the realm of religion is based on the unchanging and inscrutable commands of God. The realms of politics and the marketplace, however, are ruled by the principles humans develop within those two fields. For Luther, the individual is a citizen of all three realms. In the world of religion, the human is the corrupt agent saved before the judgment seat of God through faith in Christ. In the world of politics, the

---

5. *SHE*, 122.
6. *SHE*, 122.
7. *SHE*, 126.
8. Cf. Osborne, "Faith, Philosophy, and the Nominalist Background," 63–82 for a discussion of Ockham's influence on Luther.
9. *SHE*, 123.
10. *SHE*, 121.
11. *SHE*, 122.

person is a subject who must obey the state. In the world of economics, a person is an agent who can enter into legal contracts. MacIntyre characterizes the history of Calvin's thought, in particular, as the liberation of all things economic.[12]

The ethical principles that emerge from the Reformation, according to MacIntyre, are threefold. First, religious moral precepts are unconditional and do not admit of rational examination. The commands of God are good because they are what God commands, period. Second, the moral agent is sovereign in her or his choices. It is the individual and the individual alone who will face God at the end of her or his life. Lastly, the secular realm has its own norms and provides its own justification for how one ought to behave in the political environment and in the marketplace.[13] It is in the political and economic orders that secular theorists will have much to say about ethics, and it is in these two settings that the intellectual developments of the Renaissance overlap and forward the focus of morality on the individual found in Reformation thought. The secular context finds its own champion of the individual in the writing of Niccolò Machiavelli, and it is in his thought that we can find some of the most distinctive ethical and political innovations of the Renaissance.

Ethics in Machiavelli's *Realpolitik* of the Modern State

The Renaissance was a movement that affected virtually every aspect of European culture from the fourteenth through the sixteenth centuries. Beginning in Italy in the late 1300s, Renaissance thinking spread throughout the continent and affected areas of European society ranging from art, architecture, music, science, philosophy, literature, and politics. Ironically, the Renaissance is the period that marks the cultural transition from the Middle Ages to modern European society, yet much of its inspiration is drawn from humanistic intellectual interests that focused on retrieving ideas from ancient Greece and Rome.[14] The thought of Niccolò Machiavelli (b. 1469) was no exception to this trend. Influenced by a broad range of ancient thinkers, Machiavelli's career looks a lot like the ancient Roman statesman and philosopher Cicero as both thinkers were

---

12. *SHE*, 124.

13. *SHE*, 126–27.

14. Cf. Baker, *Italian Renaissance Humanism in the Mirror*, 36–89 for a thorough description of the humanist currents in fifteenth-century Italian Renaissance culture.

active in government through their middle years but found themselves on the wrong side of powerful leaders (Caesar Augustus for Cicero and Lorenzo de Medici for Machiavelli), which forced them to retire from politics and take to their pens as writers of philosophy.

Although primarily known as a political theorist, Machiavelli articulated a number of moral principles that were in continuity with aspects of classical philosophy and the Reformation, while also previewing ideas that would become prominent in the ethics of nineteenth-century Europe.[15] MacIntyre observes that Machiavelli is the first ethicist since the Sophists who judges the whole of moral choices on the basis of consequences.[16] What mattered in ethics for Machiavelli was the external effect produced by one's choice. In addition, similar to the ancients prior to Socrates, Machiavelli assumes that human nature in its motives and aspirations is unchanging.[17] Machiavelli also shares with his Reformation contemporaries a focus on the individual and an assumption that most people are relatively corrupt.[18] In his most famous work, *The Prince*, Machiavelli observes that the ruler who tries to live according to virtue will soon come to misery among so many who are vicious. A realist in his approach to ethics and politics, Machiavelli asserts that one must plan and make choices not on the basis of how people should behave, but on the basis of how they actually behave. The person or ruler who assumes morally righteous behavior on the part of others will soon come to ruin.[19] In *The Prince*, Machiavelli presumes that the goals of social and political life, like human nature, are unchanging. Those goals consist in the attainment and holding of power, the maintenance of political order, and the general prosperity of the citizenry. It is also clear in his view that order and prosperity are goals only because the primary goal of attaining and holding power is impossible without them.[20] The ethics of the individual then finds its path and goal in the pursuit and achievement of power. For Machiavelli, moral evaluation is not concerned with questions about how to live or what to do in general. In the simplest terms, moral evaluation is seen as a means to influence others so as to accrue power.[21] In mak-

15. *SHE*, 128.
16. *SHE*, 128.
17. *SHE*, 128.
18. *SHE*, 127.
19. Machiavelli, *Prince*, 32.
20. *SHE*, 127.
21. *SHE*, 128.

ing morality about power, Machiavelli is reaching back to the Sophists of fifth-century BCE Greece and anticipating the morality of Karl Marx and Friedrich Nietzsche in nineteenth-century Europe.

Similar to Luther's approach, the individual takes center stage for Machiavelli. For both thinkers, the individual is unconstrained by any social relationships. In the world of Machiavelli, the accrual of power, glory, and reputation are the only criteria guiding a person's moral choices. His ethics produce a view in which the individual is sovereign in her or his choices, and those choices are made in the context of unchanging laws.[22] MacIntyre asserts that following these two thinkers one might expect the rise of a moral theory where the individual is the seat of power, power is the ultimate concern of the individual, the idea of God is pushed to the sidelines of moral discussion, and the pre-social human (a focus we remember from the Sophists who saw the aggression and selfishness of the Homeric noblemen as humanity's pre-social/natural state) is the context in which to understand changing social forms. All of these elements are in play in the ethics of our next philosopher, Thomas Hobbes.[23]

The Moral Thought of Thomas Hobbes

In the time of Thomas Hobbes (b. 1588), we again see the forces of history impacting the way people understood ethics and politics. Hobbes was alive in England during the transition from the Renaissance to the Scientific Revolution and an economic period called the Price Revolution. Both revolutions were to have a significant impact on the thinking of Hobbes and the rest of European society. As heirs to the Scientific Revolution and practitioners of its methods, many of us have heard of and are familiar with the thinking associated with Europe's transition to modern scientific techniques and research. Europe's Price Revolution, which lasted from the late fifteenth through the seventeenth centuries, is less familiar, however. The Price Revolution refers to the marked increase in inflation felt throughout Europe as the result of the large influx of gold and silver into European economies due to Spanish mining in the New World (Mexico and Peru providing the majority of the precious metals). As a result of that influx, Europe experienced an inflation rate of 1 to

---

22. *SHE*, 128.
23. *SHE*, 130.

1.5 percent per annum over a 150-year time period.[24] What seems like a modest rise in inflation for contemporary economies represented a sixfold increase over the relative inflationary stability of the Renaissance.[25]

It might be surprising, but the impact those economic changes had on the ethical and political thinking of the time was significant. The societal institutions of Europe, and particularly England where Hobbes was active, were being rethought as the continent began the transition from feudal society to a market economy. The roles in English society, such as servant, nobleman, and king, were not changing, but the understanding of the relationships between these members of society was changing due to the influence of money.[26] Fortunes were made and lost, as MacIntyre asserts, through the adroit use of money, which begged the question of how a self-made person should relate to the established aristocracy, especially in the completely new development where the self-made person had more money than the aristocrat.[27] The questions even extended to the authority of the king. These questions were asked in the context of the king's claim to collect tax revenues from his subjects, who were at the same time making claims about their own rights in relation to the king.[28] How should these questions and claims be understood? What is the relationship between the king and a populace that was increasingly concerned with the protection of its own rights, even against the power of the king? Here is where the thinking of Thomas Hobbes comes to bear. The answers Hobbes provides to the questions of authority come on the basis of his work as both a historian and a scientist, a combination that results in a recovery of ancient thought and significant innovations compared to other thinkers of his time.[29]

One of Hobbes's important early works is his translation from Greek to English of Thucydides's *History of the Peloponnesian War*. This history chronicled the downfall of Athenian society through what Hobbes sees as the corruption that inevitably springs from democratic government. Democracy breeds political corrosiveness due to the grasping desire of

---

24. Levack et al., *West*, 96.

25. Cf. Munro, "Money, Prices, Wages, and 'Profit Inflation,'" 12–71 for a detailed description of the Price Revolution.

26. *SHE*, 131.

27. *SHE*, 131.

28. *SHE*, 131.

29. *SHE*, 131.

politicians aspiring to greatness.[30] Hobbes observed many envious and grasping people in his own culture and sought to reinforce the rights and privileges of the English monarchy as a way to stave off societal corruption that would result from envy and greed. What makes Hobbes's contribution unique is his scientific background and his willingness to use the ideas of science to justify the power of the sovereign. MacIntyre observes that up to this point, theories of the king's authority centered on the divine right of kings (the model of which is King David in the Bible) and historical precedent.[31] Hobbes discards history and Scripture in his arguments and turns to the scientific method of Galileo to make his case. The pursuit of knowledge in the scientific method of thinkers such as Galileo and Frances Bacon (Hobbes served as Bacon's secretary as a young professional) took the form of breaking down complex entities into their most basic parts to first understand those entities, and to then reconstruct them in an improved form.[32] By using this process to examine human society, Hobbes sought to improve the understanding of society so that people could refine their understanding of how they should behave.[33] In examining the state from a scientific perspective, Hobbes could offer insights on how ethics could be understood in that scientific context as well.

So, what did Hobbes discover when he broke society down to its most basic elements? He found the individual person (much like Luther and Machiavelli) whose most fundamental goal is self-preservation. Hobbes proposes that the only desires shared by all humans is the desire to dominate others and the desire to avoid death. These two desires are related in the fact that the only limitation in one's quest for power, in Hobbes's view, is death or the fear of death.[34] The individual person moved by these desires only acknowledges the rules that support self-preservation. The state of nature prior to the establishment of society is a constant competition for power. It is a state of constant warfare that in the words of Hobbes is likely to be "solitary, poor, nasty, brutish, and short."[35] It would be a lawless and hopeless existence were it not for human reason, which can discover a way out of the natural situation where

30. *SHE*, 130–31.
31. *SHE*, 132.
32. *SHE*, 132.
33. *SHE*, 132.
34. *SHE*, 132.
35. Hobbes, *Leviathan*, 185.

one is more likely to die than to dominate. Reason in the natural state recognizes three laws that enable the individual to avoid death. First, one should strive for peace where possible, and where peace is impossible, wage war effectively. Second, a person should allow other people the same liberty the person desires for himself or herself. Third, a person should keep and honor her or his covenants.[36]

MacIntyre points out for us, however, that the laws of nature are not self-enforcing. What is one to do if others do not honor these laws or the agreements people make with one another? Hobbes's answer is that enforcement of nature's laws requires an initial contract that can be backed up by the power of the sword. Individuals must transfer their own power to a common power, a state power that can physically enforce the social contract.[37] This transfer of power creates "that great Leviathan . . . that mortal God, to which we owe under the immortal God, our peace and defense."[38] The giving of power to the state marks the transition from the state of nature to civilized society. Here we have the scientific explanation for why the king should still be sovereign. It is not because God has appointed the king, nor because of the historical precedents that had established a person or family as royal. The science of politics and human nature reveal that the authority of the king is necessary to enforce the social contract that keeps the peace between humans who are naturally nasty and brutish. Those humans are bound by both the laws of nature and the laws of the state. The laws of nature guide the desire to survive and dominate. The laws of the state are obeyed because state power enforces them and because humans, due to their nature, do not want to be killed by the state.[39] The sovereign, therefore, can make other societal laws that must be obeyed by the individual. The only reason not to obey a law of the state is if it will lead to a person's death. Since the purpose of the state is to protect the individual from dying, the individual is not obligated to obey a law that will kill her or him.[40]

---

36. *SHE*, 133.
37. *SHE*, 133.
38. Hobbes, *English Works of Thomas Hobbes*, 73.
39. *SHE*, 134.
40. *SHE*, 133.

MacIntyre's Criticism of Hobbes

Hobbes's use of the scientific method to develop a theory of political authority is novel, but in MacIntyre's view, it also produces significant mistakes that make the political and moral thought of Hobbes quite problematic. According to MacIntyre, the conceptual problems for Hobbes's account of these phenomena can be seen in Hobbes's description of human desire and the way that description relates to his social contract theory.

To begin his critique, MacIntyre relates a story about Hobbes giving alms to an old man outside of St. Paul's Cathedral in London. Aubrey, a churchman at the time, approaches Hobbes and asks him if he gave the alms because Christ tells us that it is good to give alms to the poor. His question is relevant because Hobbes was known as an impious atheist. Hobbes responded by saying that he gave alms not to obey Christ, but because it pleased the old man. The fact that the assistance made the old man happy also made Hobbes happy, and that was the real reason he gave alms to the man. The altruistic act of giving to the poor is, in Hobbes's view, really an act of self-interest because it made him, as the giver of the alms, happy. This vindicates Hobbes's position that all human desires are self-interested. MacIntyre's reaction to this description is quite pointed, and interestingly enough, his criticism is not due to Hobbes's alleged atheism but was a result of Hobbes's status as a philosopher. MacIntyre asserts that Hobbes's argument is not just wrong, but it is also a lie that Hobbes had to tell. The idea that concern for others is always secondary to concern for self is false in MacIntyre's view because we experience these two motives coexisting in ourselves all the time, and while self-concern is often the primary motive, it also frequently takes second place to the concern for others. But why would Hobbes assert self-regard as always primary when clearly it is not? He does so because the question lies at the root of what is wrong with his social contract theory. In MacIntyre's view, Hobbes had to lie for the sake of his overall theory. The lie is necessary because, as MacIntyre puts it, "Human nature and human motives are not and cannot be what (Hobbes) says they are."[41] Three problems of Hobbes's thought come to the surface in the context of this discussion, which are his narrow reliance on the scientific method to justify the social contract, the historical incoherence of his social contract theory, and finally, the narrow view of human desire advanced by Hobbes. We will

---

41. *SHE*, 135–36.

look at MacIntyre's historical and scientific concerns first, before turning to the issue of desire.

Hobbes asserts that self-preservation and the pursuit of power are the two motivations that drive all people. One implication of this argument is the idea that all motivation is self-regarding or self-serving. Given this background, it might appear that people are performing acts that place regard for others above self-regard, but that is merely an appearance. In the calculation of Hobbes, people obey the rules society puts in place to help others only as a means to their own survival. MacIntyre questions the basis for this assertion. What evidence does Hobbes provide that this is actually the case? This is where the reliance on the scientific method becomes problematic because that method makes Hobbes's argument entirely independent of human history. Hobbes provides no historical evidence for his assertions, since such evidence is not part of the scientific arguments Hobbes uses to support his claims. This significantly undermines the credibility of Hobbes's argument because he cannot point to any historical examples of his theory. MacIntyre asserts that no society has ever established a social contract in the manner Hobbes describes. Given that reality, the best we can do is read Hobbes's story of the social contract as a metaphor through which to understand the authority of a ruler.[42]

MacIntyre goes further in his criticism, however, saying that no society has ever been formed the way Hobbes describes because that description is logically incoherent. The incoherence lies in the fact that Hobbes makes two incompatible demands in formulating the idea of the social contract. He claims the contract is the foundation of all common rules and standards that govern a society, but as a legally binding agreement within a historical society, a contract must depend on common standards and rules that already exist. Hobbes says that such standards do not exist without the contract, but the contract cannot exist without the rules and standards.[43] A further question can be asked of MacIntyre's argument, however, which is what rules and standards have to exist before the contract? Certainly, the rules of language are presupposed by a contract, as are the rules without which human social life cannot exist, such as norms for truth telling, promise keeping, and basic fairness.[44] This blind spot in Hobbes's analysis highlights what MacIntyre describes

42. *SHE*, 136.
43. *SHE*, 137.
44. *SHE*, 103.

as a curious mistake Hobbes makes throughout his argument, which is to equate a society with the state. Hobbes makes political authority not the product of a community's prior social life, but as the structure that makes a social life begin to exist. Here we see Hobbes's lack of historical evidence returning to bite him because history shows that it is possible for a community to have an orderly social life without the existence of state or political power.[45] Much of the history of the Middle Ages is a history of small feudal communities that have little resemblance to the complexity of the sovereign state described by Hobbes. In MacIntyre's view, the social contract as proposed by Hobbes cannot even serve as a metaphor to describe a ruler's source of authority.[46]

So, does that mean that Hobbes's entire political project fails? MacIntyre's answer to that question is yes.[47] MacIntyre stakes his position not only on the basis of the lack of historical evidence and the logical incoherence of Hobbes's analysis, but also on the moral implications put forward by Hobbes's description of human nature. MacIntyre asserts that Hobbes's picture of human motivation is defective on multiple levels. First, the description is in some ways inaccurate and is entirely too narrow. MacIntyre sees Hobbes's own behavior as an illustration of the inaccuracy. Hobbes seems to fear death (as most people do), but his behavior as a scientist and a philosopher shows no sign of the intrinsic desire to dominate others.[48] Fear is the only motivation that seems to consistently drive human behavior in Hobbes's world. In addition, Hobbes's limited view of motivation provides the basis for his limited account of why people accept political authority.[49] Political authority based on fear is a low standard for the emotional connection between a state and its subjects. Nations attempt to foster a positive patriotism and love for country among their populations, and many nations are quite successful in this endeavor. People often do love their country, which serves the goal of rendering a population obedient to societal laws more effectively than a society in which the only motivation to obey is fear. Limiting human motivation to fear also limits Hobbes's ability to provide any positive guidance to living a productive life. The state can make us secure from attack and death, but how should we live our lives in the context of safety?

45. *SHE*, 134.
46. *SHE*, 136.
47. *SHE*, 137.
48. *SHE*, 140.
49. *SHE*, 138.

Hobbes does mention a continuous process of acquiring things in one's life, but the question of how one is to live does not merit any significant analysis in his thought. Most of the pursuits that are important to human life, things like friendship, love, art, etc., go unmentioned by Hobbes.[50]

The narrowness of Hobbes's view of human desire presents further problems that MacIntyre highlights. Since fear is the only operative desire in Hobbes's analysis, he fails to examine other desires. This is in part due to the fact that Hobbes sees human desire as a given and does not entertain the idea that one might be able to alter her or his desire. People simply pursue their self-interest, pursue what they want, and the most basic thing they want is self-preservation. The notion that a person can criticize his or her own desires and then rationally shape them does not appear in his writing.[51] Desires cannot be shaped to achieve a particular kind of life because they cannot be shaped at all. In addition, Hobbes views the pursuit of other desires or ideals with suspicion. Pursuing high-minded ideals was for him simply a mask for the otherwise straightforward pursuit of power.[52] There is little doubt that Hobbes is right in asserting that people often deceive others and even themselves about their selfish motivations by wrapping them in the cloak of noble ideals. But again, that is not always the case. It is possible for a person to be motivated by a noble goal or love for another rather than love for self.

Hobbes's reduction of human motivation to fear and the search for power also prevents him from examining an emerging idea that will become crucial to modern ethics, which is the idea of freedom. In the end, Hobbes does make a significant contribution to moral thought by showing how a theory of morality is inseparable from a theory of human nature.[53] The content of Hobbes's own view of human nature, however, prevents him from commenting on an idea such as freedom. That commentary does come from one of his contemporaries, though, a philosopher named Baruch Spinoza.

---

50. *SHE*, 138.
51. *SHE*, 139.
52. *SHE*, 139.
53. *SHE*, 139.

Spinoza on Reason, Freedom, and Happiness

Baruch Spinoza (b. 1632) was a member of the Jewish Portuguese community located in Amsterdam in the seventeenth century. A brilliant student, Spinoza was also no stranger to controversy. MacIntyre describes him as an atheist who believed in a single order of nature and who also ruled out the possibility of miracles.[54] Espousing such radical ideas in seventeenth-century Europe typically carried significant risk for controversy, which was certainly part of Spinoza's experience. In 1656, at the tender age of twenty-four, Spinoza was issued a writ of harem, which in Christian terms is the rough equivalent of excommunication, as the result of his scandalous ideas. The writ expelled him from the Jewish community in Amsterdam and to this day has not been rescinded. Although at this point in his life Spinoza had no publications that allow historians to examine the positions so problematic to the Jewish community, those positions became clear in his future writings. Spinoza's later views that the soul was not immortal, that a provident God did not exist, and that the Jewish Law was neither promulgated by God nor binding on the Jewish people, were obviously incompatible with the orthodox Judaism of the time.[55] And like Hobbes, Spinoza was nothing if not innovative in his thinking. This innovation, along with the fact that Spinoza's thought was an origin of the focus on freedom in modern ethics, makes a brief examination of his moral thinking important.

MacIntyre tells us that Spinoza departs from Hobbes's view of the state and human motivation in a couple of key respects. For Spinoza, the state exists to promote positive human good and is not merely a defense against the calamities that life may present.[56] He sees the primary motivation to form communities not as the fear of death, but as a desire to pursue knowledge and liberation. Given his view of the twofold drive for knowledge and liberation, Spinoza becomes the first philosopher to place reason and freedom at the center of moral philosophy, which helps to propel the two ideas to the center of the values that distinguish modern society from its predecessors.[57] To see how Spinoza lands on the ideas of

---

54. *SHE*, 141.

55. Cf. Don Garrett, "Spinoza on the Essence of the Human Body and the Part of the Mind that is Eternal," in Koistinen, *Cambridge Companion to Spinoza's Ethics*, 284–302 for an overview of Spinoza's beliefs.

56. *SHE*, 140.

57. *SHE*, 145.

freedom and reason as central to morality, we have to look at his view of the universe and how it relates to a human nature that encompasses the ideas of not only freedom and reason, but desire as well.

Spinoza was an atheist who believed in a single order of nature. Recalling some aspects of Stoic thought that saw reason as the force that made the universe operate in the way that it did, Spinoza saw the universe as a system, a single whole that determined every part that comprised the whole. To attempt to understand any part of the universe outside of the entire system was to misunderstand that part because it is the system that provides the context in which to understand the parts of the universe. Rather than the Logos, Spinoza calls the system God, which he equates with nature.[58] This background is important to understanding the ethics of Spinoza because the implication of seeing God as nature is that ethics becomes not an exercise in examining the commandments of God, but an effort to understand nature—specifically human nature—in order to see what moves humans to make moral choices.[59] MacIntyre notes that at times Spinoza's moral thought gets sidetracked by his understanding of geometry of all things, but if we get beyond that aspect, we find an important examination of the relationship between reason, freedom, and human passion.[60]

MacIntyre describes for us Spinoza's assertion that as we examine our passions we cease to be passive in relation to them. Although a person cannot be other than herself or himself, a person enables a type of self-transformation by developing one's self-understanding. For Spinoza, accurate self-knowledge is an engine of liberation.[61] This is the case because as we examine what we desire, love, and hate, we conclude that many of those passions are merely the result of accident—that is, the result of being conditioned by living in a particular environment or setting. Freedom is achieved through this knowledge because by knowing the origins of our passions, we can disrupt the environmental associations that caused our passions to develop in the way that they did. This enables a person to make choices that break those associations and thus relocate the origins of our passions in our own self-directed decisions. Through self-examination, the person recognizes that passions (as well as pleasures and pains) arise from our power as self-moving and

58. *SHE*, 141.
59. *SHE*, 142.
60. *SHE*, 143.
61. *SHE*, 144.

self-preserving creatures. Armed with this self-knowledge, a person can see external phenomena not as hindrances, but as necessary to our self-empowerment.[62] A person who develops authentic self-knowledge will experience joy as the result of the liberation self-knowledge provides. The self-reflective person can guide his or her passions and choices towards goals and ends that are truly rewarding. Spinoza finally adds the idea of virtue to this mix, saying that the person of genuine virtue exists in a state where knowledge, freedom, and happiness meet one another.[63]

For MacIntyre, Spinoza's great contribution to the emerging modern dialogue on ethics is his retrieval from ancient thinkers that emotions, desires, and passions are not static, but transformable.[64] The most significant transformation a person can undergo is passage from the state of being a victim with no control over one's passions to that of an agent. Humans are capable of controlling their wants and desires, and in exercising this power, they become molders of the self. In this context one does not obey political authority because the person wants to be protected from the aggression of others, as Hobbes would assert. In Spinoza's calculation a person obeys a sovereign because political authority establishes the civic order that enables each person to pursue self-knowledge and the liberation produced by that knowledge.[65]

It is clear that Hobbes and Spinoza see ethics and politics quite differently. MacIntyre observes, however, that they play a similar role in channeling some of the most important questions of their time to a new generation of thinkers. The social contract, freedom, and rationality will be central to the discussions of ethics in some of the most significant Enlightenment moral thinkers, which include famous names such as John Locke and Immanuel Kant. Before getting to the big-name, Enlightenment philosophers, however, MacIntyre will stop to examine a number of seventeenth-century thinkers whose names few people remember, but who played a crucial role in shaping the moral concepts that would later be the focus of Enlightenment ethics.

62. *SHE*, 144.
63. *SHE*, 144.
64. *SHE*, 144–45.
65. *SHE*, 145.

Leadership Reflection: Freedom and Desire in Relation to Leadership

Given Spinoza's insights, one can argue that effective leaders will support the satisfaction of their followers' desires. In doing so, the leader should leverage a follower's freedom in support of the leader and the organization. So, how does this work? In 2008, the *Harvard Business Review* published an essay summarizing research on what authors called the service-profit chain, which highlights the important relationship between customer satisfaction and employee satisfaction.[66] It turns out that as followers assume a role within an organization, their desires are shaped by that role. Their desires are shaped by their working environment and circumstances. Unsurprisingly, they want to be successful in their job, and one of the most powerful indications of success is when their work produces satisfaction in the customers they are employed to serve. Customer satisfaction and loyalty to a business is produced by a high level of value offered to the customer by an employee. A virtuous cycle for an organization can be seen in the interactions between satisfied customers whose satisfaction produces fulfilled employees, who then pursue further fulfillment by serving the needs of their customers even better.

So how might leaders impact and foster this cycle? By focusing on whatever is necessary to support their followers in providing outstanding service to their customers. It is an assertion so obvious it seems silly to say. What else would a leader be doing besides supporting their followers in doing the work of the organization? A leader with any experience will tell you that a million different tasks outside the support of their followers can claim a leader's attention. Sometimes those tasks are superfluous and unimportant, but often they are also crucial to the good of the organization. Leaders are responsible for strategic planning, public speaking, reporting to their own leaders, setting goals, attending and running meetings, providing reports, and a myriad of other important tasks that are not directly related to supporting their followers. It takes discipline for a leader to focus on the crucial task of enabling followers to do their job well, and that work is often quite difficult. The problems followers bring to leaders are the hard ones, as they can usually take care of the easy problems by themselves. The challenges followers seek help with can be quite complex and often concern issues that they do not have the authority to address because they impact other aspects of the organization or aspects

---

66. Heskett et al., "Putting the Service Profit-Chain to Work."

of the mission that fall under the responsibility of the leader, but not the follower. What does a leader do when presented with such problems? Ineffective leaders often ignore them or procrastinate, putting off the hard work necessary to overcome challenges in the hope that the problem will solve itself or that easier solutions will present themselves over time. Effective leaders, on the other hand, focus on these tasks, which are many and diverse. The tasks can range from providing equipment necessary to complete the job, to giving time off to recharge a follower's energy, to simply offering a kind word of encouragement during the routine of an ordinary day. These tasks are typically the behind-the-scenes work that leaders must prioritize to make their followers successful.

Researchers label the environment produced by leadership's focus on support of employees as internal service quality. Internal service quality describes the work environment that contributes most to follower satisfaction. This satisfaction can be measured by surveying the feelings followers have toward their job, their colleagues, and their organization as a whole. And the research data reveals that follower satisfaction is impacted most by their ability to serve the needs of their customers.[67] Followers place significant value on achieving excellent results for their clientele. Thus, the leader's primary task in this context is doing whatever is necessary to help followers achieve their desire to provide outstanding service to their customers.

If creating a great work environment for employees is job one for the leader, one of the first steps to providing outstanding employee support is to ask employees what they need to get their job done. By listening to employees in an effort to discover their needs, a leader is already taking a significant step (which is also a step neglected by many leaders) toward creating an environment where followers feel respected and valued. Even if they cannot improve support for the follower, just the act of engaging and listening to a follower's challenges will increase the follower's commitment to the organization. A leader who provides actual results in support of followers will reap an even greater response from them. The impact of high internal service quality is greater loyalty, greater commitment, and greater enthusiasm on the part of employees. Satisfied, happy employees who recognize the important roles the organization and its leadership play in their service to their customers will be followers with measurable, positive feelings toward their organization and toward their leaders.

67. Heskett et al., "Putting the Service Profit-Chain to Work."

It is in these dynamics that we can see the insights of Spinoza at work. Human desires are not static. They are shaped by a person's environment. Follower roles shape follower desires, and when leaders help followers achieve their desires, they can also tap into the freedom Spinoza recognizes as a fundamental human drive. A follower's loyalty, commitment, and enthusiasm are always freely given; they cannot be coerced. And that committed energy is extraordinarily valuable to the leader and the organization. Leaders who recognize the importance of freedom in this process recognize that they can create the environment where followers will enthusiastically commit to their role and their organization. These are the leaders who will reap the benefits of a committed and enthusiastic workforce. Leaders who do not recognize this important aspect of freedom will not benefit from the loyalty and enthusiasm that followers will freely offer when they recognize that their leader and organization deserve their wholehearted support.

11

The Ethics of Rights and Freedom in the Marketplace

MacIntyre now turns to other European thinkers of the seventeenth century to address the next significant evolution in moral concepts, which concerns ideas that are very familiar to us as twenty-first-century Americans: individual rights. It is in the mid-to-late 1600s that the rights of individuals come to the fore as moral concepts, and these rights are considered primarily in the context of freedom and the economic marketplace. Spinoza's focus on freedom has prepared some of the landscape in which the rights associated with freedom emerge. Further background is necessary, however, to see how religious morality gives way to secular ethics, how the individual continues its move to the center of ethical attention and how rights become a primary focus for European ethics at the dawn of Enlightenment philosophy. To address these concerns MacIntyre provides an evaluative summary of the different approaches to ethics that we have covered so far, which enables us to see the transition from a moral environment dominated by religious concepts to a secular approach to ethics that continues to be dominant to this day. In light of these considerations, we will first cover MacIntyre's summary and evaluation of the different approaches to ethics. After his evaluation we will examine the transition from religious to secular ethics, explore the increasingly individualistic slant to morality, and finish with MacIntyre's description of the rights of freedom in the marketplace.

Three Answers to the Question, "Why Be Ethical?"

As MacIntyre's history has already outlined, European society in the seventeenth century is going through a series of enormous transitions. Those transitions are occurring in virtually every aspect of European culture. The Reformation and the Renaissance were the engines of change driving that transformation. For nearly one thousand years, the Roman Catholic Church not only held a monopoly on religious practice on the continent, but it also had a hand in virtually every sector of society, ranging from the arts and education to trade and politics. Religious reformers such as Luther and Calvin challenged that dominance, and the results were upheaval and conflict. Similarly, through its humanism—which was a retrieval of ideas from the non-Christian cultures of ancient Greece and Rome—the Renaissance introduced new thinking in virtually every field of intellectual endeavor. Increased trade and economic change were also rippling through seventeenth-century Europe, as the Age of Discovery brought resources back to the continent and upended the traditional relationships of aristocracy and money. Unsurprisingly, these currents had significant effect on the moral thinking of the time. Given the churning events in the background of this period, MacIntyre takes time in his analysis to recount the state of ethics in European thinking at this juncture. He notes that traditional moral criteria were falling apart under the pressure these changes brought to ethical thinking, which highlighted a number of moral questions. Most important among them was why should people follow moral rules? What evidence or motivation is required to make the following of moral laws necessary and compelling?[1]

Given the history we have covered up to this point, MacIntyre proposes three sets of answers that have been given to these questions dating from the ancient Greeks up through the thinking of Hobbes and Spinoza. Each of these approaches to ethics provides a different shape to moral ideas and different criteria for making moral judgments. The first answer offered by MacIntyre comes to us from the ancient Greeks, having been formulated by Plato and Aristotle. Moral rules in the classical Greek approach receive backing in the context of playing a specific societal role, where human desires and habits are formed to recognize and pursue certain goods. The operative ethical concept for this type of moral thinking is the idea of what is good, or more to the point, what makes a person good. The key moral judgment offered by the Greeks concerns what the

1. *SHE*, 148.

good person does in light of her or his role in society. The goodness of a person's moral character is evaluated in terms of how well that person performs his or her societal role, that performance being determined in large part by a person's virtue.[2]

A second answer to the question is founded in the religious approach to morality represented by the Jewish and Christian traditions of ethics. Moral rules are to be followed in this approach because they are part of a set of divine commandments that require obedience. People who live by the commandments will prosper, both in this life and the next, and those who disobey will suffer punishment. Those who disobey will fail to flourish in the temporal sphere, and they will suffer eternal damnation in the life to come. For this approach to morality, the key moral concept is the imperative to obey. Thou shalt conform your life to the precepts of God. The key motivations in support of this obedience come in the forms of reward or punishment.[3]

The third and last answer offered by MacIntyre is espoused by both ancient and early modern thinkers. In this view, moral rules have logical backing in the sense that they are instructions that enable a person to get what he or she wants in the most direct manner possible. This is the approach advocated by the Sophists and Thomas Hobbes. The key ethical concepts in this third approach to morality is choosing the most effective means to achieve a goal, and human goals are based on a set of desires rooted in an unalterable human nature. Human desires in this context do not change and are aimed at the power to do what one wants.[4]

Although MacIntyre does us the favor of drawing clear lines between these different approaches to morality, it is also true that the different approaches can exist in the same societies at the same time in history, and that there can also be significant overlap between them. The differing conceptions can be combined in any number of ways. For example, the Christian morality of a thinker such as Thomas Aquinas shares with the Greeks the idea that desire can be criticized and corrected. MacIntyre cites the integration Aquinas achieves between the Greek and Christian traditions as the most important historical combination of the different approaches he outlines.[5]

2. *SHE*, 148.
3. *SHE*, 148.
4. *SHE*, 148.
5. *SHE*, 148.

MacIntyre's Evaluation of the Three Approaches to Ethics

Given the differences in the approaches, how should one decide between them? Can we say that one approach is better than another? MacIntyre is quite willing to take a stand on that issue, and he says yes, some approaches are indeed better than others. MacIntyre shows us his philosophical cards here and asserts that if you examine the theories of the universe and human nature presupposed by these three different schools of thought, Aristotle's are the best.[6] They are better than those of Hobbes because Hobbes ignores the fact that our desires often need reform, and the good news is humans are able to correct and shape desires for the good. MacIntyre criticizes Hobbes in a way that will be pertinent to nineteenth-century utilitarian ethics when he observes that the bland reduction of morality to increasing pleasure and reducing pain fails to consider the fact that morally vicious people derive pleasure from doing terribly evil things.[7] Whether it is in our own personal experience or in the pages of history, we have all seen corrupt people take pleasure from doing corrupt things. The activity of a narcissist manipulating others for his or her own gain can result in real pleasure for the narcissist. There is little doubt that the sexual predators identified by the "Me Too" movement enjoyed either the power they exercised or the sexual pleasure of their attacks, or both. There were some Germans who derived pleasure from persecuting Jews. Satisfying one's own desire is not a reliable guide to making ethical choices when one's desires are thoroughly corrupt. This is a point missed by both the Sophists and Hobbes. In addition, the detachment of ideals from their social context achieved by thinkers like Hobbes, who looks only at the generic person in a state of nature or a person living under the power of the king, empties those ideals of much of their meaning.[8] Ideals associated with societal roles such as a Spartan soldier, a Roman patrician, a Jewish rabbi, or even simply a mother or father, provide a powerful backdrop for evaluating moral choices. Within their natural social environments, ideals can be used to critique actions, aims, and desires. Moral choices and attributes stand out quite clearly within the context of such roles. Where expectations for physical courage might vary widely for a generic person, there is little doubt how important a high standard for courage is to a soldier heading into battle.

6. *SHE*, 148.
7. *SHE*, 149.
8. *SHE*, 149.

MacIntyre also observes that despite the focus of religious morality on obedience to divine commands we can see the historical overlap between the Greek and Christian traditions of ethics. Common areas include the fact that desires can be the object of criticism and correction in both traditions, and the intellectual project of Thomas Aquinas is a refinement and adaptation of Aristotle's approach to the virtues in the context of biblical morality. Christian ethics also adds the crucial idea that all people are equal in the sight of God. It is a principle that harkens back to the first pages of the Bible in the book of Genesis, which tells us that all men and women are created in the image and likeness of God (Gen 1:27), and it is a principle that is quite foreign to a thinker like Aristotle, who saw people as belonging to different and unequal classes. MacIntyre goes so far as to assert that equality of rights and freedom for all humans is the achievement of Christian thought in the seventeenth century.[9]

Transitions from Religious to Secular Morality

Equality becomes a rallying cry during the English civil war that stretches from 1642 to 1649. The roots of that cry may have been religious, but claims to equality were soon articulated in a secular context. Part of this transition lies in what MacIntyre characterizes as the weakness of Christian moral thought. He asserts that since the purpose of life for a Christian is found not in this world but in the next, Christianity provides a context in which its moral ideas can gain and lose prominence quite quickly. If the prospects of people are dim and they are generally dissatisfied with their present life, Christianity gains influence through its ability to provide hope to persevere through the suffering meted out by the world. If, on the other hand, people can find interesting projects in this life and have positive economic prospects, the influence of Christianity wanes. Economic growth weakens belief in God, increases intellectual criticism of religion, and leads to social abandonment of religious practice.[10] This transition can be seen in the seventeenth- and eighteenth-century experience of the Puritan movement in both England and New England. Puritanism at its inception was a critique of the established religious order. Over time, however, it primarily became an endorsement

---

9. *SHE*, 149.
10. *SHE*, 150.

of economic activity.[11] Puritans were heavily influenced by the doctrine of predestination espoused by Calvinist theology. In the notion of predestination advocated by Calvin, every person was either saved or damned, and there was nothing a person could do to change that fact. In this context, a persistent psychological need developed where Calvinists, Puritans, and other Protestants looked for clues in their own lives as to whether they were among the elect who would be saved. One such clue was living a just life, which the Bible repeatedly suggests will be rewarded by God in this world and the next. Max Weber, in his famous book *The Protestant Ethic and the Spirit of Capitalism*, describes the link between this religious motivation to virtue, hard work, and thrifty living with the economics of the free market and capitalistic trade that had emerged in the modern world. Puritanism, which had begun as a corrective to the practices of the Anglican Church, over time became merely an inspiration for the behavior that produced economic success.

This process took some two centuries within the Puritan community. In secular society, the transition was much quicker. What was a religious morality became a frame for purely secular pursuits before the close of the seventeenth century.[12] MacIntyre points out that these processes can be seen most clearly in the popular literature of the time. Daniel DeFoe (b. 1660), author of *Robinson Crusoe* and other influential novels, is one of the writers who depicts the absorption of religious values into economic values most clearly. Writing at the turn of the eighteenth century, Defoe observes that zeal for the Christian religion was mostly dead in England.[13] Our ultimate home, as Defoe understood it, was no longer a personal union with God in heavenly glory. In his book *Moll Flanders* he asserts that a person "with money in the pocket is at home anywhere." Money, not prayer or religious practice, provides the security humans crave. Despite Christianity's death, however, Defoe still uses religious terms and ideas to further the pursuit of secular goals. MacIntyre observes that in Defoe's *The Further Adventures of Robinson Crusoe*, the wives depicted in the story are assessed by wholly economic criteria, even though those assessments are communicated through religious terms. The usefulness of the wives is their paramount value. Enjoyment is subordinate to capital, or better yet, developing capital is the greatest enjoyment. Defoe asserts that usefulness

---

11. *SHE*, 150.
12. *SHE*, 150.
13. Defoe, *Serious Reflections of Robinson Crusoe*, 325.

is seen by the wise as the most noble goal of life. It is the goal by which they come closest to imitating Jesus, who always went about being useful or doing good.[14] The secularization of religious moral norms ends up being a victory for the third approach to morality outlined by MacIntyre, which belongs to Hobbes and the Sophists.[15] Hobbes advocated a view of moral motivation in which self-interest reigned, the most basic aspect of which is the desire for self-preservation. It is a view of morality in which the desires of self-interest are unchanging and self-evident. Self-interested utility and economic advantage become the fundamental ideas undergirding morality, and those ideas are so basic and obvious they need neither justification nor explanation.[16]

Increasing Emphasis on the Individual as the Focal Point of Ethics

The absorption of economic values into a religious moral framework is only one part of the evolution of moral concepts at this point. The focus on the individual as the center of ethical analysis introduced by the likes of Luther and Machiavelli now becomes even more pronounced. It is at this time that the novel, with its emphasis on individual experience and the importance of that experience, becomes the principal literary format. MacIntyre asserts that Defoe's *Robinson Crusoe* became the bible for a generation of European thinkers ranging from political philosophers like Rousseau (b. 1712) to economic theorists such as Adam Smith (b. 1723). The first ancestor to this individualism in European literature can be seen in the character of Satan in John Milton's (b. 1608) *Paradise Lost*. Satan's motto in the poem is *"Non-Serviam"* (Latin for "I will not serve"), which is rebellion not only against God, but also the ordained and unchanging hierarchies, whether religious or secular.[17] European society is now the arena that hosts the conflict of individual wills. Within that context, English society was moving through a particularly important period of transition for moral thinking. Traditional order is being called into question and is being challenged by the assertion of rights in which freedom and economic pursuits take center stage. MacIntyre describes how the

14. *SHE*, 151.
15. *SHE*, 150.
16. *SHE*, 150.
17. *SHE*, 151.

English are pushing toward a view of ethics in which the pursuit of one's freedom is central to morality and only has meaning if it includes the economic advantage of the individual.[18]

What Do the Diggers and Levellers Have to Tell Us About Rights?

The literary currents that emphasized the moral importance of individual rights, freedom, and economic interests become crystallized in the statements of Diggers and Levellers, two obscure groups of radicals and free thinkers that participated in the English civil war between 1642 and 1649. Again, my hat is off to MacIntyre as an intellectual historian. Most people have not studied the English civil war during that time, nor heard of the groups called the Diggers and Levellers. As fighting forces, both groups are obscure because they were quickly overcome by the institutional forces of the day. Yet reading the ideas they articulated, we can see why MacIntyre asks us to stop and listen to what they have to say. In 1646, Thomas Overton asserts, "No man hath power over my rights and liberties and I over no mans; but an Individual, enjoy my selfe, and my selfe propriety and may write my selfe no more than my selfe, or presume any further; if I doe, I am an encroacher & invader upon an other man's Right, to which I have no Right."[19] Overton's view of human nature is quite different from that advocated by Hobbes.[20] The state of nature in Hobbes is the nasty brutish fight of all against all. For Overton, the principles of nature restrain a person from invading the domain of others while at the same time providing a warrant for the person to resist others who try to invade the domain of one's self. MacIntyre notes that the word propriety in the quote from Overton is the immediate predecessor of our English word property, but it does have a meaning somewhat distinct from our notion of property. Overton saw a person's freedom to act as closely tied to one's possessions. Without owning and having a right to own tools necessary for a task, the rights of freedom would be severely limited.[21]

Yet the question can still be asked, to whom should these rights be given? During the Putney debates of 1647, one of the most influential

---

18. *SHE*, 152.
19. *SHE*, 153–54. Quoting from Overton, *Arrow Against All Tyrants*.
20. *SHE*, 154.
21. *SHE*, 154.

Levellers, Colonel Thomas Rainborough, provides this answer: "I think that the poorest he that is in England hath a life to live as the greatest he, and therefore truly, sir, I think it is clear to every man that is to live under a government ought first by his own consent to put himself under that government."[22] Rainborough's statement is an assertion of the dignity of every man and builds on the rights language put forward by Overton by placing the discussion in the context of the individual's relationship to the state. MacIntyre observes that a right can only be exercised in an environment where rules enable a person to exercise that right. In a modern state, those rules exist and are understood in a system of laws.[23]

This leads MacIntyre to raise yet another question. Why should individuals obey the laws of the state, given their dignity and natural rights? Here the idea of the social contract comes back into play. The contract is a necessary idea to explain the foundation of state authority since the traditional foundations linking a monarchy to the people via social and religious bonds have been dramatically loosened by the liberty concerns and economic changes that have disrupted seventeenth-century European society.[24] The social contract, however, needs work. The version worked about by Hobbes is problematic because it is completely ahistorical and is based on such a limited view of human nature. Overton and Rainborough have set a context in which every person has natural rights and should only submit to the authority of the state through their consent, assuming the state will fulfill its obligations based on the contract. The problem with this analysis, like that of Hobbes, is that history never allows that to actually happen. Even in a democracy, individuals have no real ability to consent or dissent from state power ruling over them.[25]

The result of these ideas coming together is that natural rights become a key part of the understanding of liberty. The rights of individuals concern their ability to exercise freedom in the economic marketplace. The conceptual developments are made on the backs of names almost lost to history, but that will change with the coming of John Locke, one of the most important intellectual predecessors to the founders of the United States. Locke inherits the ideas of the contract and makes his own attempt to work them out. In doing so, he works out his own version of ethical concepts that are based on Plato's thought but are articulated

22. *SHE*, 153. Quoting from Libcom.org, "Entry on Diggers and Levellers."
23. *SHE*, 154.
24. *SHE*, 156.
25. *SHE*, 156.

in the context of Locke's political theory, which will shape much of the ethical thinking in eighteenth-century England. The next chapter will examine Locke's approach to morality and how that shapes the English thinkers that follow him.

Leadership Reflection: Follower Motivation

"It's the economy, stupid," is a famous political slogan coined by James Carville when he served as an advisor for Bill Clinton's successful presidential election campaign in 1992. Carville's succinct formulation puts into words what many of us believe about our political motivations, which is we vote our pocketbooks. We vote for what is in our economic self-interest. MacIntyre provides a nice historical summary of how the idea to pursue one's economic interest developed in Western culture. A combination of philosophy and economic development produced a context in which economic self-interest came to be seen not only as the dominant motive for human behavior, but the *only* motive of human behavior. The roots of that assertion can be found in the thinking of Thomas Hobbes, who claimed that morality is motivated by self-interest and the desires of self-interest (self-preservation and obtaining power) are unchanging, universal, and self-evident. These ideas are further developed by authors such as Defoe who place it in a context of economic self-interest and utility. For DeFoe and others, morality is based on economic advantage and utility, and again, this reality is so basic and obvious that it need not be explained. Thus, we can see that an idea most Americans take for granted as universally valid is actually the result of historical processes and the thinking that emerged as those processes evolved between the sixteenth and seventeenth centuries.

Another assertion that may be surprising to a present-day American is the fact that acting in economic self-interest is not a universal behavior. People do not always act in their economic self-interest for a variety of reasons. This is particularly the case when we examine the motives behind the behavior of followers and how financial incentives affect that behavior in a work environment. The followers or employees of an organization can be motivated by economic self-interest/financial incentives, but recent psychological research has consistently demonstrated that financial incentives are not only ineffective motivators of improved performance, but in the great majority of cases actually lead to lower employee performance. This seems counterintuitive to say the least. So how did the psychologists figure that out? Going back to psychological research conducted in the early twentieth century, we see Robert Yerkes and John Dodson (in 1908) test the hypothesis that there is an optimal level of arousal in animals for performing tasks and deviations from that arousal level, both positive and negative, will yield lower performance.[26] They confirmed their hypothesis through experiments on mice, and the hypothesis has been further confirmed in human psychological research many times over. Applying this idea in the context of financial incentives, researchers have found that more money provides good motivation for followers if the tasks those followers are executing involve virtually no cognitive dimensions. If the task is simple manual labor, extrinsic motivation such as a bonus does increase follower performance. Add even just rudimentary cognitive functioning to the task, however, and employee performance actually suffers when leaders provide monetary incentives. There are a number of psychological reasons that cause this unexpected result. People may choke under pressure or they may be distracted by the incentive in a number of different ways. The research conclusion is clear, however, that financial incentives have a negative impact on follower performance for work that is cognitively complex.[27]

Contemporary business practice has further discovered that economic self-interest, as an external motivation, is inferior in its ability to motivate followers compared to what are called intrinsic motivations. It is not just the fact that relying on economic self-interest can psychologically distract a person from focusing on a task. The real cost to that focus is neglecting to use other motivations that are simply more compelling than financial incentives. Author Dan Pink has popularized social scientific research regarding human motivation and has also surveyed corporate practices that leverage these internal motivations of behavior to great effect. Pink asserts that tapping into the intrinsic motivations of autonomy, mastery, and purpose not only lead to more ethical behavior on the part of followers, but leads to significantly greater productivity on their part, as well.[28] This is the case for two reasons. First, as the psychological research shows, if any of the work requires even rudimentary cognitive skill, the extrinsic motivation of economic self-interest will lower follower

---

26. Yerkes and Dodson, "Relationship of Strength of Stimulus to Rapidity of Habit-Formation," 459–82.
27. Ariely et al., "Large Stakes and Big Mistakes."
28. Paton, "Performance Related Pay Does Not Encourage Performance."

performance. Second, as MacIntyre makes clear in his critique of Hobbes, there are many factors in addition to self-interest that motivate human behavior and moral choice. There is no doubt, as Hobbes asserts, that people regularly make self-interested choices. His mistake is to universalize this observation. The result is a narrow and inaccurate view of human motivation. People pursue their life projects for a large variety of reasons and motivations. Pink hits on a few that are central. People see the use of their autonomy as fulfilling. Becoming masterful at a particular task or activity is a great source of satisfaction. Lastly, achieving a purpose and making a positive difference for others is one of the strongest motivations we experience as human beings. Leaders who follow the thinking of Hobbes and Defoe, motivating their followers only by means of self-interest and financial incentives, will depress follower performance and miss out on the factors that motivate followers to go above and beyond their duties. Leaders who inspire brilliance and tap into the human desire for excellence will incorporate the most powerful motivators for follower behavior into the work of the organization. This is a recipe for productivity that monetary self-interest simply cannot produce.

12

Eighteenth-Century British Ethics

OUR NEXT THREE CHAPTERS will examine the development of ethics over the course of the late seventeenth and eighteenth centuries. Testimony to the turbulence and importance of the thinking and history of this period are the revolutions that mark its beginning and end. England at the end of the 1680s experienced the Glorious Revolution, which established William and Mary on the throne of England and thrust the idea of the social contract into the practice of politics at the time. The eighteenth century concluded with two further revolutions, the American and the French. The importance of these events in shaping twenty-first-century Europe and America needs little explanation. Within the context of this tumultuous history the development of ethical thinking continues and is touched by some of the most important thinkers of the Age of Enlightenment, which is the intellectual heir to the Renaissance and the Scientific Revolution. Enlightenment thinkers shaped not only the political theory that is still dominant in Europe and the United States, but they also developed the ethical concepts and constructs that have defined contemporary ethics. MacIntyre asserts that the ethics of today have been defined by one thinker from this time period in particular: Immanuel Kant. Ironically, Kant's moral formulations influence multitudes of people who have never even heard of Kant.[1] Kant's thinking does not occur in a vacuum, however. In his own words, he was awoken from his "dogmatic slumber" by the Scottish philosopher David Hume.[2] And the

1. *SHE*, 190.
2. Kant, *Prolegomena to Any Future Metaphysics*, 7.

important moral concepts that are reinforced and developed throughout this period are by no means the product of only these two influential authors. This development is the result of a cultural dialogue that crosses the entire continent of Europe and receives contributions from authors hailing from many countries. In an attempt to bring order to this rich dialogue, MacIntyre provides a geographic focus for his analysis, examining Enlightenment moral thought first in England, then in France, and finally in Germany. Following the path MacIntyre lays out for us, we will start with the prominent English philosopher John Locke, who takes up the social contract theory of Hobbes, articulates it to a new generation of people facing political conflict, and in doing so further shapes the moral ideas that exist within that environment.

John Locke on Liberty, Property, and the Rationality of Ethics

Similar to Cicero and Machiavelli, John Locke (b. 1632) was not only an influential thinker and author, but was also active in the politics and events of his day. Educated at Oxford, Locke's intellectual interests were broad, ranging from medicine, to politics and ethics. In 1666 he met Anthony Ashley, the future Lord Shaftesbury (the title by which Ashley is known in most historical accounts of the period) who was one of the most influential men in England at the time. In 1667 Ashley invited Locke to work with him in London. Locke became Ashley's close confidant, serving as his physician, political and economic adviser, secretary, researcher, and friend. Locke's relationship with Shaftesbury proved crucial to Locke's career and experience, as it enabled Locke to participate in many of the events that marked the English political landscape in the late seventeenth century. In addition, Shaftesbury's grandson, the Third Earl of Shaftesbury, who would be educated under Locke's direction, became one of the most influential British ethicists of the early eighteenth century and also a significant critic of Locke's moral thought.[3] To examine their differences, we will start by looking at how Locke picks up where Hobbes leaves off, asking similar questions regarding the foundation of political authority, but using a different view of human nature to arrive at his ethical conclusions.

---

3. Cf. Thomas, *Routledge Philosophy Guidebook to Locke on Government*, 3–7 for a brief overview of Locke's life and career.

Locke, like Hobbes, examined the relationship between ruler and ruled so that he could defend the authority of the sovereigns of his time, William of Orange and his queen, Mary. MacIntyre relates how Locke follows Hobbes by starting with human nature and the social contract. Locke's state of nature, however, departs significantly from that of Hobbes. For Locke, the natural person is neither pre-moral nor pre-social. The state of nature is not a nasty and solitary existence, but includes families and a settled social order.[4] Despite this order, Locke justifies the need for state authority in terms similar to those laid down by Hobbes. Disputes inevitably arise in a community of any significant size. Such conflict requires settlement by means of an impartial authority if the community is to maintain peace and tranquility among its citizens. Thus, there is a need for the social contract, the aim of which is to create an authority with strength to safeguard a person's natural rights, the most important of which is the right to property.[5] MacIntyre notes how Locke links the right to property with the right to liberty in a manner similar to the view Overton advocated in the 1640s. A person's liberty and property are so closely connected that any notion of a right to freedom must carry a right to property, for without property the value of a person's freedom, especially in the economic sphere, will be severely limited. Despite the economic context for the pursuit of liberty that is part of the intellectual environment in which Locke is operating, he is speaking of the right to property as a right that exists in the state of nature before the laws of civil society have been established. The property to which a person has a right is the property produced by that person.[6] It is in protecting rights such as property that the state has a claim to authority under social contract theory. The state is the entity that has the ability to judge conflicts between individuals impartially and also has the power to protect natural rights from being trampled upon in the midst of these conflicts.

It is in his description of natural rights that Locke's view of ethics comes into focus. For Locke, natural rights are based on a moral law that humans apprehend through their power of reason. He asserts that although moral ideas derive from sense experience, the relationship between these ideas are such that morality is as clearly rational and capable of demonstration as the relationships that are examined in a field such as mathematics. Ethics for Locke is understood through the rational

4. *SHE*, 157.
5. *SHE*, 158.
6. *SHE*, 158.

scrutiny of moral terms. In examining the terms, a person is exposed to the ideas expressed by those terms and comes to understand the moral principles in question.[7] Given this background, Locke asserts that reason identifies good and evil as the key moral terms. He then provides definitions of those terms that will influence English philosophers well into the 1800s. Unlike a philosopher such as Aristotle, who says that good is the object of desire, Locke asserts that a morally good choice causes pleasure and diminishes pain. Evil, on the other hand, is what causes pain or decreases pleasure. Locke contends that these definitions are a function of the law of nature that rewards good behavior with pleasure and bad behavior with pain.[8]

MacIntyre observes that what is distinctive about Locke's approach to ethical concepts is his focus on pleasure and pain that retains a rational and Platonic view of morality. MacIntyre cites the influence of the Cambridge Platonists that precede Locke as providing the inspiration for his views.[9] Locke and the Cambridge thinkers make the claim that in grasping a moral idea or insight a person understands the criteria by which a person applies that idea when making a moral judgment. For example, evidence that you actually understand the idea of "swift" is seen in your ability to apply it to animals or humans that run fast. So, too, with moral terms. Properly understanding moral concepts includes understanding the criteria that enable these ideas to be applied to moral judgments. MacIntyre asserts that in Locke's view and that of the Cambridge Platonists, moral criteria are clear and unambiguous.[10] If you understand a moral term such as justice properly, you will be able to apply the idea of justice to your moral judgments accurately.

MacIntyre observes two effects growing out of Locke's rationalistic and Platonic approach to ethics. The first is Locke's approach makes moral judgments similar to mathematical and even empirical judgements, empirical judgments being understood as judgments made on the basis of data derived from scientific experiments. Rationality provides a clarity to moral judgments that might seem too good to be true for those of us making those judgments in the often-confusing world of ethics. In a second and related observation, MacIntyre contends that in Locke's view, the fact that people can come to the opposite moral conclusion will always be

---

7. *SHE*, 160.
8. *SHE*, 160. Cf. Locke, *Essay Concerning Human Understanding*.
9. *SHE*, 160.
10. *SHE*, 161.

the result of at least one person failing to understand the moral principle in question. In failing to understand the applicable moral criteria, that person will make a bad moral judgment; he or she will fail to apply the ethical concept correctly because of that misunderstanding.[11] Given the influence Platonic thought had on Locke, it is unsurprising that Locke's position resembles those of Socrates and Plato, who held the source of ethical failure to be a lack of knowledge on the part of the person making a moral decision. MacIntyre asserts that it is an implausible description of moral disagreement that leaves Locke's thinking susceptible to criticism.[12]

Sentimental Moral Theorists

The third Lord Shaftesbury, Locke's former student, is one of the thinkers who argues against Locke's moral rationalism. For Shaftesbury (b. 1671) and thinkers such as Francis Hutcheson (b. 1694) and David Hume (b. 1711), morality was based not on reason but on a moral sense. Shaftesbury asserts that an inward eye, separate from the power of reason, distinguishes right from wrong. In his view, a moral judgment was the expression of a feeling or emotion in response to the properties of one's own moral actions or the actions of others. He saw moral judgments as similar to aesthetic judgements that respond to the beauty of shapes and figures.[13] In addition, favorable and unfavorable responses to moral actions were not seen simply as responses to a particular action but were understood as responses to the character or the virtue of the person making the moral choice.[14] Given that background, Shaftesbury described positive moral responses in terms of a virtuous person who had shaped his or her inclinations to be in harmony with the inclinations of other people. Harmony becomes the greatest of all moral properties. In the happy situation of moral harmony, human conflict is avoided because what satisfies one person is the same as what satisfies the person with whom harmony has been established. Shaftesbury contends that such harmony is possible because humans naturally tend toward benevolence

---

11. *SHE*, 161.
12. *SHE*, 161.
13. *SHE*, 162.
14. *SHE*, 163.

to one another.¹⁵ Shaftesbury's thinking is a far cry from the nasty brutishness of Hobbes's state of nature.

Shaftesbury, and Francis Hutcheson who follows him, are classified as moral sentimentalists in contrast to the moral rationalism of Locke. In this view of ethics, morality is a function of the sentiments, feelings, or emotions humans experience when confronted with a moral phenomenon. Despite the divide between reason and sentiment, Shaftesbury and Hutcheson share Locke's view that moral good and evil are based on the human experience of pleasure and pain. It is an idea that will carry their thought through to that of David Hume and his utilitarian successors in nineteenth-century British philosophy. Although Hutcheson is considered a sentimentalist and not a utilitarian, he is the thinker who coins the principle of utility that will serve as the guiding idea for the later school of utilitarian ethics, which is, "That nation is best which procures the greatest happiness for the greatest numbers, and that worst which in like manner occasions misery."¹⁶

MacIntyre asserts that the sentimentalist approach advocated by Shaftesbury and Hutcheson leaves us with gaps that are addressed by subsequent philosophers. As was mentioned earlier, Shaftesbury and Hutcheson center their conception of morality on a moral sense, and in doing so, assimilate ethics to aesthetics. The moral sense appreciates and examines virtue in the same way the aesthetic sense appreciates beauty. Theirs is a passive approach to morality that speaks from the standpoint of a critic of moral choice, but not as the person actually making the moral choice.¹⁷ By looking at moral phenomena from the outside in, so to speak, neither Shaftesbury nor Hutcheson provides an account of how reason or motives affect the actual decision-making process. Two thinkers who address these issues are Joseph Butler, who provides an account of how reason is related to morality, and David Hume, who addresses the relationship between motives and moral choices.¹⁸ Given the different starting points of Butler and Hume (Butler was a religious thinker and Hume was not), it is difficult to integrate their insights, so we will describe Butler's approach first before turning to that of Hume.

---

15. *SHE*, 162.

16. Hutcheson, *Enquiry into the Original of our Ideas of Beauty and Virtue*, 2:3 as cited in *SHE*, 163.

17. *SHE*, 163.

18. *SHE*, 164.

Joseph Butler on Reason in Relation to Ethics

Joseph Butler (b. 1692) was an Anglican bishop who disagreed with Hutcheson's approach to ethics in two major respects. First, he denied that benevolence plays the central role in morality asserted by Hutcheson. Benevolence for Butler was one among many virtues that a person should take care to promote.[19] Second, he criticized the notion that consequences should be the primary criteria to guide moral choices. This is the case for two reasons. One, we are limited in our ability to predict future consequences, so they are not a reliable guide for moral choice and could even justify making horrible moral choices. Two, he asserted that there are classes of moral action that ought to be either done or prohibited regardless of the consequences those choices entail.[20] In making that assertion, Butler anticipated the thinking of Immanuel Kant who similarly divorced the criteria for making moral choices from the consequences produced by those choices.

From MacIntyre's perspective, the importance of Butler's ethical thought lies in how he retrieves the Greek approach to moral reasoning that sees reasoning as based on what will or will not satisfy our nature as rational beings.[21] For the Greeks, rationality or reason enables a person to determine what is truly good or what should be desired if a person is to live a prosperous and noble life. Butler takes this approach as his own with one important difference. For the Greeks, such nobility and the living of a good life happened in the context of playing a specific role, and the nature of that role was determined by the community, the Greek city-state. Butler, as heir to the individualism that had been gaining steam in European culture and thought, examines the reasoning associated with moral choice in the context of individual self-awareness.[22] Happiness is the goal to be achieved for both the Greeks and modern thinkers like Butler, but the meaning of happiness changes given the different social contexts. Happiness for the Greeks is found in living a life that is good because the necessary virtues to perform one's roles in society have been developed and are being used effectively by that person. Happiness in Butler's individualistic context becomes a function of individual psychology. Happiness is now equated with a feeling or an emotion to be

---

19. *SHE*, 164.
20. *SHE*, 164–65.
21. *SHE*, 166.
22. *SHE*, 166.

achieved, but not as a way of life that provides satisfaction in the context of the community.[23]

MacIntyre explains the development of this difference as a function of the increasing emphasis on the individual that starts with Luther and Machiavelli, is culturally reinforced through the literature of authors like Milton and Defoe, and receives further support in the connection between Protestantism and capitalism. These cultural forces made the reality of later European social life so different from that of ancient Greece that the conceptual link between happiness and the duties of a societal role is broken. As a result, the moral terms are redefined. Happiness as an emotion with no necessary relation to a community replaces the satisfaction of playing one's role well within the community. Happiness is redefined to be a function of individual psychology and emotions. MacIntyre points out that this redefinition becomes a challenge for the different moral schools that emerge in eighteenth-century Europe because the idea of happiness as a psychological feeling leads to problems when used as the foundation for moral evaluations. This is the case because many choices that lead to individual happiness are often choices that no one should ever make from a moral perspective.[24] It might make you happy to steal your neighbor's expensive car, but we know stealing from neighbors is a bad moral choice. Individual happiness has difficulty providing consistently good guidance for ethical decisions. As a result, succeeding schools of philosophy oscillate between focusing on the consequences of choices that will lead to happiness (utilitarianism) and other schools that define morality in terms that have nothing to do with consequences that lead to happiness (Kantianism).[25] Given the mixed results provided by moral analysis based on reason in the context of the individual, MacIntyre shifts his analysis to a thinker that further develops the sentimentalist approach of Shaftesbury and Hutcheson, a Scottish philosopher by the name of David Hume.

---

23. *SHE*, 167.
24. *SHE*, 167.
25. *SHE*, 167.

David Hume and the Impossibility of Deriving a Moral "Ought" from a Factual "Is"

Despite the fact that many people have never heard of David Hume, MacIntyre sees him as an enormously important philosopher whose influence on ethics and other moral thinkers should not be overlooked. In a later book, MacIntyre says of Hume, "He was identified, and rightly so, as the antagonist par excellence, the philosopher whose views had to be defeated in open philosophical debate. He became the one thinker in opposition to whom decade after continuing decade Scottish philosophers had to frame their enquiries."[26] So what is it that Hume said that so many people had to challenge? He certainly was controversial in his criticism of religious approaches to ethics at a time when religion was still a dominant cultural force in British society. We will see that Hume advocates for utility and usefulness as fundamental to moral judgment, and he argues that it is precisely in the area of usefulness where religious principles of morality fail because those principles are more akin to delusions and superstition. The following citation demonstrates the direct and pointed critique he makes of religious morality:

> Celibacy, fasting, penance, mortifications, self-denial, humility, silence, solitude, and the whole train of monkish virtues; for what reason are they everywhere rejected by men of sense, but because they serve to no manner of purpose; neither advance a man's fortune in the world, nor render him a more valuable member of society; neither qualify him for the entertainment of company, nor increase his power of self-enjoyment? We observe on the contrary, that they cross all these desirable ends; stupefy the understanding and harden the heart, obscure the fancy and sour the temper. We justly, therefore, transfer them to the opposite column, and place them in the catalogue of vices.[27]

There is little doubt that Hume's religious views brought attention and even animosity to his thinking. His more enduring influence, however, stems from the innovative way he uses the scientific method to examine human nature and the comprehensive re-thinking of morality that he develops in the wake of that examination.

Hume advocates for the importance of usefulness and utility as it is articulated by Hutcheson, the greatest happiness for the greatest number

---

26. MacIntyre, *Whose Justice, Which Rationality?*, 322.
27. Hume, *Enquiry Concerning the Principles of Morals*, 9.1.1.

of people, and links this to Locke's assertion that what makes people happy is increasing pleasure and decreasing pain. Unlike later utilitarian philosophers that follow in Hume's wake (people like Jeremy Bentham and John Stuart Mill), Hume sees utility as important but not the defining principle of ethics. Following Shaftesbury and Hutcheson on what is fundamental, Hume asserts that moral sentiment, or the moral sense, is the fundamental basis for making moral evaluations. And again, moral sentiment refers to the feelings, both positive and negative, that humans encounter when they come to grips with moral choices, whether it is their own choices or those of others. To put it in Hume's words, "Morality ... is more properly felt than judged of."[28] He further asserts that, "To have the sense of virtue is nothing but to *feel* a satisfaction of a particular kind from the contemplation of a character. The very feeling constitutes our praise or admiration."[29] Another aspect of Hume's ethics implied in this quote is that the ethical sense is not primarily focused on the specific choices or actions of a person, but on the moral character of the person making the choice. In Hume's view, moral choices are the expression of a person's moral character, and it is the nature of that character that moral sense will either approve or disapprove. This position exhibits Hume's debt to Hutcheson, who first articulates the idea that a pleasurable moral feeling is based on the perception of a benevolent moral character trait that can be observed through a benevolent action.[30]

Hume presents sentiment and feeling as the foundation of morality and as an opposing viewpoint to a moral rationalist such as Locke. For Hume, moral judgments cannot be judgments of reason because reason does not have the power to move a person to act, and the whole point of moral judgment is to guide human action.[31] In Hume's calculation, reason concerns the relation of ideas in fields such as mathematics or the understanding of facts. Neither abstract ideas nor facts move humans to action because actions are inspired by the prospect of pleasure or pain that will develop as a consequence of a moral choice. It is the passions and not reason that are aroused by the expectation of pleasure or pain. Reason can tell a person if an object of desire exists and the means to acquire an object of desire, but reason cannot judge, criticize, or move the

---

28. Hume, *Treatise of Human Nature*, III.1.2, as cited in SHE, 170.
29. Hume, *Treatise of Human Nature*, III.1.2.
30. Hutcheson, *Original of Our Ideas*, Introduction.
31. SHE, 169.

passions. The passions move reason. For Hume, reason is the slave of the passions. It can only serve and obey them.[32]

It is in the context of reason being concerned only with ideas and facts and not with moral considerations that Hume articulates his most influential moral principle. Hume asserts that moral conclusions are not based on anything that can be established by reason. Many students conclude (with good reason) that Hume thinks it is logically impossible that any factual truth can provide a basis for morality. As we noted earlier, Hume is not one to shy away from controversy, and this is no doubt a controversial assertion since it rejects much of the moral tradition to which he is heir. The Greek tradition, religious morality, and even a recent predecessor such as Locke all rely on reason and human rationality to understand ethics. Yet for Hume, to use reason and facts as the lens through which to study morality is to make an enormous mistake. No set of factual circumstances can entail a moral conclusion.[33] Humans cannot derive moral obligations from factual circumstances. You cannot get a moral "ought" from a factual "is." To do so is to commit a logical fallacy that combines two different types of knowledge, moral and factual. For many philosophers after Hume, this insight is a crucial discovery about the nature of ethics.[34]

Given the history we have been reviewing, there is no doubt Hume's idea about the relationship between facts and morality is a significant change and innovation. For the ancient Greeks it would seem ethics is all about facts. For them, the fact that you are a king, a lawyer, or a soldier holds tremendous implications for your moral responsibilities. A role-based approach to ethics makes the transition from "is" to "ought" part and parcel of ethical thinking. It seems quite intuitive, as well. The fact that a person is a father seems to lead to moral obligations that do not apply to a man that does not have children. As MacIntyre points out, the fact that our house is on fire seems to give compelling guidance for the choices we make in that situation.[35] Given this background of moral analysis wedded to facts, how should we understand Hume's assertion? How do we make sense of it? MacIntyre provides an answer to these questions and helps us understand how ethical history provides the foundation for Hume's innovative thinking.

32. SHE, 169. Cf. Hume, *Treatise of Human Nature*, II.3.3.
33. SHE, 172.
34. SHE, 172.
35. SHE, 172.

MacIntyre takes two steps in answering the above questions. First, he looks at what we mean when we are talking about a moral "ought," a moral obligation, or something that should be done from an ethical perspective. Second, he describes how the understanding of this concept changes in the context of the moral individualism of Enlightenment philosophy. Beginning with the first idea, MacIntyre contends that there are two types of moral obligations or imperatives with which people are familiar. First, there is the simple imperative in which no rationale for why a command is to be obeyed is expected or provided.[36] A military order is an example of this simple type of ought or obligation, which is so well expressed in Lord Tennyson's *Charge of the Light Brigade*. "Their's not to make reply. Their's not to reason why. Their's but to do and die. Into the valley of death rode the six hundred."[37] Military culture, where life-threatening missions require immediate obedience to orders, is an environment in which orders are expected to be followed no matter the rationale because prompt obedience can be the difference between life and death.

The second type of "ought" or obligation is the type in which the person asserting the obligation is expected to and can give a reason for saying why the command should be followed. The reasons that back up the obligation are of varying types. They might be based on the result you want to achieve, "If you want good grades, you ought to study." The reason might be based on your role: "You should do this because you are a police officer." The reason you ought to do something can also be based on your aspiration to fulfill an ideal. "You ought to do this if you want to be courageous or to be a knight or to be a saint."[38] It is at this point that MacIntyre brings in the surrounding context of individualism to make sense of Hume's assertion and demonstrate how the concepts are changing and adapting to that new intellectual context.

> As shared ideals and accepted functions drop away in the age of individualism, the injunctions have less and less backing. The end of this process is the appearance of a "You ought . . ." unbacked by reasons, announcing traditional moral rules in a vacuum so far as ends are concerned, and addressed to an unlimited class of persons. For this *ought* the title of *the* moral *ought* is claimed, and it has two properties. It tells us what to do

---

36. *SHE*, 173.
37. Tennyson, "Charge of the Light Brigade," 52.
38. *SHE*, 173.

as an imperative does, and it is addressed to anyone who happens to be in the relevant circumstances. When to this use of "You ought" the response is, But why ought I? the only ultimate answer is "You just ought" . . . Of this ought it is clear that it cannot be deducted from any is.[39]

The individualistic context in which ethics approaches only a single person outside of relationships or a societal role combined with the simple imperative that requires no rationale for a command yields moral obligations that can be asserted without relying on factual evidence. Combined with Hume's sentimental approach to ethics in which moral obligation derives from feelings and not reasons, we have Hume's rationale for asserting a divide between facts and obligation.

At this point in his analysis, MacIntyre asks an interesting question of Hume's position. Is Hume saying that it is impossible to derive a moral "ought" from a factual "is" as so many philosophers have concluded Hume is saying or should people just be very careful in doing so?[40] On the mere reading of his words, one would think Hume is saying it is impossible. Yet the reality is that in much of his ethical writing, Hume makes precisely that transition himself. MacIntyre points out that one such example of Hume going from an "is" to an "ought" can be seen in Hume's analysis concerning the basis for the rules of justice. Hume asserts that the rules of justice are necessary because without them there is no stability of property, a condition that would undermine the ability of people to live together in a community. Rules of justice are established to provide this stability, and virtues that enable individuals to abide by the rules of justice are created and encouraged so the members of the community adhere to those rules even when doing so is not in their short-term interest. Adherence to the rules of justice is in the long-term interest of all because individuals can see the harm that would ensue if other people did not abide by these rules.[41] Hume's entire analysis with regard to justice and the moral obligation to obey the rules of justice is based on the factual circumstances of communities. No one wants to live in a community where the rights to property and safety are not protected. The bad conditions (or facts) produced by rampant disregard for these rights gives rise to the obligation to abide by the rules so other people will do so as well. MacIntyre puts

39. *SHE*, 173.
40. *SHE*, 174.
41. *SHE*, 174.

the issue in terms of human nature. Human persons have certain desires and needs that are served well by moral rules and the principles of justice. In MacIntyre's view, Hume's argument regarding justice recognizes this reality, but in doing so, undermines interpreting Hume as asserting it is impossible to get a moral "ought" from a factual "is." This is the case because Hume is arguing from the "facts" of human nature and human social life and then comes to a moral conclusion about why people should in fact obey the principles of justice.[42]

MacIntyre does not reserve his criticism of Hume only to the "is/ought" issue. He also takes Hume to task for one of MacIntyre's primary moral concerns, which is the ability of humans to change their desires and passions over time. Hume treats passions and desires as merely given. Desires, emotions, and feelings are static and cannot be reformed. We have the feelings and desires that we have, and Hume provides no explanation for why human desires take the shape that they do. MacIntyre asserts that Hume fails to recognize that desires and emotions can to a certain extent be altered, criticized, and even reformed.[43] It is a failure that Hume shares with both his predecessors and successors and is an issue that will raise its head again in discussing the French and German approaches to ethics in the eighteenth century.

Leadership Reflection: Reason and Emotion in Leadership

Which human faculty is more important when it comes to effective leadership, reason or emotion? Put differently, who is the philosopher we need to pay attention to more when it comes to leadership: John Locke, whose focus is on reason, or David Hume, who says reason is the slave of emotion and that emotion is the real impetus for moral decisions? Locke and Hume agree that the goal of the moral life is to experience pleasure and avoid pain, but they offer very different accounts of how to achieve those goals.

For Locke, reason points out the path that leads to the goals of experiencing pleasure and avoiding pain. In Locke's view, moral concepts are like scientific or mathematical principles, and it is in reason's ability to understand those principles that one is able to apply them accurately when making moral decisions. When a person understands the criteria

---

42. *SHE*, 175.
43. *SHE*, 175.

that govern a moral principle, the person can then make the necessary decisions to achieve a particular goal. In this context it is a leader's job to enable understanding on the part of followers. A leader needs to be able to articulate a vision that can be understood by followers so that they can achieve the goals of the organization. By enabling followers to rationally comprehend their situation and the nature of their task, a leader enables his or her followers to determine and pursue the means most important to executing their assigned mission. The leader is an arbiter of reason, linking the rationality of followers to the task at hand, which for Locke is ultimately aimed at promoting pleasure and reducing suffering.

The 2002 book *Primal Leadership*, on the other hand, seems to take Hume's view by asserting the primal task of a leader is not rational but is an effort to drive emotions in the right direction. In the words of the authors, "Great leadership works through the emotions."[44] The book begins with a story about the closing of a news division at the British Broadcasting Corporation (BBC). The division had been an experiment and was comprised of two hundred journalists and editors. They were all called together to receive the bad news that the division would have to close down. The executive delivering the news started by describing how well rival divisions had been doing, how wonderful his recent vacation was, and then moved into the dismantling of the division. The audience became so angry that security personnel were almost called to escort the executive out of the room. It's a ridiculous, but all too common story of a leader who is utterly blind to the emotions of his or her audience. What's unique about this story is the very next day, the same group was addressed by a different executive on the same issue. The difference in reaction to the second discussion could not have been more pronounced, and that difference lay in the manner in which the second executive addressed the audience and the impact his words had on their emotions. That executive discussed the importance and meaning of journalism. He described the typical instability of journalistic careers, but referenced the high calling of public service executed by journalists. He appealed to the purpose they had followed in entering the field of journalism and inspired them to persevere in the face of their current challenges. The audience reacted not with hostility, but literally with applause.[45] Here was

---

44. Goleman et al., *Primal Leadership*, 25.
45. Goleman et al., *Primal Leadership*, 4.

a leader in tune with the emotional impact he had on his followers, and the difference in response on the part of his followers was extraordinary.

So, Hume is right. Emotions drive behavior. Leaders must therefore leverage emotions and leave the cold and impotent calculations of reason aside when motivating followers. This seems too hasty a conclusion, and likely one that even the authors of *Primal Leadership* would be hesitant to endorse. After all, the authors are writing a book about the importance of emotions to leadership. They are appealing to the faculty of reason in their effort to awaken leaders to the importance of emotion. Would that not make reason more important than emotion since it is only by means of reason that a leader can become aware of the importance of emotion to leadership? Hume would answer that question by asserting reason educates the emotions, but it is only emotion that moves a person.

So, what's the right answer? As is so often the case in philosophy, the answer turns not on an either/or basis but on a both/and foundation. This can be seen in the name of the capacity that enables a leader to be cognizant of the emotional impact she or he is having on followers, which is called emotional intelligence. A crucial aspect of emotional intelligence is the ability to recognize the effect your behavior has on the emotions of the people who observe your behavior. It turns out that reason and emotion are both crucial to emotional intelligence and the effective motivation of followers. This is no great insight. We all know that reason and emotions are important to our decisions as humans, whether we are followers or leaders. What it does point out, however, is the fact that we should be wary of thinkers who draw lines that are too bright and too narrow when discussing ideas in the context of ethics and leadership. And often this is a problem for modern thinkers. Morality is not only about reason (Locke), nor is it only about emotion (Hume), nor is it only about self-interest (Hobbes), for that matter. As moral agents playing on the dynamic playing field of life, leaders must have the judgment to focus on what is pertinent in a specific situation. Sometimes it is cold, hard reason that must drive a leader's actions and sometime it is the emotion of the situation that carries the most weight, but usually both have important roles to play.

One place where all three of our thinkers seem to be too narrow is in the areas of pursuing pleasure and avoiding pain, what might be called self-interested actions. Sometimes a leader can leverage the self-interest of their followers or even the leader's own self-interest to attack a team's mission. Often, however, the path of leadership is one of sacrifice and embracing suffering. Sometimes leaders and their followers must endure and even embrace pain and suffering in order to pursue their missions. Whether it is a platoon in combat or an organization that has to sacrifice the good of its members for a greater community (firefighters in a conflagration or health care workers in a pandemic are examples that come to mind), leaders and followers often have to pursue the path directly opposed to self-interest and pleasure. This is the complexity of ethics and leadership, whether we like it or not. The leader has to keep all these balls in the air at the same time, and philosophers who try to boil human morality down to one category or another are failing to account for that complexity.

13

Ethics in Eighteenth-Century France

MacIntyre notes that Enlightenment philosophers in both England and France analyzed similar topics, which included the existing social and political orders, concepts of law, ethics, sovereignty, and various other issues. Despite this shared conceptual terrain, the French philosophers often used that analysis to criticize the existing order, whether it be that of the church or state, while the English often used their analysis to provide a justification for the existing order.[1] And while the uniformity in concepts provides a menu of similar topics, there is no doubt that the difference in social context between the two nations shapes the thinking of French writers so that they diverge from their English counterparts in significant ways. MacIntyre begins his account of moral thought in eighteenth-century France with the sociological and relativistic view of ethics provided by Baron Montesquieu, then briefly examines the moral absolutism of Claude-Adrien Helvetius before concluding with a focus on the ethics of Jean Jacques Rousseau. Montesquieu provides us with a significantly different point of departure than what was offered to England in the thought of Hobbes, so we will begin with him to see how the story of ethics unfolds in eighteenth-century France.

Society and Relativism in the Ethics of Montesquieu

We might hope that a person named Charles-Louis de Secondat, Baron de la Bréde et de Montesquieu (b. 1689), would leave us a body of thought to

---

1. *SHE*, 146.

justify the effort in merely remembering that name. Montesquieu, as he is commonly called, does not disappoint. He was among the most popular and influential writers in the eighteenth century, and his thinking continues to influence political theory and practice to this day. Although many people do not remember him as the political theorist who formulated the idea of the separation of powers in democratic governments, few people in Europe and North America would question the importance of this political innovation.[2] Montesquieu approaches morality by starting from the perspective of the community. He sees Hobbes's starting point from the isolated individual in a state of nature as a misleading myth.[3] For Montesquieu, society is not merely a collection of individuals as it is for Hobbes, and social structures do not exist merely as structures that enable individuals to achieve predetermined psychological goals.[4] This is the case because the community not only makes an individual's goals in life possible, but it shapes and is even the creator of those goals to a certain extent. The institutions and rules of a society are the background that must be examined if one is to understand the goals and needs of individual members of that society. In Montesquieu's view, a person's goals, needs, and desires depend upon the type of social system in which the person lives.[5] The reality of this observation can be seen in the different hopes and aspirations fostered by different cultures. A person from Vienna, Austria, is more likely to aspire to perform in an opera than someone from Anchorage, Alaska, and someone from Anchorage will more likely aspire to owning a snowmobile than someone from Vienna. Likewise, a young boy from Berlin, Germany, is more likely to dream of being a professional soccer player, while a boy from Austin, Texas, may be more likely to dream of playing American football. In making this point, Montesquieu's thought is quite similar to that of Aristotle with the latter's focus on the importance of the city-state in relation to ethics. MacIntyre highlights the similarity between the two, but contends that Montesquieu goes further than Aristotle by explicitly asserting that the social environment is the setting in which ethics and politics must be understood. By placing society in the foreground of an approach to

---

2. Cf. Vile, *Constitutionalism and the Separation of Powers*, 83–106 for a summary of Montesquieu's contribution to the development of political theory regarding the separation of powers.

3. *SHE*, 178–79.

4. *SHE*, 178.

5. *SHE*, 179.

ethics, MacIntyre asserts that Montesquieu becomes the first sociological moralist.[6] Given this sociological approach to morality, Montesquieu breaks from the sentimentalist individualism of his contemporaries in England. As a result, his goal is to study human societies in order to create a science of government that will enable people to improve the human condition as it existed in the communities of his day.[7] Along the way of this political analysis, Montesquieu proposes a theory of morality that sits within the different types of government that he identifies.

Montesquieu contends that there are three basic forms of government, which are despotism, monarchy, and republicanism. The differences in these political structures give rise to differences in the motivations, desires, and moralities that can be observed on the part of the people who live under each type of government. Under the rule of a despot, the only law is the whim of the leader. The motivation guiding the behavior of the people in such a context is fear. Subjects of a tyrant obey the law because they fear the punishment the tyrant will deliver to those caught breaking the tyrant's rules. A monarchy, on the other hand, is a hierarchical society. In this context, the motivations and values of subjects are shaped by the categories of rank and status. Within those categories, honor and the rewards of landing a specific position become the most important motivation that shapes the life and choices of individual people. A republican form of government, which Montesquieu held in the highest esteem, relies on a sense of civic virtue to motivate its citizens to obey the laws of society.[8] This motivation is the most difficult for a commonwealth to achieve, so considerable resources must be invested to educate the citizenry about virtue and develop the virtues necessary for collaboration in the context of freedom.[9] Since the motivation for obedience is different in each context, the moral questions that arise become different as well. In a despotic or tyrannical government, the fundamental moral question is, "What is the most expedient or safest course of action?" In a monarchy, the question is, "What is the most honorable act?" In a republic, the question becomes "What should I do as a citizen committed to the common good of my community?" What Montesquieu seems reluctant to do is to identify which type of political and moral culture is best. What is the best

6. *SHE*, 179.
7. *SHE*, 178.
8. *SHE*, 179.
9. *SHE*, 180.

motivation for members of a society: fear, honor, or virtue?[10] It is in the context of this question that MacIntyre describes Montesquieu's thought as that of an inconsistent relativist.

In describing Montesquieu's relativism, MacIntyre starts from the Baron's simple observation that societies differ greatly over time and place. In light of this fact, lawmakers must study their society with great care to make sure laws are adapted to the circumstances of that particular community, and those circumstances are affected by many variables. A variety of factors include elements as disparate as climate, law, religion, government structures, customs, manners, and exemplars or events from that society's history, all of which impact the forms of social life for a specific community.[11] These many factors give rise to communities marked by their own ethos, their own standards and forms of justification, and their own strengths and weaknesses. Citing the Aztec King Montezuma, who said that the Spanish religion was good for Spain and the Aztec religion was good for the Aztecs, Montesquieu asserts that the king had a point. Each society can only be judged on the basis of its own principles and values.[12]

The above summary seems like a straightforward argument for moral relativism. Channeling his inner Sophist, Montesquieu asserts that it is only possible to judge the moral principles of a particular community using the values of that community as the criteria by which to judge. The reason MacIntyre charges Montesquieu with inconsistency is despite this relativistic assertion, Montesquieu does infrequently use universal values to judge the merit of different societies. At times he makes the case that the best societies allow for the political liberty of their citizens.[13] In addition, his evaluation of societies on the basis of justice is an explicit example of Montesquieu applying a universal norm to judge specific communities. Montesquieu contends that humans can formulate principles of justice outside the setting of a legal system and can then use that set of principles in order to judge whether a particular system of laws satisfies the requirements of justice.[14] How can we square this position with Montesquieu's greater emphasis on judging a community only on the basis of its own moral values? Is he being inconsistent and thus

10. *SHE*, 180–81.
11. *SHE*, 178.
12. *SHE*, 179.
13. *SHE*, 180.
14. *SHE*, 179–80.

undermining the credibility of his arguments? Somewhat surprisingly, MacIntyre does not criticize Montesquieu for this inconsistency. Rather, he provides a rationale for how the twofold approach we observe in Montesquieu's thought has merit. MacIntyre asserts that what Montesquieu is arguing is not necessarily a contradiction. Montesquieu can be read as saying that there are universal principles of justice that any system of laws must observe if the system is to be considered just, but the manner in which those principles are applied can vary in an almost infinite number of ways given the almost infinite number of human societies.[15] For example, one can assert that care for elderly parents is a principle of justice that transcends all communities. Moral traditions ranging from the Jewish Ten Commandments, to Cicero in ancient Rome, to St. Thomas Aquinas in the Middle Ages, assert the fundamental obligation of caring for one's parents. Cicero is particularly pointed on the issue, saying that caring for elderly parents is a greater obligation than caring for one's children.[16] Yet the way the obligation of caring for elderly parents is applied in different cultures can vary almost indefinitely. Neglect and abuse may be ruled out, but depending on the society, you might see physical care outweigh emotional or spiritual care, or the reverse, or another focus of care entirely. Montesquieu's position can be seen as one in which the emphasis in judging or understanding the morality of a specific community is based on an understanding of that community's values, while still recognizing the existence of a limited number of principles that can be applied to each and every community.

Helvetius: Human Nature as Determined and Transformable

MacIntyre offers Claude-Adrien Helvetius (b. 1715) as a French philosopher whose deterministic account of human nature differs significantly from the relativistic approach of Montesquieu. The thought of Helvetius came to prominence through the publication of his magnum opus, *De L'Esprit, (On Minds)* in 1758. *De L'Esprit* was immediately condemned by virtually every institution in France, including the Sorbonne, and was publicly burned in Paris. As a result, the book was translated into multiple languages and became one of the most well-read books in Europe at the time. MacIntyre tells us that the reception of *De L'Esprit* is surprising in

---

15. *SHE*, 180.
16. Cicero, *On Duties*, 1.58.

the sense that Helvetius broke little new philosophical ground, repeating many of the doctrines espoused by Hobbes and the utilitarian thinkers in England. Helvetius was a psychological materialist who saw human thought and perception as merely chains of sensation that are positive (pleasure), negative (pain), or neutral.[17] For Helvetius, all human desire is oriented toward pleasure, and anything not pleasurable that seems to be an object of desire is only desired as a means to getting pleasure. In addition, some people derive pleasure from the pleasure of others, which means they possess the virtue of benevolence. Although Helvetius begins his analysis asserting that a person's own pleasure is the criteria for making the correct moral choice, he later moves from saying that some people are in fact benevolent to asserting that the young should be trained to value benevolence. In doing so, Helvetius substitutes a new moral criterion, the idea that people should take pleasure in being benevolent to others, over his earlier conception of human desire in which people should only choose what is in fact most pleasurable to themselves.[18]

MacIntyre finds the thinking of Helvetius important due to the fact that it represents a paradox that is found in the thought of many Enlightenment philosophers. Helvetius asserts a static and determinist psychology in which everyone uniformly desires pleasure and uses that desire to direct all of their choices. Any variation from action oriented toward pleasure is only a façade in which someone is choosing something that seems to be unpleasant as a means to achieving a further pleasure. Despite the universality and unchanging nature of human desire, Helvetius also believes in an almost limitless possibility of transformation of the human person. Such transformation could be achieved through free discussion and a thorough reform of the educational system. The realities of politics and church affairs made such educational reform impossible in France at the time, and Helvetius knew through personal experience that free discussion in France was quite limited, especially compared to the freedom of his British peers across the English Channel.[19] The tension between human nature as having limitless possibilities of transformation through education and human nature as a static entity always oriented toward pleasure and away from pain remains, however, and is a staple of Enlightenment ethicists ranging from Hume in Scotland,

---

17. *SHE*, 181.
18. *SHE*, 182.
19. *SHE*, 181.

to Helvetius in France, to Kant in Germany, and to John Stuart Mill in nineteenth-century England.

Jean Jacques Rousseau: Human Nature and the Corruption of Society

MacIntyre begins his description of Rousseau's thought with high praise for Rousseau at the expense of other Enlightenment thinkers. Rousseau (b. 1712), MacIntyre asserts, must be placed in the same category as the other two great moral thinkers of the eighteenth century, David Hume and Immanuel Kant.[20] MacIntyre also places Rousseau in opposition to other Enlightenment thinkers, an example of which can be seen in the difference between Rousseau's approach to the idea of liberty compared to other French thinkers of his time. For writers such as Helvetius, Denis Diderot (the general editor of the *Encyclopdie*), and Voltaire (author of *Candide* and other works), liberty was a concern only for the privileged. The elite writers of the Enlightenment advocated for freedom, but the freedom they advocated was limited to themselves. For the rest (MacIntyre quotes Voltaire as referring to the rest as the "rabble"), obedience was still the expectation. While positioning themselves as moral innovators, many Enlightenment thinkers only questioned the status quo when it was in their interest to do so.[21] Such was not the case for Rousseau, whose political theory was aimed at constructing institutions that enabled free and equal citizens to live and cooperate in communities that were ruled by those very same citizens. Rousseau, like Aristotle and Montesquieu before him, elaborated his morality at the crossroads of human nature and society, so we will begin with his distinctive view of human nature on an individual level and then move into his view of the way individuals are affected by the communities in which they live.

MacIntyre tells us that like other thinkers before him (Hobbes and Locke come to mind), Rousseau begins describing his political and moral ideas in the context of the human state of nature. Rousseau makes clear that he does not view the state of nature he depicts as historical (there is no historical data from the primitive environment he is describing).[22] Rather, the state of nature is a useful hypothesis that helps his reader

---

20. *SHE*, 183.
21. *SHE*, 183.
22. *SHE*, 185.

understand the nature of a society, including its features and goals and the manner in which individuals behave in the context of society. His hypothesis is more sophisticated than the simple categories Hobbes applies to the state of nature. Rousseau's state of nature has more in common with Locke's version in that Rousseau does not see the state of nature as pre-social. Rousseau's depiction also differs from the grim, self-serving aspects Hobbes assigns to human nature. He rejects not only Hobbes's negative characterization of the natural person, but also challenges the Christian notion of original sin by asserting that humans in their natural state are good.[23] Despite that basic goodness, Rousseau does not deny that the natural person is driven by self-love. He does, however, allow for a degree of complexity in that self-love. Self-love for Rousseau is not intrinsically corrupt because it can inspire authentic relationships based on sympathy and compassion.[24]

Rousseau adds to his state of nature description the fact that human wants and desires are limited by the environment in which a person finds herself or himself. Rousseau confirms the view of Montesquieu when he observes that human desires are rooted not only in human nature, but in the objects of desire that are presented to a person by her or his surrounding environment. Like Montesquieu, Rousseau asserts that communities have profound, powerful, and often overlooked influence on the needs and aspirations of their members. Returning to the state of nature, Rousseau notes that there is a very limited range of goods offered to a person in that environment. The wants and needs of the natural person are quite simple, ranging from the desires for food and a mate, to the fear of hunger and pain. With the introduction of a more complex society, the person's wants, needs, and desires diversify as well.[25]

MacIntyre asserts that Rousseau's most powerful insight is the idea that social and political institutions blanket, disfigure, and even corrupt individual human nature.[26] One might ask how this can be the case if in Rousseau's telling humans are originally good? How can society as a collection of good individuals become a force of corruption? Rousseau answers the question on the basis of the complexity of human nature, and the way a basically good human nature can still give rise to injustice as complex communities develop. Rousseau notes that the selfish person,

23. *SHE*, 184.
24. *SHE*, 184.
25. *SHE*, 184.
26. *SHE*, 183–84.

despite pursuing his or her own self-interest, can still exhibit an orientation towards the interests of others. When the self-interested agent merely sees or recognizes an alternative that corresponds to the interests of others, that person is already sympathetically involved with others, if only in a marginal way.[27] True self-love, which includes sympathy and compassion for others, takes this recognition further. By entering into relationships with loved ones, a self-interested person is provided a context in which justice and concern for another person's interests can be recognized and even pursued.[28] As a result, the authentic wants and needs of the self-loving person provide a basis for that person to understand concerns about ethics and justice.[29]

Despite the seeds of justice that can be found in self-love, human nature also provides elements that lead to the corruption of social institutions. For Rousseau, that corruption is a result of the proliferation of objects of desire that social cooperation produces for individuals. Civilization, in Rousseau's view, gives rise to acquisitiveness. An advancing society will continually supply the individual with new desires and aspirations for the products and privileges provided by that civilization. People will begin to desire the property and the power that become attainable on the basis of collaborative enterprise.[30] As goods proliferate, their existence makes the possession of property possible. Concepts of "mine" and "thine" come into existence, and thus the explicit need for justice arises.[31] The need for justice is based not just on the existence of private property, but also due to the fact that moral depravity in the form of theft and cheating others of their belongings comes into existence as well. The reality of moral depravity elicits a strong desire for the establishment of political institutions that will protect the rights and property of the individual person. Rousseau follows Hobbes and Locke in his contention that such institutions ground their authority in the social contract between the citizenry and government authority.[32]

With the establishment of political institutions, we might say we have the solution to the corruption that arises from Rousseau's view of human nature. So why does he still contend that social and political

27. SHE, 186.
28. SHE, 186.
29. SHE, 184.
30. SHE, 187.
31. SHE, 184.
32. SHE, 184.

institutions distort and corrupt the very people they are supposed to protect? The state, in Rousseau's view, is supposed to provide impartial justice and rectify the moral depravity spawned by desire for societal goods through its power to enact and enforce just laws.[33] The problem Rousseau observes is that governments in the real world do not play the role of impartially dispensing justice. Rather, the state itself becomes an engine of despotism, oppression, and inequality. Instead of protecting citizens from injustice, the state is run by the rich and powerful who use the supposedly legitimate authority of the state to oppress the very people the state exists to protect.[34] It is a trenchant critique of the French monarchy of the time and one reason Rousseau was heralded as an intellectual hero of the French Revolution.

In light of the moral depravity fostered by the goods of society and the alienation induced by corrupt political institutions, Rousseau contends that the reform of social institutions is the necessary precondition for ethical reform, and that reform is made possible by the resources latent in Rousseau's positive view of human nature. It is in the context of reforming social institutions as the means to reforming individual morality that we can see a similarity between Rousseau and the ancient Greeks. This similarity lies in the close relationship they see between politics and ethics. Rousseau asserts the importance of the one to the other by claiming, "Society has to be studied in the individual and the individual in society; those who wish to separate politics from morals will never understand either."[35] MacIntyre explains the meaning and importance of Rousseau's insight—an insight he says is missed by Kant—as Rousseau recognizing the fact that a person cannot answer the moral question of "What should I do?" without first answering the prior question of "Who am I?" And the answer to the question of my identity, in Rousseau's view, is found in the context of a person's relationships. A person's identity, a person's place in the world, is defined by the network of relationships that surround each human individual. It is in the context of these relationships that a person's wants, needs, desires, and goals take shape and can be understood. It is in light of these relationships and the aspirations they inspire that a person's moral judgment, one's practical decisions, can be evaluated as praiseworthy or blameworthy.[36]

33. *SHE*, 185.
34. *SHE*, 185.
35. *SHE*, 187.
36. *SHE*, 187.

MacIntyre then points out a troubling question Rousseau raises. What is one to do if that person finds himself or herself in a social order that is corrupt and corrupting to the individual?[37] Rousseau provides a recipe for reform that depends upon an ability to withstand the influence of corrupt political institutions, the use of a person's moral imagination, and the reservoir of good will that he sees as existing in human nature. In the face of institutions that treat individuals unjustly or even reward oppression and injustice, an individual is challenged to withstand the alienation and despair that might result from those circumstances and envision goals that lie outside the current forms of social life. The roots of such a vision lie in what Rousseau describes as the uncorrupted heart of an individual. He contends that such internal purity can be maintained in the context of institutional corruption, and that it is from the good heart of individuals that different moral ends can be envisioned and pursued.[38] In pursuing such ends, individuals can re-shape the institutions of civil society so the institutions encourage community members to recognize the common good and prioritize that good over the pursuit of individual goods that may be destructive to cooperation in a community. The people who inhabit sophisticated society and culture must be taught and encouraged to refuse the pursuit of individual interests that undermine the common interests of the community. Institutions must inspire individuals to aspire to the high standard of being free citizens who take responsibility for the common good through their own individual moral choices.

Rousseau's vision of civilization asks much of individual citizens, especially in republican forms of government. He challenges the citizens of a republic to live according to the virtues of free citizenry, which outstrip the demands of fear and honor experienced by people living under despots or monarchs. MacIntyre observes that despite his aspirational rhetoric, Rousseau was quite pessimistic about the possibility of reforming social institutions.[39] A contemporary of Rousseau who called for similarly high moral standards was the Prussian philosopher Immanuel Kant. It is to Kant's thought that we will now turn as MacIntyre closes out his examination of eighteenth-century European ethics.

37. *SHE*, 187.
38. *SHE*, 187–88.
39. *SHE*, 189.

Leadership Reflection: Honor as Motivation for Followers

Montesquieu mentions honor as the primary motivation for members of monarchical societies. He asserts that the titles of aristocracies and the benefits that flow from those titles are the social currency that people seek most in a monarchy. Although honor may be the main thing people are after in communities governed by a monarch, there is no doubt that honor also has a significant impact on the motivation of people no matter the form of government. This is the case because we can observe the impact the desire for honors has in our own lives, and we can also read a long history discussing honor as motivating human action in a variety of political and social settings. Authors such as Aristotle, Cicero, and St. Thomas Aquinas all addressed the importance of honor as a motivation for moral choice. Given the agreement on the importance of honor as motivation for human behavior, we can ask, is honor something leaders can leverage to motivate their followers? To answer the question well, we will need to describe the different senses the idea of honor can communicate and the different approaches our philosophers take in examining honor.

In our description of honor, which I will define as the praise offered to a person by other individuals or by a community, it is important to note that honor has both an internal and an external sense. People often think of honor as an internal moral phenomenon, which results in beliefs such as "One should never violate one's own honor." Honor in this sense represents an almost sacred aspect of a person's character and is usually related to honesty as a character trait or integrity as a more global description of good moral character. It seems, however, that this is a more recent understanding of honor. Going back to the classical tradition, we see honor spoken of by Aristotle not only as an external phenomenon, but as the greatest of all external goods. For Aristotle, honor is the greatest external good because it is offered to the gods, the greatest of all beings.[40] In addition, honor has an external aspect because it implies an audience. In bestowing an honor on someone, a message is communicated to an audience, even if that audience is only the person receiving the honor and the person offering it. Following Aristotle's description of magnanimity (the virtue concerned with honor), St. Thomas Aquinas asserts that the purpose of honor is to highlight the moral excellence of the person.[41] Bestowing honor on a virtuous person is profitable for the community

---

40. Aristotle, *Nicomachean Ethics*, 1123b17–1123b21.
41. Aquinas, *Summa Theologica*, II.II 103.1 and 129.1.3.

because the internal excellence of the virtuous person is made known as a good example to the other members of the community.[42] And here we have the link between the external and internal aspects of honor. Honor may be an external good that is given by one member of a community to another, but it is linked to an internal good—virtue—that is even more valuable than the honor itself. For in the thinking of both Aristotle and St. Thomas, the value of moral excellence, of virtue, is always greater than the honor itself.[43] Thus, in bearing witness to moral excellence, honors are at the service of and incorporated into an internal reality that is more significant than honor.

In addition to the internal and external dynamics associated with honor, both Cicero and St. Thomas highlight aspects of honor that warrant caution and concern. Cicero, writing in the first century BCE during Rome's transition from a republic to an empire, describes honor using the Latin term *gloria* in two of his most important works (*On Duties* and *Tusculan Disputations*) and even wrote an entire book on *gloria*, although that work has been lost to history.[44] In his writing Cicero distinguished between two types of glory: false glory that consisted in the adulation of the crowds for famous individuals, and true glory that was only given by the wise to the truly virtuous person. Cicero learned through his own experience as a prominent Roman politician that the lure of false glory is indeed powerful, but is empty in the end due to the fleeting memory of human beings. Likewise, St. Thomas saw in the desire for honor a risk to which Aristotle was for the most part blind. As an heir to the Jewish and Christian intellectual tradition, St. Thomas was familiar with the value of humility and wary of the corruption associated with pride, pride being understood as the sin of self-love that eclipses all other loves up to and including love for God. Thus St. Thomas provides a distinction absent in Aristotle, where the virtuous person desires to be worthy of honor, but does not desire honor itself. In St. Thomas's thinking, those who do good merely for the sake of the honor good actions will bring are not truly virtuous.[45] Our authors therefore teach us that honor is the praise that is given to the virtuous, but that praise can be misunderstood, wrongly

---

42. Aquinas, *Summa Theologica*, II.II.131.1.

43. Cf. Aristotle, *Nicomachean Ethics*, 1124a7 and Aquinas, *Summa Theologica*, II.II.129.3.3.

44. For a reference to this work see Cicero, *On Duties*, 2.31.

45. Aquinas, *Summa Theologica*, II.II.131.1.3.

given, and even if correctly given, can lead to the pride that corrupts even the most virtuous person.

So how does all of this apply to our practice of leadership? First, we must recognize that leaders should look to honor the excellence of their followers. Such honor has multiple good effects for an organization. It is a work of justice that will increase the loyalty of the followers being honored because they will know when they are doing excellent work and will appreciate their excellence being recognized. As St. Thomas points out, honoring excellence will also enable others to see, understand, and be inspired by that excellence. Honoring and rewarding superior performance in a public manner makes known what otherwise may have gone unnoticed were it not for the rendering of the honor. Organizations and leaders will get more of the behavior that they reward, so by honoring the good work of their followers, leaders will encourage further good work by others in the organization.

Despite these good effects, our philosophers help us to understand that honor can also have a downside when it comes to motivating followers. St. Thomas tells us that a person motivated only by honor and not by the excellence for which honor is bestowed is not fully virtuous. Likewise, followers motivated to do good work due to their desire for honor rather than a desire for excellence may end up causing problems for the organization in both the short and long term. An example of this can be seen in the book *What It Is Like to Go to War*. In the book, author Karl Marlantes describes two extraordinary acts of courage he executed while in combat during the Vietnam War. The first he did out of a selfish desire for honor. He risked his life in a hail of machine gun fire to save a man who was likely already dead in the hope of getting a medal. One thing we see here is the effectiveness of honor as a motivation. Marlantes was literally willing to risk his life for the honor it might bring. Although he survived the encounter, he did not win the admiration of the one witness of his act of valor because his action was poorly motivated (to get a medal), unnecessary, and truly reckless. The desire for honor produced his action, which was no doubt ridiculously brave. It was only luck, however, that enabled him to walk away from his reckless decision. Had he been motivated purely by excellence, Marlantes would never have taken the unnecessary risk in the first place. Later on, however, Marlantes describes a situation in which he leads a charge up a hill, again in a thicket of bullets, because that was the only thing to be done to achieve the mission in those circumstances. The mission and concern for his troops was the motivation the second time around, motivations we might describe as a desire for excellence, and his actions resulted in his soldiers literally following him through a valley of death, which was also the only hope for surviving the terrible situation in which they found themselves.[46]

Honor as a motivation can also be problematic with respect to selfishness and the desire to win at all costs. As a recent article in the *Harvard Business Review* points out, most companies create work environments where employees compete for honor or recognition, bonuses, and awards. Yet the desire for honor can elicit different emotional responses and different types of behavior. Through surveys that gauged the emotions of employees under such incentive systems, authors Steinhage, Cable, and Wardley found that if the incentives created positive emotions such as excitement, followers tended to pursue morally positive methods to accomplish their goals. When those honors caused follower anxiety, which happened in cases where failing to achieve an honor would have produced negative repercussions, followers had a tendency to use unethical methods in their goal achievement.[47] Behaviors such as lying, withholding information from customers, or even cheating other employees become legitimate ways to compete and may even be incentivized by the organization's recognition system when honors are not designed properly by the leadership of the organization. As leaders deliberate about how to honor their followers, they should keep in mind the fact that the desire for excellence over honor will produce the best results in the long run. Leaders should therefore design and deliver honors in such a way as to incentivize the desire for excellence without provoking anxiety or an inordinate desire for the honor itself.

---

46. Cf. Marlantes, *What it is Like to Go to War*, 155–175.
47. Steinhage et al., "Pros and Cons of Competition Among Employees."

14

The Ethics of Immanuel Kant

IMMANUEL KANT (B. 1724) has been described as the central figure in modern philosophy, the period of Western philosophy that begins in the seventeenth century and ends in the twentieth century.[1] The centrality of Kant's thought refers to its importance to virtually all subsequent branches of European philosophy, not least of which was the field of ethics. As MacIntyre puts it, whether a philosopher supported or criticized Kant, ethics has been defined by the terms that Kant formulated ever since his groundbreaking writings in the early 1780s.[2] As we examine Kantian moral thought exemplified in a work like his book *The Groundwork of the Metaphysics of Morals*, we will see that Kant provides a narrower view of morality than the classical ethics of the Greeks or the utilitarianism of nineteenth-century England. MacIntyre sees Kant as both a typical and the preeminent Enlightenment philosopher. He was typical because of his unshaken belief in the power of reason and the ability of humans to reform social institutions. And Kant was preeminent in MacIntyre's view because he was able to solve many recurrent problems in Enlightenment thinking or reformulate them in more fruitful ways.[3] An example of such reformulation provided by MacIntyre is the reconciliation Kant achieves between two dominant Enlightenment thought patterns, which were the

---

1. Many authors, including MacIntyre, see Kant as the most significant modern philosopher. Cf. Scruton, *Kant*, and *Stanford Encyclopedia of Philosophy*, "Immanuel Kant" for just two assertions on the preeminence of Kant's thinking in the modern period.
2. *SHE*, 190.
3. *SHE*, 190.

empiricism of David Hume and the laws of science proposed by Sir Isaac Newton. These two approaches to knowledge seemed completely at odds with one another. The empiricists asserted that all authentic knowledge must be linked to sense experience. Nothing can be known outside the data provided to humans by the senses. Newton's laws of science, however, purport to cover every instance of particular scientific phenomena, whether the phenomena are captured by human senses or not. In his book *The Critique of Pure Reason,* Kant asserts that all of our experience, including sense experience, is law based, not because of the nature of the world, but because of the nature of the human mind.[4] Sense experience for Kant is not merely the passive reception of data, but an active organization of data by the human mind. The mind gives shape to and organizes the data of sense experience.[5] Laws represent a primary way the mind accomplishes this task. Laws are a function of the interior mind, not the exterior world. Laws play a fundamental role in Kant's thinking because they are a staple of the mind's process for making sense of the world. As we examine Kant's moral thought, we will see that law-making, or the formation of moral principles, will play an extraordinarily important role in his approach to ethics.

Kant's Ethics of Duty

MacIntyre points out that, for Kant, ethics is a function of the human mind. Unlike other thinkers of the time who are continuously searching for the basis of fundamental principles, Kant starts by assuming moral conscience exists, and in doing so, makes moral conscience the object of his analysis.[6] Given that existence, Kant examines the ideas that arise from that consciousness in the hope of describing them to provide an accurate picture of morality.[7] It is through understanding these ideas—ideas Kant sees as unchanging and objective—that humans can figure out how to guide their moral choices. Kant asks the questions, what are the human ideas that can be characterized as moral ideas and how do those concepts guide our moral actions? To get at Kant's answers we need to examine how rationality and freedom shape the formation of moral

4. *SHE,* 190.
5. *SHE,* 190.
6. *SHE,* 191.
7. *SHE,* 191.

principles (laws), Kant's notion of a good will, and lastly, how a good will is related to Kant's understanding of duty.

Kant is a product of the individuality MacIntyre observes coming out of the Reformation and the Renaissance, and Kant adds to the importance of an individualistic approach to ethics as well. The starting point of Kant's ethical thought is human reason or rationality, which is a capacity held by each and every individual. Reason is the foundation of moral law/principles[8] because it is the rational function of the human mind that enables the mind to formulate moral principles. Since every human has the ability to reason, every individual is therefore able to formulate moral principles for herself or himself. The foundation of this moral thinking has two parts for Kant. Ethical cognition has both a legislative function and an executive function. The legislative function refers to the human person's rational capacity to formulate moral principles. The executive function follows the legislative function and refers to the ability of every person to apply those principles to his or her behavior.[9] Although the legislative and executive language is different than the terms offered by Aristotle in his analysis of voluntary action, the thought of both share much in common. The reason and rationality Kant associates with the legislative function is the same reason that Aristotle describes as producing the knowledge necessary for a person to be held accountable for her or his moral actions. The executive function identified by Kant likewise aligns with the freedom Aristotle says is necessary for moral accountability. In executing or applying the moral principles a person has formulated to that person's own behavior, the person is freely choosing to make a choice in conformity with that moral principle. Kant describes the combination of the legislative and executive functions as the human capacity for autonomy (again recalling notions of freedom). Kant is precise in the choice of the word autonomy, which draws its roots from the Greek words *autos*, meaning self, and *nomos*, meaning law. Each person is autonomous because each person can produce moral principles that can guide her or his life.[10] Kant goes on to say that autonomy is not only the foundation of morality; it is also the foundation of human dignity.[11]

It is this dignity that enables Kant to identify one of his most enduring moral formulations, which is the idea that no person should ever

---

8. Kant, *Groundwork of the Metaphysics of Morals*, 4.411.
9. Kant, *Groundwork*, 4.435.
10. Kant, *Groundwork*, 4.433, 4.436.
11. Kant, *Groundwork*, 4.435, 4.436.

be used as a mere means to an end, but should always be treated as an end in herself or himself.[12] In Kant's view, the reason it is always wrong to treat a person as a mere means is the fact that in doing so, one will always violate a person's moral autonomy. There are two primary ways in which a person's autonomy can be violated: manipulation or coercion. One treats a person as a mere means through manipulation by lying to that person in order to get him or her to do something. By withholding relevant information from a person as she or he formulates a moral principle, one is depriving that person of the ability to rationally examine the relevant circumstances to make the correct moral decision. In the case of coercion, the person is treated as a mere means by depriving the person of his or her executive function. The person is not free to follow the principle she or he has formulated and therefore has become a mere tool in a particular situation. In either case, the person is not given the dignity that rightly belongs to all rational and autonomous moral agents.

Having identified the rational process through which humans formulate principles, Kant then addresses the question of identifying laws or principles that pertain to ethics. For Kant, the natural world is non-moral, so when it comes to morality, he is unconcerned with principles such as Newton's laws of physics.[13] As heirs of modern philosophy and Kant's approach to morality, many twenty-first-century Americans might find this assertion obviously true. It is certainly a different approach from many of the philosophers we have discussed thus far who typically start from an initial state of human nature. Yet upon further reflection, many also question Kant's abrupt division between the natural and moral world. I have often asked students in class whether there are any implications for morality in the law of gravity. Reflecting the influence of Kant on our moral thinking, their immediate and nearly universal response is no. Yet when I ask if it is morally neutral to push someone off a cliff, given gravity and the squishiness of human nature, they usually step back from the stark divide between nature and morality Kant describes. Kant, however, would argue against that analysis by asserting pushing someone off of a cliff is not wrong because of gravity or the consequences of a person hitting the ground but because it would violate a duty of the person doing the pushing. So, let us take a close look at Kant's conception of duty.

12. Kant, *Groundwork*, 4.429.
13. *SHE*, 191.

To understand the role of duty in Kant's thought, we have to place it in the context of his description of a good will. Breaking down the terms, Kant describes a will not as merely a choice, desire or wish, but as the straining of every means within one's control to strive for a particular goal.[14] The goodness of a good will is defined by the will's relation to duty, and that relationship is fundamentally important for Kant who sees the good will as the only thing that is truly and unconditionally good. Intellect, virtues, wealth, and any other asset a person might have can be used for good or for ill.[15] For example, courage as the ability to act in the face of danger is normally considered a good characteristic. Courage, however, can be used to bad ends, which can be seen in the courage necessary to commit a crime in the face of severe punishment. Unlike other traits or assets, Kant asserts that a good will is intrinsically good, or good in itself. It is a shining jewel and is good even if it is completely ineffectual, never actually achieving what it intends.[16] A will is made good not by the effect it achieves, but by being motivated only by concern for duty. In light of this emphasis, Kant's morality centers on a person's motives and intentions rather than on the effect the person's choices have in the world.[17]

It is in the good will's motivation by duty alone that we can see one of the most distinctive aspects of Kant's morality. In Kant's system of ethics, an act only has moral value if it is motivated by duty.[18] If an act is motivated by any other inclination, that motivation places the act outside of the moral sphere. For example, a person might tell the truth to another person on the basis of many different motivations. A person might be motivated by self-interest in telling the truth because he or she has a need for an open and honest relationship with another person. A person might also be motivated to tell the truth because that is her or his habit, and the person likes to tell the truth. Another motivation to tell the truth might be love or altruism. Even in a difficult conversation one might tell the truth to another because it will be helpful to that other person. For Kant, such inclination-based motivations make those choices non-moral. As MacIntyre observes, Kant's ethics is always a negotiation between duty and inclination. We can distinguish between those two categories, but Kant

14. Kant, *Groundwork*, 4.394.
15. Kant, *Groundwork*, 4.393.
16. Kant, *Groundwork*, 4.393.
17. *SHE*, 192.
18. Kant, *Groundwork*, 4.399.

never examines or distinguishes between the inclinations themselves.[19] The contrast is between duty and any other motivation to make a choice. If the choice is made for duty, it is a moral choice, and if it is made out of an inclination of any other kind, it becomes non-moral. This is not only a radical narrowing of moral motivation; it also makes the idea of duty the crucial concept in determining the nature of ethics. Kant's notion of duty is the lynchpin of his ethics and has become enormously influential not only to succeeding generations of philosophers, but to the moral culture that we as twenty-first-century Americans inhabit.

So now we can finally address what Kant actually means by duty. There is both continuity and difference between Kant's notion of duty and that of his predecessors, particularly the view of duty in the classical Greek tradition. The continuity lies in the fact that both Kant and the Greek tradition see duty as an important moral criterion that guides what moral choices people should make. Both approaches recognize the importance moral obligation plays in the life of the human person. Despite this important similarity, the differences are significant as well. The first difference lies in the social context in which the two approaches tackle moral obligation. As MacIntyre has frequently pointed out, moral obligation in the Greek tradition is understood on the basis of a person's role in the community. Moral obligation for Enlightenment thinkers, on the other hand, is understood in the environment of the individual detached from society. Kant is not only representative of this approach, he is preeminent in detaching the individual from society because of his method and his conceptual goal for morality. The individuality implicit in Kant's moral thought is in clear view in his description of how a person uses reason to develop the moral principles that will guide her or his ethical life. The legislative and executive functions of morality described by Kant are done by the individual for the individual. In addition, Kant's goal in approaching ethics—and duty in particular—is to provide criteria that is always applicable no matter the time, place, or circumstances a specific person might inhabit. The goal of Kant's ethical analysis is to provide moral principles that transcend every social order and are applicable to each and every individual no matter what role a person might play in his or her community.

---

19. *SHE*, 192.

Given that background, Kant asserts that a duty is an obligation that applies to everyone all the time.[20] The question then becomes, how do we know what duties are binding on all people? To answer that question, Kant says that one must first isolate a principle that guides a person's moral intent—what he calls a maxim—and test that principle to see if it meets the criteria for a duty. Such principles are formulated through a person's rational/legislative capacity to develop moral principles. Once the maxim has been formulated (but before using the executive function and applying it to one's behavior), Kant says one should test the maxim to see if it is universally valid—that is, to see if it is a principle that should be obeyed by all people at all times. The test of a principle that is truly applicable to everyone consists of being able to apply that principle to every situation in a consistent manner. Kant provides a number of examples of such principles, the most intuitive of which concerns promise keeping. We can see if breaking a promise is morally acceptable by turning the idea into a maxim and seeing if the maxim for promise breaking can be consistently applied to everyone. So, what happens when we try to universalize a maxim such as this, "I can always break a promise when it is in my best interest to abandon that commitment"? Applying that principle universally would prevent anyone from making promises in the first place because it destroys the trust necessary for promises to be believable. That fact will yield inconsistency in the universal application of promise breaking because in desiring to be able to break a promise, the person still desires to be able make a promise so that you can take advantage of the person to whom you have made the promise. Thus, promise breaking is not a principle that can be applied without contradiction on a universal basis and therefore cannot be considered a valid moral principle or a duty that must be adhered to by every person.[21]

The name given by Kant to universal duties such as promise keeping is the categorical imperative.[22] Like much of Kant's writing, categorical imperative is not the easiest formulation to understand. Yet if we take the time to break the term down and look at its parts, we can see why he uses it and why it is an accurate way to describe his understanding of duty. The definition of categorical is the part of the phrase that is less familiar to most people. The primary meaning/function of categorical as an adjective is to describe something that is without exception. For example,

20. Kant, *Groundwork*, 4.421.
21. Kant, *Groundwork*, 4.403.
22. Kant, *Groundwork*, 4.421.

a categorical denial to a criminal charge is a perfectly complete denial. Such a denial has no exceptions. Imperative, on the other hand, is a little more familiar to most people. Simply put, an imperative is something that must be done. Putting the two together we get a phrase referring to things that must be done without exception. This is Kant's meaning of duty. From the Kantian perspective, if a duty does not require obedience by all people all the time, it is not really a duty.

MacIntyre highlights Kant's contrast between categorical imperatives and what Kant calls hypothetical imperatives to emphasize the impact Kant's thought has had on the moral thinking of people today. Categorical imperatives have no exceptions, but not all moral obligations are exceptionless or obligatory all the time. A moral classification related to the categorical imperative is what Kant calls a hypothetical imperative, which are obligations that do have exceptions.[23] Hypothetical imperatives concern things people should do if certain circumstances are present. For example, people should usually prevent other people from drowning. Preventing someone from drowning, however, is not something that is necessarily in one's power. If a person who is unable to swim witnesses someone drowning, that person is not obligated to save the person by swimming because it is impossible for him to do so. The obligation to save a drowning person varies depending on the circumstances and thus is not an exceptionless or categorical moral duty. Not everyone has to do it all the time. MacIntyre observes that there are hypothetical imperatives of skill (like our drowning example) where you should do something if you want to produce a specific result. There are also hypothetical imperatives of practical wisdom where you should do something because it is in your interest or because it will make you happy.[24] In comparison, categorical imperatives do not have any such limits. They are universal in scope, such as the duty to tell the truth. So, in practice the practical reasons to tell the truth drop out of the calculus. Here we see a distinction that marks one of the biggest differences separating Kantian and contemporary moral thought from classical ethics. Classical ethics considers itself to be the science of practical reasoning, while Kant sees morality as the adherence to principles that are often the antithesis to what is practical. One should tell the truth because everyone should tell the truth, no

---

23. Kant, *Groundwork*, 4.428.
24. *SHE*, 194.

matter the practical considerations. Everyone has a duty to tell the truth, and the rationale behind the duty becomes unspoken.[25]

A familiar phrase in contemporary military culture reflects the effect of Kant's thinking. People in the military are often told and often say a person should do the right thing because it is the right thing to do. The assertion is helpful in a psychological sense because there is still a concern and commitment to doing good. It is, however, a statement almost entirely empty of meaning and provides very little guidance for how to figure out what the right thing to do is or why one should do the right thing. There is a significant cost to this lack of meaning, too. If you do not know why you are doing something, you will stop doing it as soon as that action becomes hard to do, and we all know that morally admirable actions are often the most difficult to undertake. Specifying why a person should do something provides the motivation, often the strongest motivation, to pursue that action.

Impact and Power of Kant's Ethics

There are few philosophers who would argue with MacIntyre when he asserts that Kant's ethics are enormously influential. MacIntyre's analysis regarding the impact of Kant's ethics focuses on Kant's replacement of previous criteria for moral judgment,[26] after which he highlights why Kant's moral thinking became particularly powerful as modern European society emerged in the eighteenth, nineteenth, and twentieth centuries.

MacIntyre notes that Kant's impact can be seen in the way his rational moral analysis displaces two traditional and influential criteria for moral judgment. Kant's goal is to provide a purely rational and therefore truly objective moral criteria to decide what are authentic moral obligations. This rational basis is intended to replace what Kant sees as the false and problematic criteria for making moral judgments based on religion and the idea of happiness. MacIntyre turns to the relationship of ethics to religious authority first where Kant contends that any attribution of moral authority to the divine is simply a misunderstanding of the roots of moral authority. Kant asserts that humans as rational beings inescapably define morality for themselves. The rational moral agent obeys no one

25. *SHE*, 194.
26. *SHE*, 194.

but himself or herself.[27] As a religious believer, a person might provide authority to a divine figure such as Jesus, but the roots of that authority lie in the person's rational decision to imbue that figure with authority rather than the authority of the divine figure. A person may decide to observe the moral precepts of Christianity, thus giving authority to Jesus as a moral teacher, but that authority is a function of the person's reason, which has decided that those teachings are worthy of obedience because they conform to the rational moral principles one has already developed.[28] Put another way, in Kant's view, a person should only conform to divinely inspired moral precepts if one judges those precepts to be right and good. It is the rational capacity of the human person that makes a judgment as to what is right and good, and so the decision to follow a divinely revealed morality is always based on human reason. For Kant, the authority of human reason is inescapably the final arbiter of moral principles.[29]

MacIntyre then points out that for Kant the concept of happiness based on the natural inclination to fulfill human needs and desires similarly fails to be an authentic guide to ethics for two reasons. First, Kant asserts that the world of inclinations is part of the natural world, which he considered to be non-moral. Morality is always a function of human rational capacity, so to place the guide for moral choice in the realm of human inclination (which is a function of human biology among other factors) is to misunderstand the nature of morality.[30] Second, happiness as a concept to guide moral choice is no guide at all because the idea of happiness is subjective and infinitely variable. Infinitely malleable moral principles go against Kant's notion of morality as the formulation of moral principles that are entirely fixed. When a person formulates a categorical imperative, that person is identifying a moral principle that is constant. Categorical imperatives are exceptionless rules and as such are unchanging. The idea of happiness, on the other hand, varies from person to person and can even vary in the same person depending on the situation or the passage of time. Rational and unchanging moral principles provide the stability necessary for sound and consistent moral judgments, and notions of happiness are simply unable to provide this stability.[31] By anchoring moral principles in human rationality, Kant sees

27. *SHE*, 194.
28. *SHE*, 194–95.
29. *SHE*, 195.
30. *SHE*, 195.
31. *SHE*, 195.

himself as identifying their true nature and providing the clarity and stability necessary to identify authentic moral obligations.

MacIntyre further asserts that the power of Kant's analysis is undeniable, and that power increases for two reasons when Kant's ideas are applied in the individualistic context of modern moral thought. First, Kant's ethics make the individual person morally sovereign. As rational agents, humans unavoidably formulate moral principles and apply them to their moral judgments. When it comes to Kantian morality, neither God nor human inclination is in charge. Human rationality rules morality, and thus every individual human has the capacity and the responsibility to define morality for herself or himself. No external authority can displace the autonomy and entitlements of the individual will.[32] Second, Kant's morality not only gives the individual the power to define morality, but it also provides considerable space for an individual to live life in the way he or she sees fit. Categorical imperatives tell people what not to do, but they do not provide guidance for what a person should do in a positive sense. Positive direction in life is the grist of contingent hypothetical imperatives, and as such, lie outside the realm of morality. Again, only choices based on duty, understood as adherence to a categorical imperative, represent the moral realm for Kant. As a result, a person is able to pursue whatever type of life he or she may desire as long as that life conforms to the relatively narrow restrictions imposed by categorical imperatives, such as telling the truth and keeping our promises. The categorical imperative can sanction any way of life that does not break universal rules.[33]

MacIntyre's Critique of Kant

Although Kant's ethics are powerful and influential, that does not render them beyond MacIntyre's criticism. One concern MacIntyre raises is the fact that Kant's thought depends heavily on the formulation of maxims to be tested, but Kant does not provide guidance on how to develop maxims in the first place. As a result, MacIntyre asserts that Kant's ethics is dependent upon some previous system of values that enables maxims to be developed. Once the maxim is formulated, Kant's thinking then provides the method by which maxims can be evaluated as worthy of universal

32. *SHE*, 197.
33. *SHE*, 197.

application or not. In this sense, the categorical imperative is secondary to the values that a person uses to formulate the maxim in the first place.[34] For example, individuals might be guided by very different philosophies when confronted by people who have wronged them. A person who believes in the "eye for an eye" justice articulated in the book of Leviticus is likely to formulate a different maxim than someone who is guided by the New Testament Sermon on the Mount, which asserts one must love an enemy and offer the other cheek to be struck after being hit a first time. The different philosophies yield different maxims to be tested, thus placing Kant's method in that secondary role.

The secondary aspect of Kant's method is not the only problem MacIntyre sees with the testing role of the categorical imperative. It would be helpful if the universalization of the categorical imperative served as a reliable test to discover exceptionless moral obligations, but MacIntyre contends that Kant's method is not a reliable test at all. The categorical imperative fails to discern universal moral principles because it is quite easy to formulate maxims so that any of them can be universalized. If the maxim is articulated in a way that is narrow, making it applicable in only a few circumstances, it is likely to pass the universalization test.[35] Such a maxim might look like this, "I can lie only when my child is in danger of being killed by Nazis." Or, "I can lie only when it is necessary to avoid being fired by a malicious boss who has proven he will stop at nothing until I am destitute." The potential for the manipulation of maxims is great, which renders the categorical imperative a restriction only to people who lack creativity.[36] And when it comes to rationalizing normally unethical behavior that is in one's own interest, humans tend to be quite creative. MacIntyre's critique makes the charge that instead of a process establishing an objective morality for all people, Kant has established a subjective test of morality that can be manipulated to justify virtually any moral position. MacIntyre later uses Nazi Germany to provide us examples of how this plays out in history, but we will only examine them after further exploration of nineteenth-century German ethics.

Lastly, MacIntyre contends that the susceptibility of maxims to manipulation results in an easy capitulation of those adhering to Kantian ethics to whatever power holds sway in a particular society. Kantian notions of duty, he says, are so formal they can be given virtually any

34. *SHE*, 197.
35. *SHE*, 197–98.
36. *SHE*, 198.

content.³⁷ Since duty is detached from all other criteria such as purposes, wants, or needs, once a person is given a proposed course of action by her or his authority figure, the follower can only ask if the order can be universalized. No other criteria can be applied to deter the authority because the only criteria preventing execution of a maxim is the maxim's failure to be universalized. Thus, in a community governed by Kant's ethics a person can only protest against the norms asserted by authority figures in cases where those norms fail to be universal. And as we noted earlier, such failure is unlikely with a little ingenuity on the part of authorities when they formulate the maxim. Kant was not looking to create sheep who were willing to follow a corrupt social order, but MacIntyre thinks that is precisely what Kant's thinking inspires. If anything, Kant was likely looking to empower individuals to stand outside of a social order in order to correct it when necessary. MacIntyre concludes that Kant's search for a universal moral perspective that stands outside of any specific community is the search for an illusion.³⁸ Rather than creating autonomous moral agents, Kant's ethics creates servile followers of the existing social order. An approach to morality that recognizes the importance of wants and needs of people in the context of a specific community is one that MacIntyre sees as much more likely to avoid the conformism that results from Kant's ethics. Two Germans following in Kant's wake that turn back to the importance of society for ethics are Hegel and Marx, and it is to them that MacIntyre turns next.

Leadership Reflection: Treating Followers as Ends Rather than Means

The writing of Immanuel Kant is as dense and complex as it is influential. A quick example of that complexity can be seen in Kant's first formulation of the categorical imperative where a person determines whether a maxim can be universalized or not. Often both the identification of the maxim guiding a person's choice and the attempt to universalize that maxim are not in the least intuitive. Thankfully, Kant's thinking is not always that complicated, and an example of an intuitive principle of his is the second formulation of the categorical imperative, which states that no person should ever be treated as a mere means to an end. People should, at a

37. *SHE*, 198.
38. *SHE*, 198.

minimum, give their consent to being used as a means to a particular goal. An example of this can be seen in the consent necessary in trials for experimental medical treatments. It would be highly unethical for a patient to be enrolled in a trial without telling that person the risks associated with participation in the trial. Including someone in an experiment without their informed consent would truly be treating the person as a mere means to the experiment's end. One might say that Kant's second formulation of the categorical imperative is a rational description of the golden rule—to treat others as one wants to be treated—because virtually all people want to be given the respect not to be instrumentalized and used as a thing to accomplish some further goal. And if history is any guide, the golden rule does seem to be the type of universal moral principle that Kant asserts should be a duty—that is, a moral principle that merits obedience by all people in every situation. Such universality is likely the reason the golden rule is enshrined in virtually every society and religious tradition in the history of mankind,[39] and the practice of leadership is no exception to Kant's insight regarding means and ends.

The wisdom of never treating people as a mere means to an end is crucial to effective leadership. This idea is important to effective leadership because the temptation to treat followers simply as means to an end is great. Followers can become mere instruments of an organization and its leaders quite easily. Instrumentalizing followers happens as the result of numerous factors. The fact that followers can often be easily replaced and the fact that they lack standing and influence compared to the leaders of an organization is one set of factors supporting their treatment as objects rather than as persons. There are two other dynamics that also contribute significantly to instrumentalizing followers, which are the desire of leaders to pursue self-interested goals and the arrogance of leaders.

Examining the tendency of leaders to seek self-interested goals first, we can say that the power given to leaders often presents a strong temptation to either forget the importance of followers or to think of followers as expendable pawns in the pursuit of organizational goals. Leaders often exercise power irrespective of the interests of followers. Giving such power to leaders is frequently necessary, but also entails organizational hazards. For example, in the military, a unit's mission may call for risking the lives of its members. That risk is intrinsic to the nature of combat operations,

---

39. Cf. Porter, *Philosophy Through Fiction and Film* for a list of the various cultures and intellectual traditions that have articulated similar notions regarding the golden rule of treating others as you would like to be treated.

so a military commander is given the authority to make decisions that may literally kill his or her followers. It is an awesome responsibility and one that must be used with extreme care. Most leaders do not have life-and-death decisions at stake in their daily deliberations, but similar to combatant commanders, they will frequently have the authority to make decisions that prioritize the mission of the organization over the interests of its followers. There is a logic to this prioritization. The reason leaders and followers are part of an organization is to accomplish a particular purpose, and that purpose may indeed run athwart the interests of both leaders and followers. It is here that we can see one of the most important aspects of ethics to leadership. Leaders have the responsibility to put their interests last—to put their interests behind those of their followers and behind the organization's mission. The sad reality is many leaders are simply unable to do this. Putting one's own interests after those of the organization and its followers takes a degree of wisdom (leaders will often rationalize "win-win" solutions in these circumstances that really do not benefit their followers or team) and a level of self-discipline that is beyond the moral capacity of many leaders. The power leaders exercise and the desire to pursue self-interest is a combination that tempts many (most?) leaders to treat followers as mere means to the leader's or the organization's goals.

Another aspect of leadership that contributes significantly to the temptation to treat followers as mere means is based on the impact success has on the leader's mindset. The success typically required to achieve a leadership position and the fact of being named to a leadership position itself will make leaders prone to ignore follower interests on a psychological basis. Simply put, people who experience repeated success often become arrogant. Leadership hubris is such a consistent phenomenon that it was highlighted by Cicero more than two thousand years ago. Cicero asserts that the more successful a leader becomes the more that person is in need of humility.[40] Humility in this context is seen as a source of wisdom that enables a person to overcome the ignorance that builds up over time due to lack of failure. It is almost funny to put it that way since most people would die to have that kind of ignorance. It also sounds strange since leaders are usually highly intelligent people, but there's little doubt that the most brilliant leaders are often the most at risk of believing they are above making mistakes and therefore need

---

40. Cicero, *On Duties*, 1.90.

not be concerned with the thinking of followers. And it is when leaders believe in their own press clippings the most that they are at the greatest risk of overlooking or discounting the needs of their followers. Hubris, arrogance, and self-importance are not the character traits that help leaders focus on follower concerns.

Having a moral principle at hand that protects against treating followers as mere means is therefore helpful to leaders, followers, and organizations as a whole. It helps leaders because no matter how powerful one becomes, few leaders want to be a person who uses other people without respecting their dignity. Likewise, no follower wants to be treated as an object, so a moral principle that reminds leaders that followers are autonomous moral agents whose dignity demands respect will support an environment where concern for followers is integrated into an organization's culture. Lastly, a community or team that reduces followers to the status of mere tools will have a wretched organizational climate. Such climates produce demoralized workforces whose members will head for the door as soon as another opportunity materializes. Treating followers as valued members of a team where their hopes, dreams, and aspirations are demonstrably important to the organization's leadership will build a team culture that will not only retain its talent but will also get the most out of that talent. Followers whose leaders treat them as persons with intrinsic value will respond to that treatment with loyalty to the leader and to the organization the leader represents.

15

Hegel, Marx, and the Historical Nature of Ethics

GEORG WILHELM FRIEDRICH HEGEL (b. 1770) is a person quite familiar to philosophers, but he is not a household name for most twenty-first-century Americans. Hegel is no doubt an important philosopher in his own right, being one of the most systematic thinkers in the school of philosophy know as German Idealism that emerged in the seventeenth and eighteenth centuries.[1] In addition to his own thought, Hegel is important to MacIntyre's historical analysis for two reasons. First, Hegel is one of the most significant philosophers to advocate for MacIntyre's thesis that to understand philosophy one must understand the history through which philosophy has developed. Second, although the influence of Hegel's own thinking has waxed and waned in the centuries since his death, the influence of his thinking over that of Karl Marx is quite significant, and it is through the legacy of Marxism that the thought of Hegel has made its most potent impact on the world. In order to see that impact, we must first describe some key elements of Hegel's thought, which include his descriptions of master and serf relations (a theme further developed by Marx and Friedrich Nietzsche), freedom, and false conceptual schemes. In doing so, we will be able to appreciate not only Hegel's original contributions to European thought, but we will also be able to see how those ideas inspired the nineteenth-century thinkers that followed in his wake. After that description, we will examine the moral thought of Karl Marx as

1. Cf. Beiser, "Hegel and the Problem of Metaphysics," 1–19 for an overview of Hegel's thought and impact on contemporary philosophy.

the most significant of those followers. Marx ends up repudiating much of Hegel's thinking, but he nevertheless charts a new course in economic theory that owes a significant debt to the categories developed by Hegel.

History, Hegel, Rousseau, and the Engagement with Christian Ideals

MacIntyre begins his analysis of Hegel's thought by noting how MacIntyre's own analysis covers similar ground with respect to the significant role history plays in understanding philosophy. Hegel asserts that the history of philosophy is at the core of philosophy and that the key element to understanding ethics lies in this history as well. This is the case because Hegel sees the role of philosophy as clarifying and articulating the concepts that guide the rhythms of ordinary life. Since communities have contact with one another in both time and place, philosophy will be shaped as ideas are communicated from one community to another.[2] Early in his career Hegel questions why modern Europeans are not more like the ancient Greeks when it came to the moral rules that guided their ethics. He turns to history for his answer and asserts that the coming of Christianity, the epoch that separates modern Europe from ancient Greece, sets a new context for the rules that differentiated modern European ethics from that of its ancestor in classical Greece. The *polis* set the context for morality in ancient Greece, providing a shared political structure for the citizens of the Greek city-state, which produced goals, aspirations, and desires that were shared by those citizens. With the breakdown of the city-state and the coming of Christianity, Christian believers look to an eternal destiny and a transcendent God who provides the rules that guide moral choices rather than taking their moral cues from the earth-bound city of man (to use the language of St. Augustine).[3] As a result, Hegel contends that the primary driver for the way people live and make their moral choices is no longer the societal roles that played such an important part in Greek ethics. Rather, ethics had become a function of the relationships surrounding the individual that enabled each man and woman to recognize themselves as persons whose dignity was supported

---

2. *SHE*, 199–200.
3. *SHE*, 199.

by both the religious ethics of Christians and the rational morality of a thinker like Kant.[4]

Hegel centers his moral thinking on the person, but does so in a way that moves away from the individualistic context for morality common to most Enlightenment ethicists. MacIntyre repeatedly points out that many Enlightenment thinkers viewed modern communities merely as collections of individuals.[5] Hegel, on the other hand, provides a more substantive role for the relationships that bind an individual to his or her community. In taking this approach, he applies a view of the community that has much in common with Rousseau's approach to the relationship between a society and the moral ideas of the individuals living within that society. Like Rousseau, Hegel asserts that the choices available to individuals living in primitive communities are relatively limited. As societies get more complex, however, the choices available to individuals multiply. Multiplication of opportunity has an impact on what a person actually chooses, as do the criteria that are generally used to make such choices. Social practices have a significant impact on the acceptability or unacceptability of the choices available to each person.[6] MacIntyre returns to the Sophists to explain this point. The Sophists (like Hobbes and others) see the goals and desires of each person as fixed, which results in a predetermined range of options that are offered to a person within a particular society. Hegel sees such an approach as profoundly mistaken.[7] Following Diderot and Rousseau on this issue, Hegel asserts that societal structures affect and provide people living within those societies with their goals and passions. A person cannot desire to be a Tik-Tok influencer unless the community has the technology, infrastructure, and audience to enable that influence in the first place. Desires are elicited by the objects a community presents to the individual.[8]

Hegel also asserts that the desires elicited by a society may be very difficult to attain in that society. A community in which fame is a fundamental value will likely fail to provide the opportunity for all of its members to be famous. In light of the power of the community to shape the desires and goals of its members, Hegel describes societies in terms of the transitions between stages of a society where different objects are offered

4. *SHE*, 200.
5. *SHE*, 199.
6. *SHE*, 200.
7. *SHE*, 200.
8. *SHE*, 200.

and then desired and pursued by the people inhabiting those societies. Those transitions again point to the importance of history and its stages to understanding the nature of ethics.[9] Hegel focuses on one stage in Roman antiquity, which he describes as the master and serf relationship, as particularly important for the understanding of ethics. The master and serf dynamic became central to Hegel's approach to ethics and later became paradigmatic for Marx's approach to economic concepts as well.

Masters and Serfs, False Solutions, and Freedom

Hegel describes the human condition in the context of freedom, and MacIntyre notes that Hegel's conception of freedom may be the most significant innovation he offers to philosophy.[10] Hegel asserts that to understand a concept such as freedom—or any belief for that matter—one must first approach it within the backdrop of the social system of which it is a part.[11] A social system is visible both in the way people live in that system and in the thinking that articulates the beliefs and concepts imbedded in the system. In other words, by examining a social system one can understand the ideas that direct not only the system as a whole, but the behavior and the relations of the people living within it.[12] Hegel approaches the idea of freedom through one relationship that seems to represent a profound limitation of freedom, the master-serf relationship. The master-serf relationship bears examination if for no other reason than the fact that it appears over and over again in various social systems throughout history. In addition, it has a profound effect on the thinking and behavior of the people who inhabit the relationship, an examination of which enables us to understand not just the relationship itself, but also the nature of freedom and even the human condition more generally.

In MacIntyre's recounting Hegel asserts that the master-serf relationship is bad not only for the serf, but for the master as well. The degradation of the serf is clear from the outset. The serf is reduced to the level of a thing, a tool to be used to accomplish a particular task. The serf is deformed because he or she has little ability to assert any autonomy whatsoever. The aspirations and purposes of the serf are dominated by

9. *SHE*, 201.
10. *SHE*, 203.
11. *SHE*, 203.
12. *SHE*, 203.

the commands of the master.[13] The degradation of the master is less obvious, but even more radical from Hegel's perspective. This is because the relationship between the master and serf is defined by the material things produced by the work the serf does for the master. Although serfs are deformed by the subjugation experienced in coerced labor, there is also a dignity to their work in producing a thing of value. In addition, the serf can look up to the master as one who has the autonomy the serf would like to experience. For the master, the relationship involves only corruption. The things produced for the master by the serf serve as only transient enjoyments. The master has diminished another person to the status of a thing to serve his or her self-interested needs.[14] Lord Acton's famous quote comes to bear within the relationship. "Power tends to corrupt and absolute power corrupts absolutely. Great men are almost always bad men."[15] In Hegel's analysis, the power of the master over the serf serves to corrupt the master, making the person a tyrant capable of using another person for no good reason. In addition, the master is isolated. By degrading other people, the master is left with no one with whom the master can establish an authentic relationship. The self-consciousness of the master is stunted because the master can find no other person to be an object of regard on the same level as the master. There is no friend in which the master may find a mirror for the self.[16] By their own actions, masters are cut off from the relationships that make it possible to grow and flourish. They become the Scrooge of Dickens's novel, experiencing the impoverishment of loneliness and isolation even in the midst of material abundance.

Since the master-serf relationship deforms both master and serf, Hegel asks how people in the relationship cope with its circumstances. He turns to the history of the Roman Empire, a society dominated by the master-serf relationship, to provide three false answers to the predicament. The first answer is given by Stoic philosophy. For Stoicism, each person is a citizen not of the *polis*, nor even of the empire, but is a citizen of the entire universe. Emperors, senators, plebes, and slaves are all equally citizens of the cosmos. This, Hegel contends, is the assertion of a false equality. Such an approach merely masks the true nature of the master-serf relationship rather than doing anything to actually

13. *SHE*, 201.
14. *SHE*, 201.
15. Acton, "Letter 1."
16. *SHE*, 201.

transform the relationship or mitigate its debilitating aspects.[17] A second false solution is provided by the Skeptic school of philosophy that also existed during the years of the Roman Empire. Skepticism (from the Greek *skepsis* for investigation) is a philosophy that investigates all received beliefs and concepts.[18] While investigating a topic, the method of the Skeptics included suspending belief or putting a received doctrine into doubt until the investigation and interrogation of the idea is complete. In the context of the master-serf relationship, the skeptical serf doubts and even rejects the ideas forced upon the serf by the master. The serf's attitude produces two frames of mind: one in which the serf intellectually defies the ideology of the master, which stands in contrast to the serf's frame of mind in the real world where the behavior of the serf must conform to the reality of the master's ideas or commands.[19] The Stoic and Skeptic methods of dealing with the master-serf relationship lead to what Hegel calls the state of unhappy consciousness, where the social forms in which the person exists deform a person's relationships and even the personality of each individual. The state of unhappy consciousness comes to fruition in the epoch of Catholic Christianity.[20] In the context of ancient Catholicism, the deformity of human life is recognized as a lack of freedom, which is intrinsic to a fallen world. Christianity offers a means to overcome the fallen world, the City of Man, by transitioning to the City of God, which represents the divine realm that offers a perfection of life not accessible to the fallen world. In Hegel's view, the mistake for many Christians is the belief that the redemption and atonement offered by Christ is a reality of history rather than a symbolic message through which a person can understand the nature of one's slavery in the fallen world. For Hegel, Christianity describes the human condition well but is itself part of the false consciousness when it is taken to be literally rather than figuratively true.[21]

So, if Christianity is only a symbol, how can it help the serf in his or her condition of slavery? The symbolism of Christianity enables a person to see and understand the form of life, the social structure of which he or she is a part. In recognizing the structure, a person can see the

17. SHE, 202.

18. Cf. Popkin, *History of Skepticism From Savonarola to Bayle* for a thorough treatment of skepticism and its historical impact.

19. SHE, 202.

20. SHE, 202.

21. SHE, 202–3.

boundaries that limit his or her freedom. The social forms or structures set the limits and obstacles that each person must overcome to escape whatever slavery is imposed by that person's society. The barriers the social forms placed in the path of the individual form the horizon over which they must leap. And it is in defining the horizon and boundaries of each person that social forms and relationships play a positive role, according to Hegel. It is in marking the horizon that must be transcended to achieve liberation that the human person can conceive of the freedom that can be gained by breaking the fetters of their particular community. Hegel sees freedom as the core of human existence, and freedom, simply put, is achieved by overcoming the barriers a community places in the way of its members.[22] Structural relationships in societies can deform and degrade the individuals that comprise the society. It is in escaping these deforming and degrading relationships, whatever their form in the infinite variety of historical communities, that a person achieves his or her freedom. MacIntyre points out that the limiting factor, the role of the horizon, is what is original in Hegel's thought, and Hegel uses the idea to evaluate societies from different epochs in history.[23] To identify the aims and goals of the people who comprise a historical community, one must discover what the people in that society saw as the obstacles in their path. Once you have done this, you have identified the meaning of freedom for that community.[24] Hegel's articulation of his notion of freedom may seem quite abstract, but Marx makes use of this abstract idea in a materialistic and economic context that had an extraordinary impact on history. Before turning to Marx and the use he makes of Hegel's ideas, however, it is important to spend some time with a last aspect of Hegel's thought that MacIntyre uses to criticize Kant's thinking and the motivations of Nazi behavior in the twentieth century.

False Consciousness and the Ethics of Bureaucracies

According to MacIntyre Hegel describes a false consciousness as a theory of life that both educates people on significant aspects of life and simultaneously obscures other important parts. A false consciousness can be misleading in two ways. First, as already mentioned, it hides aspects of

22. *SHE*, 203.
23. *SHE*, 203.
24. *SHE*, 203.

society and morality that are important to moral deliberation. Second, a false consciousness will often misrepresent itself as universal in scope rather than focused on one aspect of human experience. What may be true in a narrower context is not necessarily true of all humans, but the false consciousness will often claim that its perspective is universally applicable.[25] For example, as an American I may think that a democratic republic is always the best form of government, but others in different cultures and living under different forms of government may say otherwise. The false consciousness of this example lies not in a discussion of what is the best form of government, but in the idea that an American might falsely universalize his or her experience and think democratic republics are always the best form of government.

Hegel sees the modern attachment to individualism as an obvious example of a false consciousness.[26] An individualist approach to ethics is a false consciousness because it represents features of individualism as universal aspects of human experience. MacIntyre provides a thorough review of Hegel's point, the highlights of which are as follows. The first individualist doctrine is that of a moral hedonism where the fundamental moral principle is looking out for one's own interest. Here the moral imperative is, "You better look out for yourself because if you do not, no one else will." The problem with this approach is that as a collection of individuals pursue their own desires and happiness, those purposes and aspirations come into conflict with one another.[27] Disharmony is a quick product of moral hedonism, which leads to disillusionment with one's peers and society in general. This causes an individual to quickly recognize that impersonal forces rule one's life, and the person therefore must develop an inner nobility through which she or he can rise above an indifferent and hostile world. A person is then able to overcome the world through his or her virtue and can execute necessary worldly duties on the basis of virtue even for a world whose values the person disdains. This is the stage of individualism that Hegel calls the "spiritual zoo," where each person has limited his or her own scope of responsibility to only the specific task at hand. The broader context is not the concern of the individual. The individual takes pride in minding his or her own business. They remain in their cage.[28]

25. *SHE*, 206–7.
26. *SHE*, 207.
27. *SHE*, 207.
28. *SHE*, 207.

Hegel has brought us to the social setting of bureaucracy, and MacIntyre provides a powerful critique of Kant's thought in the context of bureaucracies and the horror of the Nazi regime. In a bureaucracy, the good bureaucrat is concerned with the immediate task at hand and not with the broader context that might give meaning to her or his actions. The bureaucrat accepts a limited vision for his or her behavior and therefore limited responsibility. MacIntyre applies Kant's thought in Hegel's social context by examining the ethical motivation and behavior of the notorious Nazi, Adolph Eichmann, who organized the transportation of countless Jews to their deaths in the Holocaust. MacIntyre references Hegel's analysis in relation to bureaucratic behavior and asserts,

> (The bureaucrat) boasts of minding his own business. He is the outcome of all good bureaucrats, of those technical specialists such as Eichmann who boasted that they merely discharged their function in arranging for so much transport to be provided between point X and point Y. Whether the cargo was sheep or Jews, whether points X and Y were farm and butcher's slaughterhouse, or ghetto and gas chamber was no concern of theirs . . . . The worst of it is that in its devotion to the affair-on-hand the individual reason now presents itself as a moral legislator: the task before you is your duty. First uttering imperatives to us and then offering us a test of self-consistent universalizability, as we have already noted in discussing Kant, lets in almost any action.[29]

MacIntyre goes on to observe the relevance of Kant's thought to Eichmann's defense at his 1962 trial in Israel for crimes against humanity. Eichmann defended himself by asserting he was merely following the rules of his organization, and that the moral basis he used for making his determinations was the categorical imperative, Kant's fundamental moral principle. Critics of Eichmann, Hannah Arendt foremost among them, assert that Eichmann twisted the categorical imperative to his own profoundly warped ends.[30] It's a charge with which MacIntyre might readily agree, since his critique of Kant is that the categorical imperative is distinctly vulnerable to such twisting.

The bottom line for Hegel and MacIntyre in this analysis is that in the false consciousness of individualism, a person supplies a moral code that is of his or her own making and claims that it is universally binding.

---

29. *SHE*, 207–8.

30. Cf. Arendt, *Eichmann in Jerusalem*, for the full version of Arendt's reporting and analysis regarding Eichmann's trial.

Hegel asserts that this is to deceive oneself and therefore be self-defeating. What gives sanction to our moral choices is in part the fact that the criteria governing moral activity are not chosen but given to each individual. Moral criteria made up by the individual are a counterfeit morality.[31] It is radical individualism masquerading as an objective and universal moral code.

It is in this context that Hegel asserts the origin of moral principles, which in his view lies in the community. A person finds the criteria for moral judgments in the time-honored moral practices of a well-formed community. A person forms their subjective choices in accordance with such principles, but the authority of the principles resides in the authority of the community and not in the fact that the person chooses to follow those rules or practices.[32] Given the differences in communities over time and place, Hegel's approach sounds relativistic. MacIntyre points out that despite the fact that Hegel does recognize some virtues as important to every community, his method emphasizes the variety of moral cultures and gives credence to a relativistic description of his moral thinking.[33] Yet while these values may vary from community to community, Hegel still asserts an objective approach to morality where objective (i.e., impersonal and external) moral rules are based on specific values that are indispensable to a life well lived in a specific community.[34]

For Hegel, the community is the authority that defines moral principles for the individual. This moral foundation seems shaky, however, in light of the fact that historical communities are highly imperfect. Recognizing this problem, Hegel uses his understanding of reason and freedom to critique existing communities. Hegel asserts that through the process of that critique an ideal, true, and finally satisfactory social order can be established. When this occurs, what Hegel calls the Absolute will have been achieved in history. And by the Absolute Hegel means that the reconciliation of God and humans, symbolically represented by Christianity, will finally be achieved.[35] In addition, the Absolute will be achieved through the progression of history as a whole and is not to be confused with any finite part of history. For Hegel, the whole of history exhibits a logical evolution in which one stage succeeds another, and the

31. *SHE*, 208.
32. *SHE*, 208.
33. *SHE*, 206.
34. *SHE*, 208.
35. *SHE*, 209.

different stages are linked by the evolution of ideas as thought moves through various historical periods. The movement between stages of history is thus a movement of thought in which successor stages replace their predecessors by thinking more effectively. This conclusion was retained by Hegel's followers, in particular the group called the Young or Left Hegelians. These followers saw themselves as obligated to surpass their philosophical mentor by thinking more effectively than Hegel. Their object was to purge Hegel's thought of its primary weakness, which was its religious aspects.[36] The most influential Left Hegelian is none other than Karl Marx, and it is to Marx's use of Hegel's thought that we will now turn.

The Influence of Hegel on the Morality of Marx

Although a German by birth, Karl Marx (b. 1818) spent much of his adult life outside of Germany due to the controversies surrounding his writing and advocacy. Following his philosophical studies at the universities of Bonn and Berlin, Marx moved to Paris and Brussels before settling in London in 1849 where he remained until his death.[37] In examining the aspects of Marx's philosophy that engage ethics, we will see many of Hegel's primary themes. Marx uses Hegel's notion of freedom, the master-serf antagonism, the individualistic critique, and the idea of a false consciousness to great effect. Given the extensive use Marx made of Hegel's ideas, it is helpful to first start with the differences between their thinking to see the novel ways in which Marx applies the thought of Hegel.

Hegel has been described as one of the most systematic German thinkers in the school of idealism. The focus of Hegel's idealism, as the name implies, are the ideas or concepts that lead to the progression of history. MacIntyre asserts that unlike Hegel, who focused on the ideas that formed a society, Marx turns his focus to the work or labor necessary to support a society as the key to understanding different social structures. Where Hegel describes history as the development of the Absolute idea in time, Marx sees the development of history in economic and social terms.[38] Change in history is not an evolution in thinking for Marx, but an evolution in the manner of work undertaken to support a society

---

36. *SHE*, 210.
37. Cf. Patterson, *Karl Marx, Anthropologist*, xi–xiii for a chronology of Marx's life.
38. *SHE*, 211.

and in the way a society organizes itself to support that work. According to MacIntyre, Marx asserts that the economy emerging in eighteenth- and nineteenth-century Europe is a bourgeois economy that is driven by technical innovation. The bourgeois economy destroyed the bonds of feudalism through the economic transformation accomplished by the use of technology in service of the goal of accumulating capital. It is in the context of human mastery over nature by means of technology and the spirit of enterprise unleashed by these processes that Marx examines the idea of freedom. MacIntyre then tells us that freedom and Marx's approach to morality can be analyzed in the economic and social context in which the individual is liberated to participate in the free market economy.[39] It is in this markedly different context, one focused on economic and material categories rather than categories concerned with ideas, that Marx puts the concepts of Hegel to work.

Freedom is perhaps the best place to begin when examining the similarities between the thought of Hegel and Marx. MacIntyre asserts that the central concept of Marx's philosophy is Hegel's sense of freedom, and there is no doubt their formulations are quite similar. Where Hegel asserts that freedom "is the actuality of men—not something which they have, as men, but which they are," Marx describes it thus: "Freedom is so much the essence of man that even its opponents realize it . . . . No man fights freedom; he fights at most the freedom of others."[40] For Marx, like Hegel, freedom is the overcoming of limitations, the transcendence of horizons. The horizons, however, are not conceptual for Marx as they are for Hegel. Rather, they are economic. In pursuing one's freedom, a person overcomes the constraints of one social setting by establishing a new social setting with less limitations. The limitations Marx sees for the laborer are those imposed by the bourgeois economy of the nineteenth century. And similar to Hegel, Marx puts striving for freedom in the context of a conflict between superiors and inferiors. Where Hegel describes this conflict on the individual level of master and serf, Marx describes it on the communal level between bourgeois capitalists and laborers. For Marx, nineteenth-century history should be examined in the context of the progress that is possible through class conflict in which laborers throw off the yoke of their capitalist masters.[41]

---

39. *SHE*, 211–12.
40. *SHE*, 211, citing Marx from *Discussion of Press Debates*.
41. *SHE*, 211.

It is also in his description of the alienation of laborers in the bourgeois economy that Marx makes significant use of Hegel's view of both individualism and Hegel's concept of a false consciousness. Hegel and Marx see individualism as a false consciousness emerging in nineteenth-century Europe. As a false consciousness, individualism is both an achievement of and a barrier to freedom. In the eighteenth and nineteenth centuries, the citizens of Europe had been liberated from their former bonds as serfs to pursue the accumulation of capital as a result of their own individual enterprise and labor. According to Marx, it is an achievement that has grave costs because it is a liberation that is only partial and to a large extent illusory.[42] For Marx, the social and economic structures of bourgeois society also imprison the individual in a set of relationships that cancel the freedom of individuals and stunt their growth as members of the labor class. Those relationships prevent each individual from coming to a self-understanding that is not warped and full of distortion. Marx asserts that under the bourgeois economy people find themselves in the grips of impersonal powers that are actually the fruit of their own labors, which are then falsely objectified and given a counterfeit independence of their own. For example, the capital or value produced by a laborer is used by the bourgeoisie in the establishment of a banking system that leverages the work of the laborer but is inaccessible to that worker and thus a barrier to his or her liberation. In addition, workers may see themselves as free agents, but they are in reality being forced to play roles not of their own choosing by the social and economic forces that direct society as a whole. Marx contends that it is in these twin illusions that the alienation of the human person consists. The worker is unable to escape and sometimes unable to see their new serfdom. This alienation, Marx says, is brought to its climax in the institutions of private property.[43] The capital making these institutions possible is produced by the worker, but the benefits capital can confer are often denied to the working class. The result is not only the impoverishment and disempowerment of the working class, but an environment that prevents workers from seeing and understanding the possibilities that await them beyond the walls of bourgeois economic structures.[44] For Marx Hegel's view of a conceptual limit or horizon as the border between captivity and

---

42. *SHE*, 211–12.
43. *SHE*, 212.
44. *SHE*, 212.

freedom becomes the economic and social horizon the worker must cross to achieve his or her freedom.

It is in the context of his view of alienation and the separation of the bourgeoisie and workers that Marx articulates his understanding of ethical principles. Recognizing the divide between the classes, the divide between workers and the bourgeoisie, Marx asserts that morality cannot transcend the gulf that separates each class.[45] The working class is dominated and pillaged by the bourgeoisie, but that domination is precisely the result of capitalist bourgeois morality. No appeal to justice can be made in defense of workers because the bourgeoisie is merely acting upon the capitalist morality embodied by their societal class. The job of the bourgeois class is to accumulate capital, and the workers are a means to that end. The only solution that can enable or empower the moral principles of the working class—that can enable workers to pursue their hopes, dreams, and aspirations—is to abolish the bourgeois economic and social structures that subjugate workers.[46] Those structures limit the freedom of workers and must therefore be transcended to achieve the liberation of the working class.

In his critique of Marx, MacIntyre points out that Marx never addresses the important question of what moral principles should actually guide workers and guide socialist and communist societies once those societies are established. MacIntyre acknowledges that Marx does discuss the issue in the context of Kant's hypothetical Kingdom of Ends, which is a thought experiment Kant used to illustrate how a society of autonomous moral agents guided by universally valid moral principles would operate. Marx's discussion on this front is quite limited, however, and yields meager conclusions.[47] Marxist ethicists have attempted to fill this void in a variety of ways. Eduard Bernstein (b. 1850), a Marxist theorist and politician, tried to establish a Kantian basis for the moral principles that should guide the labor movement. Bernstein's thought was criticized by other Marxists such as Karl Kautsky (b. 1854), who asserted that Bernstein's appeal to universally valid moral principles that transcended economic classes was exactly the type of morality Marx would condemn. Rather than Kant's thought, Kautsky offers what MacIntyre describes as a crude utilitarianism to guide worker morality.[48] As a result, despite being

---

45. *SHE*, 213.
46. *SHE*, 212.
47. *SHE*, 214.
48. *SHE*, 214.

the preeminent voice to champion the values of workers, Marx ends up being strangely silent about the actual moral principles workers should hold. Silence about the reform of public institutions is not an issue for the British Utilitarians of the nineteenth-century and it is their significant innovations that MacIntyre examines next.

Leadership Reflection: Leadership in the Bureaucratic Zoo

Hegel came up with the idea of the "Spiritual Zoo" in the early nineteenth century, which MacIntyre recognizes as having particular relevance to the corporate and governmental bureaucracies of the twentieth and twenty-first centuries. The zoo refers to the cages we humans construct for ourselves and inhabit in reaction to the realization that we live in thoroughly corrupt societies. In Hegel's telling, individuals recognize the corruption of their surrounding society and realize their only choice is to rise above that corporate vice through their own individual virtue. The result is people who mind and take care of their own business and do not worry about the malice and corruption that surrounds them. They do their jobs to the best of their ability even in the context of a community or organization whose values they disdain. This is the spiritual zoo. It is the environment where people (leaders and followers) keep their heads down and focus only on their task, the task at hand. Do not worry about the big picture. Mind your own business. Stay in your cage.

It sounds realistic, admirable, and depressing all at the same time. Realistic because it describes the experience of alienation so many members of mediocre organizations endure. Admirable because it makes the best of these difficult situations. Depressing because of the powerlessness of the individual. But we are not talking about followers in this essay, we are talking about leaders. Surely leaders do not have to stay in their cages. They are the ones who can prevent the cages from being built in the first place. Leaders should be working to create an organizational environment where followers will be empowered to share their ideas on whatever is important to the life of the organization. Right? Alas, such is not always the case. Leaders not only may not have the power to prevent the formation of cages; they may be the people most comfortable staying in the cage. Such is the case because bureaucracies value efficiency in getting things done. Calling out the moral faults and corruption of an institution will not only be viewed negatively by those at the top of the organization, but it will also engender inefficiency. Confronting moral ills will cause controversy, and controversy will distract from the work at hand. Efficiency requires smooth sailing over unperturbed waters, and confronting a corrupt organizational culture will make waves that distract, depress morale, and cause friction between different members of the organization. The leadership of bureaucrats is most efficient when they stay in their lanes and do not cause controversy. The cage can be a wonderfully comfortable place to stay, for both leaders and followers.

Sometimes the cage is the right place for leaders and their followers to be. Leaders must be guided by practical wisdom when confronting the failures of their organizations. Not all problems need be addressed. Sometimes a failure is not significant enough to warrant the attention or energy to correct it. Sometimes a corrupt practice can be too risky to address. For example, the leader or followers could end up getting fired or suffering some other punishment that outweighs the value of correcting whatever the deficiency might be. Similarly, it might be completely futile to address a problem because it is impossible to make the changes necessary to correct it, or those changes could even yield the destruction of the organization. These are mountains not worth dying on.

Yet these legitimate considerations can also distract from the situations when leaders are presented with corruption that must be confronted. And those same considerations can serve as rationalizations for not addressing moral wrongs that should be addressed come what may. Often the refrain is "Nothing you do will make a difference. It's not worth the trouble or risk." Yet we all know that there are moral mountains where leaders have to take risks and be willing to sacrifice their own good for that of their followers, their organizations, and even their community. A stark example of this is the leadership provided by Martin Luther King Jr. during the civil rights struggle in the mid-twentieth century. King was a pastor at Dexter Avenue Baptist Church in Montgomery, Alabama. It was a church that could have served as King's cage had he decided to focus only on his ministry at the church rather than the injustice that stalked the streets outside his church. We all know that King did not stay in his cage and instead took up the fight against segregation which disfigured the broader American society surrounding his church. A leader in the fight against segregation through nonviolent protest, King penned his famous *Letter from a Birmingham City Jail* in 1963 during one of his many incarcerations. King's letter described a way to get out of the spiritual cage and fight for the justice so desperately needed in the local and even national community. In his letter, King described the nonviolent tactics of direct action and addressed the concerns of the white Protestant ministers of the south who said King's tactics were too extreme. These ministers felt that King should be more patient and pursue the change he sought through legal means. History has confirmed the righteousness of King's actions, however, and it is King himself who explains why he had to step out of the spiritual cage society had built for him, while simultaneously stepping into the physical cage of the Birmingham City Jail. The injustice of racism in the United States could not be corrected via legal means if the laws themselves were corrupt. Making a natural law argument, Dr. King asserted that any law that did not conform to the law of God was no law at all and must therefore be resisted. He was not, however, advocating for chaos or the abandonment of a society based on laws. If there was an unjust law, King argued, then it must be resisted, but those resisting the law must also be willing to pay the cost of respecting a lawful society and be willing to suffer the consequences of breaking the law, even if that meant going to jail.[49]

King's experience and the history of the civil rights movement teach us that leaders who stick their heads out of the spiritual or bureaucratic cage must be willing to suffer the costs. And sometime those costs will accrue and are never paid back to the people, to the leaders, who put their lives on the line. This is the risk and cost of living in any human society. There has never been a perfect human society. Injustice rears its head in every community. This means sometimes leaders and followers must be willing to suffer so that others may flourish. Without leaders willing to make that sacrifice, whether it be in corporations, in government, in the military, in religious institutions, or civil society, injustice will eventually reign. At some point, injustice must be confronted, and both leaders and followers must emerge from the safety of their cages to put an end to that injustice. Such leadership requires both wisdom and courage, but without wise and brave leaders, there is little hope for a community to overcome the injustice that will inevitably threaten it.

---

49. King, *Letter From a Birmingham City Jail*.

16

Nineteenth-Century Utilitarianism

WE WILL NOW HAVE to turn the clock back a little to examine the genesis of utilitarianism, a school of thought that became prominent in eighteenth- and nineteenth-century Great Britain and remains one of the most influential moral theories today. The term utilitarianism was coined by Jeremy Bentham (b. 1748). As a legal theorist, reforming political and social structures was the cause most dear to Bentham's heart, but his broad approach to this passion enabled him to innovate in other intellectual areas, including ethics. Bentham detailed the basic elements of utilitarianism in his work *An Introduction to The Principles of Morals and Legislation*, initially published in 1789.[1] Bentham built on the thought of earlier sentimental moralists such as Francis Hutcheson. Hutcheson is the first thinker to articulate what would later become known as the principle of utility when he asserted that good actions are actions that provide the greatest happiness for the greatest number of people.[2] Bentham laid out the basic terms of utilitarianism early in his career, and then sought to use the principle of utility to reform many of the political and social institutions of nineteenth-century England throughout the remainder of his life.

MacIntyre observes that British society owed reformers such as Bentham and his collaborators a debt for the important economic, legal, and political reforms that they pursued.[3] The most significant of Bentham's collaborators were a father and son duo named James and John

1. Cf. Schofield, *Bentham*, 1–18 for a brief biography of Bentham.
2. Hutcheson, *Inquiry into the Original of Our Ideas*.
3. *SHE*, 237.

Stuart Mill. Bentham met the father, James, in 1808, and James became one of Bentham's closest associates, serving almost as an aide-de-camp for Bentham until Bentham's death in 1832. John Stuart Mill (b. 1806), born only two years before Bentham met James, was destined to be not only the greatest defender of Bentham's views on utilitarianism, but he also became the most influential English-speaking philosopher of the nineteenth century. J. S. Mill was brought up by his father from his earliest years to be a philosopher. Educated in both Greek and Latin by the age of eight, J. S. Mill had read most of the great philosophical treatises of European history before his twelfth birthday.[4] His father's grooming was the perfect preparation for Mill to assume the mantle of leadership for the next generation of British reformers. According to the younger Mill's autobiography, however, his preparation to carry on the work of societal reform did not prepare him well for the living of his own individual life. Under the weight of his scholarship and the expectations thrust upon him, Mill discovered at the tender age of twenty that even if all the reforms that he thought necessary for the transformation of society were implemented immediately, he would find no joy in the implementation.[5] This realization led to a mental crisis with which Mill struggled for the remainder of his life. Despite that crisis, Mill would go on to write works such as *On Liberty* and *Utilitarianism* that would make him one of the dominant voices in modern British ethics.

The Utilitarianism of Jeremy Bentham

In his passion to reform the ills of British society, Bentham sought a moral principle that would provide a clear measure to guide those changes. In devising a systematic approach to reform, he concluded that ethics had to be defined in terms of pleasure and pain. In Bentham's view, the rational assessment of the pleasure and pain caused by a choice was the only consistent criteria to determine whether a choice was good or bad. According to Bentham, the morality of an action can only be judged by examining its consequences to see if those consequences produced happiness by either increasing pleasure or decreasing pain.[6] He came to this conclusion on the basis of his critique of theories of morality based on

---

4. Schultz, *Happiness Philosophers*, 115–17.
5. Mill, *Autobiography*, I.139.
6. *SHE*, 233.

human nature and his understanding of psychology. In his description of Bentham's thought MacIntyre turns first to moral theories based on human nature and Bentham's assertion that they could not provide consistent guidance to point out what was right or wrong. He made his case in the context of the large diversity of laws based on natural moral principles. Bentham observed that when tasked to provide laws to govern human society, natural theorists would come up with sets of laws that were not only different, but contradictory. In addition, the natural theorists could provide no consistent criteria for choosing between the contradictions. Bentham thus asked the question, how can human nature provide a foundation for law if its theorists could not formulate either a consensus for those laws or a process by which a consensus might be achieved?[7] For Bentham, that failure was not merely a bug for a natural theory of ethics, but an intrinsic problem of such theories. In his view, the nature of logic and the way words and sentences define ideas prevent humans from taking the abstractions of nature and applying them to the ideas of morality and law.[8]

Since natural theories cannot provide a basis for ethics and law, Bentham turns to psychology for that foundation. In Bentham's view the psychological motivation for moral choice was always the human experience of pleasure and pain.

> Nature has placed mankind under the governance of two sovereign masters, pain and pleasure. It is for them alone to point out what we ought to do, as well as to determine what we shall do. On the one hand the standard of right and wrong, on the other the chain of causes and effects, are fastened to their throne. They govern us in all we do, in all we say, in all we think: every effort we can make to throw off our subjection, will serve but to demonstrate and confirm it. In words a man may pretend to abjure their empire: *but in reality he will remain subject to it all the while.*[9]

For Bentham, pleasure and pain were the inescapable realities that drove all moral choices.

---

7. Cf. *SHE*, 233–34 for MacIntyre's summary of the logical critique Bentham offers against natural law theories as well as Bentham's pragmatic assertion that even if one could logically devise such a set of natural laws there is no consensus on what principles should actually be included in that body of law.

8. *SHE*, 233–34.

9. Bentham, *Principle of Utility*, 1.1.

MacIntyre characterizes Bentham's moral psychology as associative and mechanistic. His psychology is associative because not only are pleasure and pain the sole motivators for human choice, but anything associated with each will also provide such motivation. Things associated with pleasure will draw humans, while things associated with pain will repel them. Bentham's psychology is also mechanistic because, as is indicated in the above quote, it is not possible for humans to do anything but pursue pleasure and flee from pain.[10] MacIntyre further describes Bentham's view of pleasure and pain as simple and unitary correlates, which is to say that humans experience pleasure and pain together and that experience can be defined in clear scientific terms as a result of this simplicity. Bentham can thus identify more than fifty synonyms for the experience of pleasure, and treats many of these terms—words such as happiness, enjoyment, and pleasure—as naming precisely the same phenomenon. In Bentham's understanding, pleasure (and pain) can be quantified and compared. The subsequent analysis of pleasure and pain admits of such transparency that it enables a moralist to compare quantities of pleasure and pain between individuals and across a society. These psychological principles enable him to assert that the quantity of pleasure or pain resulting from a specific choice is the only criteria by which humans should judge whether a choice is good or bad.[11]

With Macintyre's description of Bentham's moral psychology as a backdrop, we can see why Bentham concludes that the greatest fulfillment available to the individual is pursuing happiness (increased pleasure and decreased pain) for the greatest number of people.[12] Choices whose consequences produce more happiness in more people are the morally correct choices to make. As a result, Bentham offers a moral theory that situates public welfare as the greatest moral good, which enables him to pursue the reform of institutions such as hospitals, prisons, and political constitutions, which are all institutions that have an enormous impact on the happiness of many people in society.

Bentham's approach to ethics is both influential and controversial. Its influence can be linked to the simplicity of its core assertion (moral choices should increase the happiness of the people affected by those choices) and the importance pleasure and pain clearly play in moral calculations. This importance can be seen in the history of ethics stretching all

10. *SHE*, 234.
11. *SHE*, 234.
12. *SHE*, 235.

the way back to Aristotle and the classical tradition, which also acknowledges the importance of pleasure and pain to moral decisions. Despite those strengths and the significant impact of utilitarianism, controversy has stalked the discussion of utility ever since Bentham formulated his views. This is the case not only because Bentham was offering a conception of moral principles that was at odds with other moral traditions, but also because the implications of his thought posed the rethinking of even the most basic ethical assertions.[13] The only moral standard left standing by Bentham was whether the consequences of an act made the most people happy. In this context, general moral prohibitions, such as those condemning lies or the killing of the innocent, could not be pronounced morally bad until the specific consequences of each choice were evaluated to see how they impacted the happiness of the greatest number of people. Bentham's assertions were quickly attacked and even ridiculed. The responsibility of defending those assertions fell to Bentham's protégé, John Stuart Mill.

Mill's Defense of Utilitarianism and MacIntyre's Critique

In his book *Utilitarianism*, Mill takes up the defense of Bentham's utilitarian formulations, and it is in the context of this defense that MacIntyre provides his own criticism of both Bentham and Mill. MacIntyre begins that critique by noting that Mill, like Bentham, sees no other alternative to a clear understanding of ethics outside the principle of utility. This is despite the fact that the crisis of Mill's own life disproves one of the central assertions of Bentham's system: that the greatest happiness of the individual is achieved by promoting the greatest happiness of the greatest number of people. As we mentioned earlier, Mill realized in his youth that the execution of his entire reform agenda would not bring him personal satisfaction or happiness. MacIntyre thus characterizes Mill's defense of utility as an attempt to justify a philosophical narrative that Mill himself finds both inescapable but is also beset in Mill's own view with unsolvable problems.[14]

MacIntyre describes Mill's proof and justification for using the principle of utility as "unimpressive" and "necessarily ineffective," which

---

13. Cf. *SHE*, 240–41 for MacIntyre's discussion of how the principle of utility challenges basic moral intuitions.

14. *SHE*, 235.

seems quite negative given the stature and influence of both Mill and utilitarianism in general.[15] So, what is the argument MacIntyre finds unconvincing? Mill asserts utility is the fundamental criteria to make moral judgments because philosophy cannot arrive at a consensus concerning the ultimate goals of human life.[16] Mill asserts, however, that despite the absence of agreed upon human goals, there is a universal motivation for moral choice recognized by all, which is the desire for pleasure. All people desire pleasure, and it is in the context of this universal desire that humans can discern the principle of utility as the guide for moral choice. Increasing happiness by increasing pleasure through moral choice is a clear and simple criterion by which people can make moral judgments. In addition, Mill observes that the pleasure of another person is naturally pleasurable to anyone making a moral choice.[17] The pleasure produced by observing the happiness of others becomes the basis for the idea that the greatest pleasure is making choices that produce pleasure in the greatest number of people. Given this chain of reasoning, it is difficult to disagree with MacIntyre's dissatisfaction. It is no doubt true that seeing the happiness of others can make a person happy, but Mill's assertion that this is always the case is clearly false, as is the idea that observing the happiness of the greatest number of people is the greatest pleasure to be pursued. It is true that pleasure, happiness, and the happiness of the greatest number of people can be worthy moral goals, but Mill's arguments fail in their effort to make those ideas universal and fundamental to all moral choices.

MacIntyre also takes aim at one of Mill's arguments that seems to be a strategic retreat from Bentham's assertion that the comparisons of pleasure can be accomplished on a purely quantitative basis. Bentham's critics assert his quantitative focus on the accumulation of pleasure presents an ethic of crude hedonism. Utilitarianism in this context becomes a moral theory fit for swine because, as the saying goes, a pig satisfied is seen as happier than Socrates dissatisfied. To counter the criticism, Mill moves away from purely quantitative comparisons of pleasures and introduces a distinction between higher and lower pleasures. In his view, utility need not and is not solely concerned with pursuing any lowly or base pleasure. Pleasures of the body, pleasures that humans share with other animals, are recognized as inferior to intellectual and aesthetic pleasures. Utilitarianism allows for discernment between higher and lower pleasures

15. *SHE*, 238–39.
16. Mill, *Utilitarianism*, 1, 4; *SHE*, 238.
17. *SHE*, 239.

because knowledgeable moral agents have experienced both types and recognize that higher pleasures are more substantive, more enjoyable, and more durable.[18] They are therefore more worthy of pursuit than mere bodily pleasures.

MacIntyre is not convinced by Mill's line of reasoning. He asks how Mill could know what it is like for a fool to be satisfied any more than a fool could know what is like to be a wise person dissatisfied.[19] The argument, however, raises broader concerns for MacIntyre than just trying to compare the subjective aspects of human fulfillment. He contends that Mill's reasoning is still trying to shore up Bentham's effort to align all objects of human pursuit under the single category of pleasure. In so doing, Mill continues to treat pleasure as a simple, unitary concept in the same way as Bentham. If his efforts were successful, it would enable utilitarianism to place all objects of desire on a single scale in which higher and lower pleasures could be evaluated and compared.[20]

MacIntyre then steps back from Mill's assertion and says we need to take a look at how utilitarianism was changing the moral use—and therefore the meaning—of the term pleasure. This change was taking place in the context of a history similar to the history MacIntyre has already recounted concerning the idea of duty. To briefly review that story, we can say that duty made the transition from referring to specific actions that had to be accomplished to fulfill a particular role in a community (the classical morality of the Greeks) to a general notion of what any person should do given the fact that the person is a member of the human species (the deontological or duty-based ethics of Kant). Duty in the latter context has virtually no meaning because each individual has the authority, indeed the responsibility, to figure out what is the duty of every human. Duty in this light becomes radically subjective and loses its force and meaning as a moral term. MacIntyre asserts that a similar emptying of meaning for the moral category of pleasure is underway in utilitarianism. Instead of being one specific goal that is pursued through moral choice, pleasure becomes every goal and the only goal of moral striving.[21] MacIntyre notes that the changed meaning of the term pleasure is reinforced by the arguments of widely varying groups. On one side, hedonists and utilitarians like Mill assert that pleasure refers not only to bodily

---

18. *SHE*, 235.
19. *SHE*, 236.
20. *SHE*, 236.
21. *SHE*, 236.

pleasures, but to goals that require serious strain and education to appreciate. Studying quantum physics has a pleasurable aspect, and for a utilitarian like Jeremy Bentham, this pleasure can be compared to the pleasure of eating a great piece of pizza. On the other side, Puritans assert that they are not against pleasure in itself, just the wrong types of pleasure. They contend that only the true and lasting pleasures associated with religious practice should be sought. The combination of these varied approaches to the idea of pleasure results in pleasure referring to whatever goal a person might desire.[22] MacIntyre sees problems for the general understanding of ethics when pleasure becomes the only goal of moral choice. This is a problem because moral evaluation entails the grading and comparison of objects we already desire, but also includes the grading and comparison of desires themselves. The cultivation of desire by means of developing dispositions or habits is a crucial issue for moral evaluation. When happiness and pleasure are given the broad meaning assigned to them by the likes of Bentham and Mill, those ideas are merely telling us to pursue whatever object that we happen to already desire. However, when confronted with rival objects of desire or with the challenge of determining if we have good desires to begin with (two activities essential to living a good moral life), the ideas of pleasure and happiness offer no guidance because they no longer have any specific meaning. MacIntyre ends his critique by asserting that this absence of meaning applies whether we are examining our own individual choices or those of the greatest number.[23]

MacIntyre also observes that one argument offered by Mill to defend utilitarianism undermines Mill's core claim that the principle of utility is the source of all moral obligation.[24] Mill's answer to the question of how a person should make a moral judgment when it is impossible to figure out how to increase the happiness of the greatest number of people claims that there are other criteria for moral judgment that can supersede the principle of utility. MacIntyre provides a general example of this problem when he raises the question of what would provide a greater general level of happiness for a society: applying resources to the reform of the healthcare system or the reform of a penal system. Certainly, the evaluation of such a question would differ under different circumstances, but the point is that utility would be a very poor guide for such decisions because it

22. *SHE*, 236.
23. *SHE*, 236.
24. Mill, *Utilitarianism*, 4.

is impossible to answer the question before the decision is made. The general impact of the decision would likely defy prediction, much less the specificity necessary to compare how much happiness would be produced for how many people. Given that ambiguity, other criteria, such as justice or efficacy, would be invoked to make the decision. MacIntyre observes that Mill fully agrees with making decisions in accordance with these other criteria because Mill asserts that utility only applies when you can actually determine what choice would increase the happiness of the most people.[25] MacIntyre points out, however, that Mill's concession undermines the argument that utility is the principle that guides all moral decision-making if it does not apply in some situations. The concession renders utilitarianism inconsistent on one of its most fundamental claims.

While Mill explicitly refers to the importance of other moral criteria when the impact of a choice is difficult to predict, MacIntyre points out that an even greater difficulty for utilitarianism is its implicit reliance on other moral principles even when you can figure out the impact a choice has on happiness. MacIntyre contends that it is only in societies where other basic norms of ethics are observed that the principle of utility, the greatest happiness of the greatest number, can be a significant guide for moral choices. This is the case because utility could be used to justify actions that any rational person would see as morally horrific. Utility proclaims that an action is morally good if it leads to the happiness of the greatest number of people. What would that look like in a society where most people take pleasure in the appalling treatment of a minority group?[26] Unfortunately, MacIntyre's question is not academic nor merely hypothetical. If we look to history, especially the history of the last two centuries, we see example after example of societies subjecting some of their members to the most cruel and horrific treatment, the institutions of slavery and the genocidal actions of the Nazis being some of the most extreme examples. These large-scale moral crimes are theoretically supported by utilitarianism. As long as the most people are made happy by whatever the horror might be, the actions can be sanctioned by utilitarianism. MacIntyre observes that such a conclusion could not be further from the minds of reformers such as Bentham and Mill, but it does point to a weakness in their thinking. If the basic standards of ethics

---

25. *SHE*, 237.
26. *SHE*, 238.

and decency—the basic standards of treating others in a humane manner—are not already present in a society, the principle of utility will lose its credibility.[27] How could the pursuit of pleasure and the minimization of pain be the primary criteria in a social setting where people are being brutalized? In addition, the principle of utility could be used to justify crimes that any basic standard of morality must reject. Utilitarian moral considerations can only become justified in communities where the basic standards of morality are already respected and used to guide the life of that community.

A last critique MacIntyre raises is the risk of using the modern psychological view of happiness as the sole guide for moral evaluation. MacIntyre maintains that psychological happiness is an unsure guide for ethics and politics because humans are so malleable. They can be conditioned to accept and even be satisfied with almost any set of circumstances. The fact that people are happy with their set of circumstances does not mean those circumstances are good.[28] No doubt there were some slaves in the pre-Civil War South that were content and even happy with their living arrangements. Such happiness, MacIntyre points out and most would agree, is not a vindication of slavery as an institution. A biblical example can be seen in the Old Testament book of Exodus where the Israelites complain to Moses, saying it is better to remain in bondage serving the Egyptians than to die in the wilderness.[29] It is in contexts such as these that the greatest happiness for the greatest number of people as a principle can be used to support the worst types of paternalism and even totalitarian rule. MacIntyre cites the nineteenth-century Fabian socialist movement (which advocated for a gradual transition to a socialist state rather than the revolutionary transition advocated by Karl Marx) as an example of an intellectual reform movement in which the enlightened few dictated what ought to be done to the unenlightened many.[30] A more extreme example of the domination of happiness over freedom can be seen in the communism in twenty-first-century China. The Communist Party of China is committed to raising the living standard of its citizens, one might say committed to their material happiness, but has long been criticized for its neglect of its citizens' rights and freedoms. MacIntyre asserts that a utilitarian approach to ethics would struggle to criticize

27. *SHE*, 238.
28. *SHE*, 237.
29. Exod 14:11–12.
30. *SHE*, 238.

such an approach as long as most people considered themselves happy with the status quo. This, combined with the human ability to adapt to current conditions and the all-too-common fear of the risks associated with changing unjust conditions, makes utilitarianism a powerful way to justify the corrupt machinations of a totalitarian state.

Despite recognizing the importance of the historical reforms that Bentham and his peers achieved in eighteenth- and nineteenth-century Britain, MacIntyre clearly has concerns about the abuse to which utilitarian principles are susceptible. He also has concerns about the moral thinking of the dominant ethicists in continental Europe during the nineteenth century. It is to those philosophers and MacIntyre's trepidation about their thinking that we will turn next.

Leadership Reflection: Utility or Virtue? Tasks or Follower Development?

Utilitarian ethics focuses on consequences to determine whether a choice is morally good or bad. For a utilitarian, the choice that leads to greater happiness for the greatest number of people is the right choice to make. This is different from classical ethics, which offers a virtue-based approach that focuses on the habits that are developed as a result of moral choice. Despite this difference, the two schools share significant features that make them seem quite similar. The first is the fact that each school asserts that ethics is about human happiness (although the concept of happiness is somewhat different in each school). For each approach, good moral choices will support the happiness that humans desire and pursue. The second commonality concerns virtue itself because habits (virtues being good habits) are the consequence of moral choice. One can therefore argue that a utilitarian approach to ethics accounts for a virtue-based approach to ethics because the habits resulting from moral choice are a crucial consequence of such choices. This is precisely the argument that John Stuart Mill makes in his essay *Utilitarianism*. In Mill's words, "The utilitarian standard . . . enjoins and requires the cultivation of the love of virtue up to the greatest strength possible, as being above all things important to the general happiness."[31] Yet despite these common touch points, differences between the two approaches to ethics are so significant they should indeed be considered separate schools of thought, and

---

31. Mill, *Utilitarianism*, 37.

it is by examining those differences that one can see how a virtue-based approach offers a better understanding of both ethics and leadership.

The first difference between the schools lies in utility's focus on the external environment of consequences as opposed to the interior focus of classical ethics on habits. Utilitarians examine the consequences a choice has on the environment of the external world and how that environment impacts the subjective happiness of the people affected by the choice. Although virtue is theoretically captured by this outlook, virtue rarely plays a role in utilitarian moral analysis. Instead, the analysis proposed by Bentham and Mill evaluates the magnitude of the pleasure and pain resulting from the decision as well as the number of people who feel pleasure or pain due to a decision. Classical morality, on the other hand, recognizes the link between moral choice and the formation of moral character and is primarily concerned with the dynamic between choice and habits. The moral question in this context is what kind of person do I want to be and will this moral choice bring me closer to that goal or further from it? This is not to say that classical morality is unconcerned with the impact a choice has on the external environment and other people affected by the choice. In the thought of a classical thinker such as Aristotle, the consequences or the goal pursued through moral choice provides the context in which virtues are measured and given value. The goal to win a battle makes the virtue of courage valuable. And winning the battle is the goal for which a courageous choice is made. The primary criteria for a soldier's individual choice, however, is the virtue or vice, the courage or cowardice, that is engendered by the choice. Moral choices in this view are primarily measured as praiseworthy or blameworthy on the basis of what habits they produce, and only secondarily on whether the ultimate goal of winning the battle is achieved.

One might ask at this point, why is focusing on habits better than focusing on consequences? It seems like the less important issue, a person's habit, is being placed above a more important issue, whatever consequence is at stake in a particular choice. This perspective seems to be backed up by our intuitions and experience as well. The primary driver for many of our moral choices is the consequences we will face as a result of the choice. No doubt prospective failure on a hard test is a consequence that drives many students to cheat, and many a lie is told in an effort to avoid pain and suffering. Yet we all know that choices made to avoid short-term pain, which utilitarian ethics encourages, are often the choices we should shun. Those choices and the utilitarian perspective that promotes them should be rejected for a couple of reasons. First, as a utilitarian supporter like David Hume fully admits, humans tend to be concerned with short-term, obvious results rather than long-term concerns.[32] Yet long-term concerns are often more subtle, more powerful, and more enduring in nature, as Aesop's fable on the ant and the grasshopper teaches us so well. Second, we often are so fearful of the pain a choice may engender or anxious to reap the positive benefits of a choice that we choose according to irrational desire rather than reasons that can provide substantive guidance in perilous or promising situations. Third, we humans are limited in our ability to predict the future. We know from experience that our choices can result in things we would have never predicted in a million years. Utilitarianism makes us prone to fear and anxiety of consequences that may or may not come to fruition. A virtue-based approach avoids many of these pitfalls. We may not know the long-term impact a lie may have on our circumstances, but we do know the impact it will have on our character. It will promote and establish the habit of dishonesty as part of one's moral character. This is a fancy way of saying when I lie, I am turning myself into a liar. And the saying, "Honesty is the best policy" points to the truth that despite the short-term costs honesty may sometimes impose, honesty as a habit will lead to better long-term results. This can be linked to a further truth, which is virtue, i.e., morally excellent habits, will lead to the best consequences over time. Ironically John Stuart Mill recognizes this fact but does not seem to realize that the utilitarian reasoning he champions with its narrow concern about pleasure and pain does not promote the cultivation of virtue.

The paradox of this discussion can be seen in the reality that a virtue-based approach to ethics produces better external consequences by not focusing on those consequences, while utilitarianism produces worse consequences by exclusively focusing on them. How does that make sense? It actually makes a great deal of sense if we look at two other aspects of classical ethics. The first aspect is the realism of an ethics whose focus is habits. Habit-based moral thinking accounts for the fact that humans are animals—biological beings—that exist across a span of time. A consistent weakness of Enlightenment moral thinking, and utilitarianism is no exception to this weakness, is a blindness to biology. Moral deliberation for modern thinkers focuses on rationally determining what is right or wrong in a specific situation with little regard for the facts that

---

32. Cf. Mcintyre, "Strength of Mind," 393–401 for a description of the short-term focus Hume provides to his moral analysis.

moral choice inescapably becomes part of a person's experience (modern neuroscience shows us that moral choices literally become embedded in our neurophysiology)[33] and that experience will drive our decisions in the future. Habit-based ethics accounts for these aspects of our moral existence. Ethical behavior, both good and bad, has always occurred in the context of human biology and the existence of humans as timebound creatures. Any approach to ethics that does not account for those facts will be inaccurate and misleading.

The second aspect of classical ethics that leads to better results can be found in a concept that we have not mentioned since the beginning chapters of this book, which is the idea of *areté* the idea of moral excellence. A habit-based approach to ethics tends toward a morality of excellence. This is the case because, generally speaking, humans desire what is good for them. As this book indicates, there are many ways to describe and understand what is good for humans, and we may often be confused about what is good, especially when thinking about ethics abstractly. When it comes to seeking what is good in our concrete actions, however, the desire to acquire what is good is a strong impulse, as is the desire to be a good person. A virtue-based approach to ethics leverages these desires in a powerful way. When a person recognizes she or he has the power to shape his or her own moral character through the moral choices one makes, the person will naturally focus on excellence. Excellence, no matter its form, is attractive to people. People pursue excellence for themselves and their loved ones. When the result of an ethical choice is understood to be what makes a person either good or bad, there is a strong impulse to choose what is good, or even excellent. When we see that the primary thing at stake in our ethical choosing is our own moral character, we tend to raise our standards. Instead of ethics being about "what I can get away with without hurting anyone," which is often the standard of utilitarian analysis, classical ethics provide a context in which the standards of excellence are pursued. The goal of a virtue-based approach to ethics becomes what is praiseworthy, what is noble, what is excellent, because in the end, the most important consequence of a person's moral choice is his or her own character.

So how does all of this apply to leadership? There is a direct parallel of the paradox that in ethics we get the best results by not focusing on results in the relationship between followers and leaders. When

---

33. Cf. Duhigg, *Power of Habit*, for an overview of contemporary psychological and neurological research concerning the nature of habits.

leaders guide followers, they often do so in a utilitarian fashion. To put it in Kantian terms, they use followers to achieve a particular task. Kant's insight guiding us not to treat followers as mere instruments helps us to see that developing followers, like developing virtues, is more important in the long run than achieving a short-term task. This does not mean that a leader should neglect the task at hand. By devoting themselves to follower education and improvement, leaders will develop their followers through the education provided by doing the work of the organization. The work still needs to get done, and it is by means of doing the work that followers will develop the skills to do that work by themselves, without the supervision of leaders. This means that leaders should put a different lens on their interactions with followers than the utilitarian lens. The primary goal is the development of a follower into a person who can operate independently to accomplish whatever work needs to be done. And just as in the development of virtue, the focus on developing followers engenders higher standards of treatment for those followers. Leaders who are concerned primarily with their followers will treat them better. They will praise them when praise will further that development. They will reward followers when rewards will further follower development. They will correct and even punish followers if those actions serve the long-term development of the follower. Leaders will do what's in the long-term interest of the follower because that long-term interest serves the leader's team better than a focus on short-term tasks. This insight is leveraging an experience that every parent has had. It is always easier to do a task yourself than to train your child to do it. The parent will do it more efficiently and more effectively, and that is precisely the path to take to make sure your child will never learn those tasks. By taking the time to train the child, painful as that process may be, eventually the parent will not have to take out the garbage or mow the lawn. That benefit, however, can only be achieved if the parent takes the time and energy to invest in the development of the child. The fact that followers are not children makes the insight even more fruitful. As mature adults, followers are capable of developing extraordinary skills. Leaders who invest their time in developing those skills will reap the benefits of followers who will grow to do the task as well as—and even better—than the leaders can do it themselves. If the follower under development is also a leader, the investment will provide even further benefit because that leader development will have a multiplying effect. Enhancing the leadership of one's follower advances the productivity of all the followers under that person's supervision. Investing in the effectiveness of one person who then does the same for multiple followers can have an explosive effect on a team's productivity. So, leaders who want efficient and effective long-term task accomplishment should have a laser-like focus on the development of their followers and use the tasks at hand as a means to that development, rather than focusing on the task as the ultimate goal.

17

Danish and German Ethics in the Nineteenth Century

ETHICAL THINKING IN MAINLAND Europe during the nineteenth century was heavily influenced by Kant and Hegel, with thinkers reacting both positively and negatively to their thought. Germans such as Heinrich Heine, Arthur Schopenhauer, and Friedrich Nietzsche were both prophetic and profoundly influential to the historical developments that would mark nineteenth- and twentieth-century Europe. Before examining their thought, however, MacIntyre begins his analysis with the writing of Soren Kierkegaard (b. 1813), a Danish thinker. Kierkegaard was an extraordinary author whose writing crossed a multitude of disciplines, including philosophy, theology, psychology, fiction, and even literary criticism. Educated in Denmark and the recipient of a significant inheritance from his father, Kierkegaard remained a bachelor his entire life after breaking off an engagement to marry. Kierkegaard's writings were significantly affected by his status as a person outside the typical experience of the bourgeois married life of his time. His thought and written work were also impacted to a large extent by his mentors, F. C. Sibbern and Poul Martin Moller, who were both philosophers and fiction writers.[1] A deeply religious thinker who sought to invigorate Christian belief in Europe, Kierkegaard embraced the ethics of Kant while rejecting the philosophy of Hegel. In looking at his thought, we will first examine Kierkegaard's assertion that choice lies at the foundation of ethics and will subsequently address his

---

1. Stewart, *Kierkegaard and His Contemporaries*, 8–9.

comparison between what he calls the aesthetic and ethical ways of life, before finishing with how he applied these ideas to Christian belief.

Choice, Ethics, and the Irrationality of Christian Faith

MacIntyre frames his analysis of Kierkegaard's moral thinking by comparing it with the thinking of Kant and Hegel. Kant bases his approach to morality on the reason of each individual person and asserts that the test of morality can be found in using categorical imperatives, or universal duties, as a way to find the ethical norms that should guide moral choices. Hegel, on the other hand, finds the norms to guide the ethical thinking of the individual in the established practices and customs of a free and rational society. Kierkegaard sides with neither of these alternatives, asserting that there are no normative tests for morality at all. In his view the rules people use to guide their ethical deliberation are simply chosen.[2] For Kierkegaard, the only sanction and authority for moral rules is the fact that a person has made the choice to observe those rules. Kierkegaard asserts that rational argument reigns supreme in mathematics and the natural sciences, but outside those fields reason can only present the human person with alternatives, and it is up to each individual to decide between them. MacIntyre observes that Kierkegaard is not advocating for an arbitrary irrationality but is making his assertion on the basis of what reason shows us when we examine the manner in which we make choices. It is rational argument itself that shows us how the choice of each person is the most sovereign authority. This is the case because on the one hand, moral arguments can be rationally justified on the basis of specific premises, while on the other hand, rational justification cannot be an infinite process. In Kierkegaard's view there is no doubt that a moral conclusion can be rationally justified, which means a moral conclusion can be validly made through a process of reasoning that begins with fundamental principles. To justify using those principles as premises for a conclusion, one would also have to show how those premises are reasonable to hold. This process, however, cannot go on forever. Humans are finite creatures living finite lives. From a practical perspective, the chain of reasoning cannot be interminable. Humans have lives to live and decisions that have to be made, so at some point they must simply make a choice as to what fundamental premises will provide the foundation

---

2. *SHE*, 215.

to their moral thinking. The chain of reasoning must have an endpoint, which is the point where one simply chooses to stand by specific premises. It is at this juncture, according to Kierkegaard's thinking, that choice displaces rational argument.[3]

This is the framework Kierkegaard applies to the contrast between the aesthetic and ethical ways of life in his famous book *Either/Or*, which provides us a literary example for Kierkegaard's description of how choice shapes a person's moral life. The aesthetic life is the life centered on satisfying one's desires. Pain and boredom are the enemies to be fought or avoided in the aesthetic way of life. MacIntyre points out that romantic love is the paradigm Kierkegaard uses to describe the aesthetic life. Romantic love seeks to satisfy the passion of the moment and is always looking for new satisfactions.[4] The ethical way of life, on the other hand, is represented by the institution of marriage. Marriage models lifelong commitments and inescapable duties. It is the sphere of obligation and rules. Kierkegaard asserts that there is no way to rationally compare these alternative ways of life. They are modes of life that use different and even incomparable criteria for making moral choices. One first chooses the aesthetic or the ethical way of life, and in doing so, that person obtains a specific set of criteria with which he or she can make moral choices.[5] In addition, the characters in *Either/Or* demonstrate the futility of attempting to use rational arguments to make the choice between each form of life. The person arguing for the ethical, Judge Wilhelm (a fictitious character in the book), uses ethical principles to evaluate the two forms of life. A is the person ("A" is the actual name of the character in the book) who champions the aesthetic way of life, and he uses aesthetic criteria as the basis for his arguments. The criteria each character uses to make his judgments are chosen before reason can be used to apply the criteria to make practical choices.[6] One first chooses the criteria, and then uses reason to apply those criteria to moral deliberation.

MacIntyre makes two observations regarding Kierkegaard's presentation. First, he notes that the style of presentation in *Either/Or* purports to be neutral, merely describing the criteria of moral choice operative in both ways of life. MacIntyre asserts, however, that one comes away from the description with the feeling that Kierkegaard sees the aesthetic

---

3. *SHE*, 216.
4. *SHE*, 216.
5. *SHE*, 216.
6. *SHE*, 216.

manner of life as problematic. The aesthetic life is portrayed as a state of permanent dissatisfaction in which a person travels, hopefully so as to never arrive at one's destination.[7] It is a description that recalls the argument of Socrates who criticized the Sophist assertion that the greatest good is getting what one wants because the Sophist formulation does not recognize the ever-expanding appetite that is the product of constantly getting what one wants. The ethical way of life, on the other hand, is portrayed as the way of life that yields a peaceful soul who achieves peace through the meeting of one's obligations and the successful completion of one's duties.[8] Given the slant provided by Kierkegaard, MacIntyre asks how Kierkegaard could have made a truly neutral presentation between the two lifestyles. MacIntyre proposes that a truly neutral presentation would be based on a person who had no preexisting wants, needs, desires, or aspirations. It is a picture of an individual who stands outside of society and has no personal characteristics. The person then acquires characteristics on the basis of the fundamental choice between the ethical or the aesthetic way of life.[9]

MacIntyre's analysis begs the question, does such a person exist? It seems that for Kierkegaard, the answer is yes, and it is here that we move from Kierkegaard's ethical thought into his religious thought. Kierkegaard was an adherent of a strict Lutheran and pietistic approach to Christian faith that held much in common with the religious upbringing of Immanuel Kant. Recalling the hallmarks of Martin Luther's ethics, we saw a focus on the individual who is naked before the judgment of God. It is this individualistic ethic that is operative in Kierkegaard's thinking as well, and that ethic is shaped by Kierkegaard's notion of fundamental choice. Following Luther's rejection of the Aristotelian Christianity of a thinker like St. Thomas Aquinas, MacIntyre tells us that Kierkegaard saw Christian faith as fundamentally offensive to human rationality.[10] It made claims to truth that were not accessible to human reason and were objectionable to the long-standing philosophical tradition (dating all the way to Plato's dialogue *Euthyphro*) that saw philosophy as the arbiter of moral truth rather than religion. Christian faith therefore could not be based on the reason of philosophers. And in Kierkegaard's view, objections to Christianity were not made on an intellectual basis anyway. Rather the

---

7. *SHE*, 216–17.
8. *SHE*, 216.
9. *SHE*, 217.
10. *SHE*, 217.

fundamental objection to Christianity was made on the basis of whether a person would submit to the commands of God or not. In Kierkegaard's telling, Christian faith was not a function of rational argument; it was a function of obedience. It was based on a person's fundamental choice to obey the commands of God as they came to be understood through God's revelation.[11]

In his book *Fear and Trembling*, Kierkegaard presents the example of Abraham's willingness to sacrifice his son Isaac due to God's command as the paradigm for this obedience. From an ethical perspective, God's command to kill Isaac is simply a command to do what is morally evil. God is commanding murder, the killing of an innocent, and rationally based human morality can do nothing but condemn such a command. God's command is a scandal because it is immoral and absurd; an offense to the rational morality virtually every human society espouses. There is a clear break between the rational conclusions of human morality and the ethics commanded by the God portrayed in Genesis. With this backdrop in mind MacIntyre asserts that Kierkegaard provides two lenses through which one can understand the relationship between ethics and Christianity. The first is for Christianity to accept the terms of secular reason as the final arbiter of ethics (similar to Kant's view of ethics). This will make Christian moral thought entirely rational, which leads to Hegel's conclusions that the Christian religion is one stage in the evolution of the Absolute Idea.[12] Kierkegaard rejects Hegel's project of rationalizing Christian religious thought. The second alternative is one in which Christianity insists on being judged by its own ethical standard, the will of God, which results in Christianity being reduced to an isolated and self-enclosed system of thought that is unintelligible to those standing outside the Christian tradition.[13] Following Luther, Kierkegaard takes this latter position, asserting that Abraham is the "Knight of Faith" who chooses to obey the will of God not only in the face of human morality, but even to the point of denying his love for Isaac and his desire to be a father of a great nation through his son.

Despite the coherence and power of Kierkegaard's analysis, MacIntyre provides a series of observations that puts Kierkegaard's analysis within a broader philosophical and theological perspective and in doing so, raises questions about its validity. Kierkegaard's thought regarding Abraham

11. *SHE*, 217.
12. *SHE*, 218.
13. *SHE*, 218.

and Isaac fails to account for an interpretation of that passage asserted by Old Testament scholars who see the story as a critique of human sacrifice, an all-too-common phenomenon in the ancient world. In this context, the point of the story is not to describe a God making morally incoherent commands, but to highlight the idea that human sacrifice is not the will of God. The revelation provided by the story can be seen as progressive; it is suited to, but slightly ahead of, the moral norms of the culture being addressed by the story.[14] MacIntyre also notes that Kierkegaard's analysis is not entirely consistent. Kierkegaard moves between two positions: one in which God's will provides a criterion for choice and a second position of the lonely individual, perhaps a person without Christian faith, who truly lives in a world offering no criteria for fundamental choice. Kierkegaard's individualism appears to be consistent, but it yields a situation in which the criterion-less choice, the choice that cannot be judged by reason, is contradicted by the all too human experience of pain that results from poor choices.[15] If the results of a bad choice can be rationally evaluated once its effects have been experienced, why not use rationality to evaluate the choice before it is made? A last thought regarding Kierkegaard's moral conclusions is they represent only one part of the larger tradition of Christian ethics. The individualism and rejection of rational morality Kierkegaard advocates are certainly consistent with his Lutheran roots, but they do not represent other Christian moral traditions (an example being the Natural Law tradition espoused by St. Thomas Aquinas) that account for the concerns of the community and the importance of reason in addition to the moral outlook of the individual.

The Darkness of Nineteenth-Century German Ethics: Heine, Schopenhauer, and Nietzsche

MacIntyre next turns his eye toward the thinkers he calls the "anti-German" German philosophers of the nineteenth century, the greatest of whom are Arthur Schopenhauer (b. 1788) and Friedrich Nietzsche (b. 1844). Schopenhauer and Nietzsche are both critics of the moral status quo of nineteenth-century Germany that is based on the thought of Kant and Hegel.[16] Before describing their work, however, MacIntyre provides

14. *SHE*, 217–18.
15. *SHE*, 218.
16. *SHE*, 220.

a fascinating prelude to their thinking in the person of Heinrich Heine (b. 1797), who was an influential German poet that lived in Germany and France in the first half of the nineteenth century. MacIntyre observes a link between Kierkegaard's irrational Christianity and Heine's thinking in Heine's essay *The History of Philosophy and Religion in Germany*, published in 1834. In his essay, Heine connects the intellectual past of Germany with a future catastrophe. MacIntyre asserts that Catholicism had overcome the ancient Nordic paganism of the Germans, but with the coming of Martin Luther, a new German consciousness is born. It is a consciousness that is spiritually susceptible to secularization, which is achieved in the thought of influential philosophers such as Spinoza, Kant, and Hegel who replace the supernatural moral principles of Christianity with the natural moral principles of human reason.[17] As of the early nineteenth century, these changes have only permeated German intellectual culture. Once the critical analysis of Kant's thought takes hold in the entire German culture, however, the power of Christian culture becomes fatally undermined. It is in this context that Heine asserts,

> Christianity—and this is its fairest merit—subdued to a certain extent the brutal warrior ardor of the Germans, but it could not entirely quench it; and when the cross, that remaining talisman, falls to pieces, then will break forth again the ferocity of the old combatants. . . . There will be played in Germany a drama compared to which the French Revolution will seem but an innocent idyll.[18]

As MacIntyre notes, Heine's prophecy comes true one hundred years later with the rise of Adolph Hitler and the Nazi horror of the twentieth century.[19] In his subsequent analysis of Schopenhauer and Nietzsche, MacIntyre asserts a further link between nineteenth-century German philosophy and the coming catastrophe of twentieth-century German culture. Let's turn to his analysis to see if it convinces.

---

17. *SHE*, 219.

18. Heine, *History of Philosophy and Religion in Germany*, 158. Also cited in *SHE*, 219.

19. *SHE*, 219.

Schopenhauer's Pessimistic Philosophy

MacIntyre describes how Arthur Schopenhauer was a contemporary of Hegel, and between 1820 and 1822 his lectures were in direct competition (literally offered at the same time) with Hegel's at the University of Berlin. Hegel was the more popular lecturer, and Schopenhauer left the university after two years.[20] Although Schopenhauer never sustained a teaching career, his writings were received with significant acclaim throughout Europe before his death in 1860.[21] Schopenhauer's thought represents a distinct departure from that of Hegel and Kierkegaard. Where Hegel sees the universe as the expression of the Absolute Idea, Schopenhauer asserts that the universe has no meaning whatsoever. Where Kierkegaard sees value in each individual, Schopenhauer asserts the opposite, claiming there is no value to the individual human being. MacIntyre observes that Schopenhauer is a corrective to the easy optimism of nineteenth-century liberalism, who offers a number of keen observations regarding human existence, but struggles to integrate those observations into a coherent whole.[22]

Schopenhauer begins with the assertion that the world is nothing but striving will. In his view humans have a direct inner experience of will, but will can also manifest itself on the outside in other disguises such as rational thought. The world is a place where striving wills come into conflict, and it is a place of human pain and suffering.[23] Human existence for Schopenhauer is blind, cruel, and meaningless, and those negative aspects of individual human experience can be seen clearly in the natural world. Humans as a species continue to thrive and reproduce, but individual humans are subject to suffering and death. Their path, their destiny, is the experience of pain and ultimate destruction. Yet despite their bleak prospects, individual humans still cling to life. This, Schopenhauer asserts, is the striving of cosmic will present in each individual, which has the goal of continuing the existence of individual humans no matter the terms or conditions of that existence. Humans reject the idea that pain and suffering will have the last word, which they do by means of their intellect using philosophy and religion to show a path beyond inevitable

20. *SHE*, 220.

21. Cf. Wicks, *Schopenhauer's The World as Will and Representation*, 1–9 for a brief overview of Schopenhauer's life and writing career.

22. *SHE*, 220.

23. *SHE*, 220.

physical death. Schopenhauer makes the interesting observation that religion is simply the human desire for continued existence, and were it not for the lack of human knowledge beyond death, religion would have no role.[24] The human will uses intellect to develop ideas that comfort each person in the face of mortality and despair.

MacIntyre points out that will and striving as the center of human experience has implications for Schopenhauer's description of morality and his view of what motivates humans to make specific moral choices. Schopenhauer sees humans as so fundamentally constituted by will that they are utterly unchanging. Human character is fixed, and there is nothing a person can do to make changes to that character. As a result, Schopenhauer asserts that much of moral philosophy is built on a mistaken idea that moral principles can shape and change human behavior. Neither experience, nor self-reflection, nor learning can change the striving that shapes and motivates moral choice. The only role for moral philosophy in this context is to explain why humans make the moral choices that they do. Moral thinking does not have the power to change the inalterable nature of human behavior. For Schopenhauer, moral philosophy can only explain what we choose, but it will never alter what we choose.[25]

Schopenhauer identifies three basic motives that shape moral choice, two familiar and one that is quite novel. The first motive is self-interest, an assertion that puts Schopenhauer in the company of the Sophists and Hobbes, and MacIntyre asserts that Schopenhauer adds little to what others have already said about the relationship between self-interest and ethics.[26] Schopenhauer's second observation regarding moral motivation is where he breaks new ground. That observation is the fact that humans are willing to act, are willing to make moral choices on the basis of malice alone. They are willing to harm other members of their species when it is in their interest to do so, or for no other reason than the pleasure that harming other people gives them. Other animals harm one another to fight for food or in a rage, but humans have an additional motivation to harm other humans in the pleasure such harming provides.[27]

The appalling record of humans inflicting suffering on their fellow humans is softened by the last of the moral motivations observed by Schopenhauer, which is compassion or sympathy. By highlighting

24. *SHE*, 221.
25. *SHE*, 221.
26. *SHE*, 221.
27. *SHE*, 221–22.

sympathy as a significant moral motivator, Schopenhauer finds common ground with sentimental moral thinkers such as David Hume and British utilitarian ethicists such as Jeremy Bentham and John Stuart Mill. Schopenhauer defines compassion as the ability to imagine the suffering of another and then working to alleviate that suffering as a result of that insight. Compassion is unique compared to the other two moral motivations because it provides a relief for the individual human from the striving of universal will. By stepping into the perspective of another and allowing that perspective to motivate moral choice, a person ceases to strive for the assertion of one's own will. In leaving aside one's own will, a person steps outside of the operation of the cosmic will driving the universe. In historical persons, such as Christ and the Buddha, Schopenhauer sees individuals who have systematically pursued compassionate activity in service to others.[28] Such cases are obviously an exception rather than a norm for human behavior, however. Self-interest and malice provide the moral motivation for the striving will that dominates Schopenhauer's ethical thinking, and it is these aspects of his thinking that inspire the thinking of Friedrich Nietzsche in the second half of the nineteenth century.

Nietzsche, The Will to Power, and the Catastrophe to Come

Friedrich Nietzsche was the son of a Lutheran minister. His father died early in Nietzsche's life (1849), and with his father's death, any positive influence of religious thinking on the philosophy of Nietzsche died as well. Nietzsche was an intellectual prodigy who at the age of twenty-four became the youngest person ever to be appointed to a chair of classical philology (the study of ancient languages) at the University of Basil. His extraordinary intellectual career was marked by both its anti-religious character (he was a critic of both Jewish and Christian morality) and its remarkable impact on twentieth-century thinkers.[29]

To understand Nietzsche's approach to moral thought, we must begin with his rejection of God and the moral traditions of Judaism and Christianity, which Nietzsche sees as closely intertwined. Following the thought of Ludwig Feuerbach (1804–1872), who asserted that God was

---

28. *SHE*, 222.

29. Cf. Conway, "Life After the Death of God," 2:103–36 for a brief summary of Nietzsche's life, writings, and influence.

a fictitious image humanity created in an effort to understand the great aspects of human nature, Nietzsche contends that humans must do away with the idea of God if they are to claim the dignity and grandeur that is their due. To put it in Nietzsche's terms, it is only by killing God that humanity can aspire to greatness. In his book *The Gay Science*, Nietzsche describes the intellectual consequences of the death of God.

> Are we perhaps still not too influenced by the most immediate consequences of this event (the death of God)—and these immediate consequences, the consequences for ourselves, are the opposite of what one might expect—not all sad and gloomy, but much amusement, encouragement, dawn... Indeed, at hearing the news that "the old god is dead," we philosophers and "free spirits" feel illuminated by a new dawn; our heart overflows with gratitude, amazement, forebodings, expectation—finally the horizon seems clear again, even if not bright; finally our ships may set out again, set out to face any danger; every daring of the lover of knowledge is allowed again; the sea, our sea, lies open again; maybe there has never been such an "open sea."[30]

MacIntyre describes Nietzsche's "open sea" as a vacuum of ethical thought.[31] Nietzsche saw the state of nineteenth-century European ethics as an empty shell that had been created by Jewish and Christian morality. Given the diagnosis, MacIntyre portrays Nietzsche's approach to morality as a threefold task. First, Nietzsche sets out to describe how the vacuum developed. Second, Nietzsche wants to identify and criticize the false solutions that are attempting to fill the ethical void. Third, Nietzsche offers his own answer to fill the void—the answer of how humans should chart their moral course on the newly open sea of ethical thinking made possible by the death of God.[32] In the next section, we will follow the schematic of Nietzsche's thought, but will also include MacIntyre's own analysis and criticism of that thinking.

Filling the Ethical Vacuum: The Will to Power

Nietzsche asserts that it is the victory of Christian morality over Greek ethics that lies at the root of the vacuum, the moral malaise afflicting the

---

30. Nietzsche, *Gay Science*, 5.343.
31. *SHE*, 223.
32. *SHE*, 223.

European culture of his time. To understand the defeat of Greek ethics at the hands of Judaism and Christianity, one must retrieve the initial content of how the Greeks defined what was morally good or morally bad. In pursuing this retrieval, Nietzsche criticizes nineteenth-century English psychologists and utilitarians who claim the word "good" originally described altruistic actions because those actions were seen to be socially useful.[33] In the utilitarian context, the divide between what is morally good or bad can be seen as actions that serve the community (good) and actions that serve the self (bad). Nietzsche asserts that their analysis is not historically accurate, and MacIntyre confirms the accuracy of Nietzsche's position.[34] The ancient Greeks did not see morality in altruistic versus egoistic terms. Rather, the original contrast between morally good and bad was seen in terms of the noble versus the lowly. The definition of good was determined by the elite, the mighty, and the highly placed. And the criteria they used to judge what was good, according to Nietzsche's description, was themselves. Greek nobles looked upon themselves and liked what they saw. They defined goodness, the concept of *agathos* in our earlier chapters, on the basis of their own character. Theirs was a morality of self-glorification.[35] In his book *On the Genealogy of Morality*, Nietzsche describes an aristocratic value chain to represent how Greek nobility viewed what was morally good: good = noble = powerful = beautiful = happy = blessed.[36] The Greeks then placed what was lowly or base as the morally bad state in opposition to what was good. The distance between the noble and good and that which was low, common, or plebeian was the original foundation for the distinction between what was good and what was bad.[37]

In Nietzsche's telling, which MacIntyre describes as a simplification of a complex historical process,[38] this aristocratic view of the good espoused by the Greeks was challenged by Jewish and Christian moral culture. The Jew, Nietzsche contends, substitutes a slave morality of envy for the Greek aristocratic morality of self-affirmation. Citing the claim of Tacitus (a first-century Roman historian) that the Jews were "a people born for slavery," Nietzsche asserts that the slave revolt in morality begins

33. SHE, 223.
34. SHE, 223.
35. Nietzsche, *Beyond Good and Evil*, 260.
36. Nietzsche, *On the Genealogy of Morality*, 1.8.
37. Nietzsche, *Genealogy*, 1.2. Cf. McInerney, *Greatness of Humility*, 144.
38. SHE, 223.

with the Jews. Jewish morality inaugurates a complete reversal in moral values that reaches its pinnacle in the person of Jesus Christ, who comes to bring salvation to the poor, to the sick, and to sinners.[39] Christianity exalts the virtues of the weak, the oppressed, the humble and the poor, not because these are truly admirable attributes, but because of the hidden hatred weak people have for the strong. The thought of the powerless is to view anyone with strength as evil.[40] In Nietzsche's view, the slave morality of Jewish and Christian culture posits the weakness of the weak as positive virtues.[41]

With the dispatch of Christianity as the primary influence in German moral culture, Nietzsche heralds a new era of moral thinking. The moral vacuum has been established. The Christian God is dead, and therefore, it is time to set sail on the newly open seas of morality. The problem, according to Nietzsche, is those seas have already become cluttered with false navigators who say they know how to cross these uncharted moral waters but are fooling themselves and whoever follows their guidance. These imposters are composed of two broad groups, Kantians and utilitarians. The confusion of these two schools is different, but stem from the same root, which is the inability to recognize the will to power as the fundamental goal driving human behavior. For the Kantians this failure can be seen in the focus Kant places on the role of reason in ethics. For Kant, moral obligation is based upon moral principles that humans formulate through their rational capacity that have no exceptions due to their universal character. Nietzsche criticizes the Kantian approach, asserting that Kant and his followers may think they are using reason to define ethics, but in reality, they are not. What seems to be an exercise in the pure use of reason is, in Nietzsche's view, an attempt to coerce others into moral behavior that is based purely upon will and not rationally constructed moral principles.[42] Nietzsche, like Schopenhauer, sees striving will as the motive for moral assertions, and Kantians disguise this motive in the garb of rational moral deliberation.

Nietzsche's attack on utilitarianism also takes place in the context of the will to power. Utilitarians make the mistake of thinking that humans desire and seek happiness. He pokes fun at the English utilitarians

39. Nietzsche, *Genealogy*, 1.8.
40. Nietzsche, *Human, All to Human*, 1.45.
41. Nietzsche, *Genealogy*, 1.13.
42. *SHE*, 224.

asserting, "Man does not seek happiness; only the Englishman does that."[43] Nietzsche contends that happiness is not the fundamental goal of the human person. Humans, above all, wish to express their power, and any moral scheme that does not recognize this reality is fatally flawed.[44]

Having described the vacuum of nineteenth-century European ethics and having discarded the erroneous attempts to fill the vacuum by the Kantians and utilitarians, Nietzsche can now propose what he calls a "Transvaluation of All Values" on the basis of the will to power.[45] For Nietzsche, the will to power is so basic to human activity it even supersedes the desire for self-preservation. He asserts that "physiologists should think twice before deciding that an organic being's primary instinct is the instinct of self-preservation. A living being wants above all else to release its strength; life itself is the will to power, and self-preservation is only one of its indirect and most frequent consequences."[46] Nietzsche is quite explicit about the difference between the path to the expression of power and the path to happiness. They can overlap to a certain extent; there can be a pleasure or happiness associated with the expression of power, but happiness is not a necessary outcome of power expression. He observes that the path to power and the mighty deeds that result from the expression of power often produce profound unhappiness. The path to power can be a path to misery.[47] Although there is an ominous implication in the path to power where the powerful might use their strength to coerce and manipulate others, sympathetic interpreters of Nietzsche note that power is not necessarily exercised over others.[48] The will to power can be seen as the need to express one's strength, a drive to act spontaneously and pursue one's projects in life with passion. The will to power can be seen in the musical genius of Mozart and Beethoven, the art of Michelangelo and Da Vinci, and in the scientific achievements of Galileo and Newton. For Nietzsche, it is only when the will to power is hidden and repressed (as happens in the Christian practice of morality) that it turns into an adversarial drive against others.[49]

43. Nietzsche, *Twilight of the Idols*, 1.2. Also cited in SHE, 224.
44. SHE, 224.
45. Nietzsche, *Antichrist*, 62.
46. Nietzsche, *Nietzsche Reader*, 318.
47. Nietzsche, *Genealogy*, 3.7.
48. SHE, 224.
49. SHE, 224.

A person with the character to express power successfully is what Nietzsche calls a higher person or the *Ubermensch*. The literal translation for *Ubermensch* is "the man who transcends," but simply (and maybe badly) put, the *Ubermensch* is a type of superman. Nietzsche's *Ubermensch* is not like most people. The *Ubermensch* is a person of virtue, which means the *Ubermensch* has the steel and the hardness to marshal his or her passions to achieve that person's highest goals.[50] Most people are incapable of this, belonging to the group Nietzsche labels "The Herd." From a moral perspective, members of "The Herd" are only capable of following the norms of society that enable them to live with a semblance of order within a community.[51] Ethics for the *Ubermensch*, the elite, on the other hand, is guided by virtue, which is the alignment of passion to the completion of great projects. Nietzsche thus asserts a double standard for human morality: a standard of rules for the commoner and the expression of power as passion for great deeds by the elite.

It is in the context of the *Ubermensch*'s expression of power that MacIntyre provides one of the most trenchant critiques of any of the philosophers he has yet covered. It is not a critique based on Nietzsche's intellectual failing or his lack of perception either. MacIntyre considers Nietzsche to be the most perceptive of nineteenth-century German philosophers and, in a later book asserts that Nietzsche's historic achievement was to see more clearly than any other philosopher the implications of Enlightenment moral thought. It is Nietzsche who understands better than any of his predecessors that Kant's moral thought was not an expression of objective reason, but was in fact an expression of an individual's subjective will.[52] Although it is Nietzsche who sees through Kant's mask of reason most clearly, Nietzsche's insights were not possible without Hegel's critique of Kant and the striving will described by Schopenhauer. And it is with the barrels of the Hegelian critique of Kant that MacIntyre takes aim at Nietzsche's concept of the *Ubermensch*. Hegel says of Kant's ethics that the conscientious moral agent who uses the categorical imperative as guide to moral action is licensed to do whatever he or she wants as long as that person does it conscientiously or consistently.[53] The only rule a person needs to obey is, "Can their action be formulated as a universal principle?" The answer to this is always yes, given the flexibility of language and the human penchant for

---

50. Nietzsche, *Thus Spoke Zarathustra*, 3.3; 3.12.29.
51. Nietzsche, *Good and Evil*, 201.
52. MacIntyre, *After Virtue*, 113.
53. *SHE*, 225.

ingenuity. The categorical imperative looks like a stringent test of morality but is in fact empty of guidance. The impact is that the determined and creative Kantian can justify virtually any action, and we recall Adolf Eichmann as the historical example of a self-proclaimed Kantian at the heart of the moral horror that was the Holocaust.

Similar to Hegel's critique of Kant, MacIntyre asks of the *Ubermensch* as a moral concept, is there anything in the name of the will to power that the *Ubermensch* ought not do?[54] And like Hegel's conclusion concerning Kant, MacIntyre concludes that the answer to that question is no. It is in this context that MacIntyre links Nietzsche's moral thought to the death and destruction wrought by the Nazis in the twentieth century. Before looking at his criticism, it is important to note that MacIntyre agrees with other authors who say that Nietzsche was not anti-Semitic and also notes that Nietzsche forcefully rejected the Pan-German nationalism and racism that was the nineteenth-century forerunner to twentieth-century National Socialism.[55] One cannot place the anti-Semitism and racism of the Nazi regime at Nietzsche's doorstep. He repudiated those two aspects of Nazi doctrine. Despite that fact, however, MacIntyre still finds Nietzsche's philosophy deeply irresponsible.[56] MacIntyre asserts that Nietzsche's thought does contribute to the catastrophe of German National Socialism in a significant manner. First, Nietzsche devised a twofold, relativistic moral structure in which the better humans can look down on other people they believe to be inferior, the herd or the masses, with contempt.[57] This is certainly a mindset manifest in the actions of the Nazis in their treatment of Jews and anyone else outside of their preferred racial categories. Second, Nietzsche's description of the *Ubermensch* has a violence of language and an emptiness of moral constraint that in MacIntyre's view provides an effective intellectual scaffolding to support the programs of the Nazis.[58] Like Kant's conscientious moral agent, there is nothing the *Ubermensch* can do that cannot be justified by the will to power. In the person of Nietzsche, MacIntyre sees the most perceptive German moralist turning his back on German society. It is a turning that MacIntyre sees as a prophetic symbol of German society turning its back

54. *SHE*, 225.
55. *SHE*, 223.
56. *SHE*, 225.
57. *SHE*, 225.
58. *SHE*, 225.

on humanity as a whole in the century to follow.[59] In his critique of Nietzsche, MacIntyre again demonstrates that moral philosophy is bound up in human history and can be quite influential in shaping that history.

Leadership Reflection: Nietzsche's Virtue and the Moral Corruption of Leaders

Nietzsche's focus on the importance of the human will has significant implications for ethics and leadership. Recent leadership research has confirmed what is intuitive to many, which is the importance of passion to leadership.[60] A passionate will is of fundamental importance to the work of a leader. If leaders have it, people will follow them and will even follow despite the other weaknesses a passionate leader might have. Nietzsche links passion with the great, with the leaders of society, by means of his distinctive view of virtue and its relationship to the idea of passion. It is an approach that emphasizes the pursuit of power, the accrual of which is the goal of many leaders. In addition to the realism Nietzsche adds to the discussion of leadership with his focus on the will and the search for power, we will also see the irresponsibility of Nietzsche's ethics that MacIntyre describes. Leaders often struggle with moral corruption as they take the reins of power, and when we examine Nietzsche's ethics, we can see how his thinking makes that problem worse.

In his book, *Thus Spoke Zarathustra*, Nietzsche discusses the idea of virtue in terms of passions and goals. He begins his description from a traditional perspective where passions are emotions that one undergoes or suffers through. Traditionally the human person was seen as passive in relation to a passion: a passion acted on a person, rather than a person acting on a passion. For example, anger might sweep over a person who has been treated unjustly. Nietzsche's description of virtue and passion reverses the relationship, however. Although he recognizes that passions can by suffered through passively, Nietzsche also asserts that when aligned with a person's goals, passions are transformed from a passive experience into instruments of power. Passions are transformed into virtues when a person's will directs those passions at his or her highest

---

59. *SHE*, 226.

60. Cf. Tan et al., "Impact of Leaders' Passion at Work on Leader Effectiveness," 1681–84 for just one among many articles on the importance of passion to leadership.

goals.⁶¹ For example, when painters apply their creativity and passion for beauty to their work, they are developing a virtue, a habitual power, to create beauty on their canvas.

Nietzsche goes on to explain two further aspects of the virtues that have bearing on the character of a great person or a leader. First, unlike the classical approach to moral character, the virtues for Nietzsche have no unity. They are adversarial in nature. Nietzsche makes this assertion in the context of his thought regarding the will in relation to meaning and interpretation. Nietzsche defines interpretation as a manifestation of will. When a person makes an interpretation, that person is imposing a meaning on a concept or a set of circumstances.⁶² For Nietzsche, interpretation represents a cognitive aspect of the will to power. To interpret is to define; it is to assert one's meaning in a specific situation. By interpreting, a person is asserting his or her will and by means of will is forcing that meaning upon a subject matter. Nietzsche links his notion of interpretation to his understanding of virtue. In the process of creating a virtue, the passion is the subject matter upon which meaning is imposed.⁶³ A person forms a virtue when he or she orders a passion toward a particular goal. Nietzsche sees the process of virtue formation as a sort of contest. Each person has different passions competing within oneself, and one set of passions will emerge as dominant in the conflict between the passions. In conquering the other passions, the virtues of a person are blind and irrational. They overcome the other passions and therefore do not take them into account, thus imposing a type of ignorance on the person. "An earthly virtue is it which I love; little prudence is therein and the least everyday wisdom."⁶⁴ Instead of the unity of the virtues preached by classical philosophers, Nietzsche proposes an enmity between the virtues in which the establishment of a virtue is the victory of one passion over another. The virtues are just one further arena where the adversarial striving of will plays out. A second aspect of virtue with implications for leadership is the fact that very few people are capable of forming virtues. Only the great have the inner strength and hardness to achieve the integration necessary for the formation of virtue. Most people belong to the herd who lack this strength and must resort to following the moral rules

---

61. Nietzsche, *Zarathustra*, 1.5. Lester Hunt, *Nietzsche and the Origin of Virtue*, 70–71.

62. Hunt, *Nietzsche and the Origin of Virtue*, 73.

63. Nietzsche, *Zarathustra*, 1.5.

64. Nietzsche, *Zarathustra*, 1.5.

that enable people to live in community with one another.[65] Nietzsche's two different standards of morality—one for the great, the strong, the hard, the leaders, and one for the herd or the followers—is a dualistic and relativistic approach to morality that presents considerable risks when applied to leaders.

Nietzsche's combination of the adversarial will to power and his two levels of moral criteria, virtue for leaders and customs and norms for followers, is troubling for leadership on two fronts. First, it is inaccurate. Nietzsche asserts that, "It is . . . absurd to ask strength not to express itself as strength, not to be a desire to overthrow, crush, become master, to be a thirst for enemies, resistance and triumphs as it is to ask weakness to express itself as strength."[66] His view that strength must express itself aggressively and always seek dominance is falsified by the daily experience of human life. The strong put their strength at the service and in the interest of others and of the weak all the time. Whether it is soldiers sacrificing their lives to defend the citizens of their community, or first responders using their strength to save others in distress, or teachers using their strength to educate young people, or parents using their strength to protect and nurture their children, we see the strong using their strength in a loving and supportive fashion on a daily basis. Examples of strength at the service of others are ubiquitous, almost infinite, and are so fundamental to human flourishing it is difficult to imagine the horrific state of a world where those acts were absent.

Yet we do glimpse the horror of a world where strength is used as a weapon in the hands of the aggressive, in the hands of the powerful, in the hands of leaders. This is where MacIntyre's charge that Nietzschean ethics are irresponsible finds its power (for lack of a better term). Nietzsche's moral thought empowers the selfish and self-serving tendencies that are temptations for all humans, and leaders in particular. Many authors have observed and written about the moral failings of leaders and the corruption that so often rears its head when a leader accumulates power. Lord Acton's assertion that power corrupts, and absolute power corrupts absolutely, again comes to mind.[67] By glamorizing the pursuit of power and its aggressive use and then placing it in the context of a two-tiered system of morality in which leaders can do anything with which their passions

---

65. Nietzsche, *Good and Evil*, 201; Hunt, *Origin of Virtue*, 141–42.

66. Nietzsche, *Genealogy*, 1.13.

67. Cf. Ludwig and Longenecker, "Bathsheba Syndrome," for an in-depth analysis of Acton's assertion.

align, Nietzsche is providing a powerful intellectual infrastructure for abuse and corruption on the part of the elite. There is a long history of leaders using their power to abuse and defraud others—including their followers—and the Nietzschean system of reducing leader moral constraints to whatever goals leaders can align with their passions douses that fire with further fuel. In Nietzsche's context, not only should leaders pursue their own goals, but they should do so with aggression and at the expense of others. For Nietzsche, power is the only criteria by which the actions of leaders can or should be judged. The pursuit and wielding of power provide the justification for any and all of a leader's behavior. Imagine the misery of a community whose leaders care only about themselves and their own goals and will mow any person down who tries to stand in their way. The problem of leader self-service, corruption, and aggression plagues every society, every community. Nietzsche's ethics does everything to inflame that problem and nothing to control it. MacIntyre's description of Nietzsche's ethics as irresponsible is really too kind. The application of Nietzsche's moral thought to leader behavior should be avoided at all costs.

18

Twentieth-Century Ethics and Twenty-First-Century Leadership

MACINTYRE'S FINAL CHAPTER STARTS at the dawn of the twentieth century. It is the century that many of us were born in, so we can say that MacIntyre's history finally touches the moral ideas of the people living today. Despite the current relevance of the twentieth-century thinkers MacIntyre covers, none are familiar names. Moore, Prichard, Dewey, Ayer, Stevenson, Hare, Foot, and Geach are all preeminent academics who had a significant impact on the ethical debates that shape contemporary moral culture in the English-speaking world, yet few remember their names. All the reasons for that are beyond the scope of this discussion, but one reason may be that they were primarily carrying forward and developing the ideas of previous thinkers, Immanual Kant being chief among those predecessors. Another reason may be that they are important not so much for the distinct ideas that they formulated, which certainly do vary, but because of the common features that their related systems of thought shared. One thing about this group of writers that is also true is their thinking was significant to MacIntyre's future research and writing. It is out of his dialogue with these twentieth-century philosophers that much of MacIntyre's work after *A Short History of Ethics* emerges. The features he observes in twentieth-century moral thought in the early 1960s become the questions he seeks to answer in the influential books that he writes in the 1980s and 1990s.

Given that background here is the plan for our last chapter. MacIntyre offers an intricate description of the developments in ethical thought during the twentieth century. I will provide a brief recap of his description that focuses on two of these thinkers, specifically G. E. Moore and C. L. Stevenson, that set up MacIntyre's conclusions at the end of the book and also provide the springboard for his future writing. We will also cover his concluding observations, which are useful not only to capture where we have arrived after this 2,500-year history but are also helpful to understand the challenges of our contemporary moral culture. Lastly, I will offer my own synthesis to make sense of what we have covered, especially as it relates to the practice of leadership. Outside of the previous leadership reflections I have tried to keep my own thought out of the equation. I wanted to let MacIntyre and the other authors speak, and have largely left the criticism of various thinkers to MacIntyre. Having done that, I will now add a few thoughts of my own to tie together the ideas that I see as the most important to our current understanding of ethics and leadership. Also, having written this book on the basis of MacIntyre's analysis, I hope it comes as little surprise that I will leverage his thinking to capture what I see as the most important points of this conceptual history for leadership.

Moore, Stevenson, and the Emergence of Emotive Moral Thought

MacIntyre begins his survey of twentieth-century moral thinkers with the work of G. E. Moore (b. 1873) and his book *Principia Ethica*, written in 1903. Moore claims that moral philosophy has struggled to answer the questions of ethics because those questions have not been formulated properly. To correct that shortcoming Moore asserts that ethics must seek to answer the question what actions should be done, and that the answer to this important question is based on the answer to an even more fundamental question, which is what things ought to exist for their own sake?[1] Moore's second question is asking about what things are intrinsically good and in answering that question we will be able to answer the question of what actions ought to be done in pursuit of those good things. Moore then explains that humans can recognize intrinsically good objects whenever they are encountered, but the idea of good is not something that can be defined. MacIntyre tells us that from Moore's perspective good is the name of a simple unanalyzable property because

1. *SHE*, 249.

it is a concept that defies definition. To define something, according to Moore, one must be able to break that thing down into its constituent parts.[2] Moore provides an analogy to prove his point. There are things that are like to the idea good, such as pleasant, in the same way that there are things that are similar to the color yellow, such as the wavelength of light that enables a person to see the color yellow. Those similarities, however, do not mean that yellow is the same as a specific wavelength of light, nor is good the same as pleasant. And we know this to be the case by examining these ideas or presenting them to our minds for observation and evaluation. We can see the difference between the concepts by means of simple scrutiny. Given what we can observe about the concept good Moore concludes that it is an idea we can build upon, but not something we can break down. MacIntyre describes Moore's analysis at this point as curious because Moore's understanding of what it means to define something is idiosyncratic; there are other ways to understand the notion of what it means to define a word or idea (for example the Oxford dictionary tells us that to define a word is to "Set forth or explain what a word or expression means; to declare the signification of a word").[3] He also sees Moore's description of good as problematic because his description does not enable a person to explain in intelligible terms what the word good actually means. Good can be recognized but cannot be described.[4] And if it cannot be described it is difficult to tell a person how to apply the idea, which is especially problematic for a term like good that is used frequently and in many ways. A further problem is the fact that the word good usually provides a reason for a person to act to attain whatever it is that is labeled as good. For MacIntyre, the person without an ability to articulate what it means to be good is deprived of reasons to act in pursuit of what is good.[5]

MacIntyre's initial description of Moore's moral thought finishes with what Moore calls the "naturalistic fallacy."[6] The idea behind the term and the term itself would have significant impact on Moore's twentieth-century heirs. Moore coined the phrase to name the mistake in which a person thinks that the word good names some natural property that can be equated to the idea of good. As we noted earlier, Moore asserts that

2. *SHE*, 249–50.
3. *SHE*, 250. Cf. *Oxford English Dictionary*, "Define."
4. *SHE*, 252.
5. *SHE*, 252.
6. *SHE*, 252.

good cannot be equated with pleasant, or any other idea for that matter, and to make an assertion along those lines is to misunderstand that good is a simple unanalyzable property. Despite Moore's definition of the naturalistic fallacy, the phrase came to be associated with the separation between facts and moral evaluations. Later philosophers used naturalistic fallacy as a label for the idea that no factual circumstance can give rise to a moral obligation.[7] Many modern philosophers assert that you cannot derive a moral "ought" from a factual "is" and naturalistic fallacy became the shorthand title for their assertion. Both ideas would have influence on thinkers following in Moore's wake.

MacIntyre covers a number of authors that are influenced by Moore and critics of those authors, to include H. A. Prichard, John Dewey, R. G. Collingwood, and A. J. Ayer. He identifies C. L. Stevenson (b. 1908) as the most powerful exponent of emotive moral thinking and thus the most significant later thinker to apply Moore's insights.[8] Stevenson, like Ayer, maintains the separation between factual circumstances and moral judgments, captured by the repurposed use of Moore's naturalistic fallacy label, and articulates his emotivism on the basis of Moore's idea that good is an unanalyzable property. MacIntyre notes that Stevenson uses moral terms as rough approximations. For example, the idea of good roughly means "I like this, do so as well."[9] MacIntyre returns to the implications of good as an unanalyzable property noting that it produces discussions that can only observe and assert rather than providing reasons for a moral position. MacIntyre notes that if one cannot use moral ideas such as good to provide the rationale for a moral assertion, moral debate is reduced to the expression of opinions and feelings and it is here that we find one of the seeds of emotive moral theory.[10] Despite the late hour we seem to be heading back to the world of the Sophists where convincing one's audience is a function of psychological pressure rather than rational persuasion. Stevenson seems to be asserting exactly this point when he moves beyond Ayre's idea that ethics is about self-expression and asserts that the purpose of using moral terms is to align the attitudes of others with one's own attitudes.[11] MacIntyre describes this dynamic function of moral terms in Stevenson's thinking as the nucleus of emotive moral thought.

7. *SHE*, 252.
8. *SHE*, 255.
9. *SHE*, 258.
10. *SHE*, 257.
11. *SHE*, 257.

Ethical terms are emotive because they produce "affective responses in people";[12] that is, they can change another person's attitude or feelings. Stevenson's position also seems in line with a Nietzschean approach to ethics in which moral assertion is merely the attempt of one person to impose his or her will upon that of another.

Following this description MacIntyre asserts that Stevenson's thinking is marked by other features that have ramifications for later twentieth-century thinkers. In addition to the above characteristics, Stevenson's thought embraces the idea that emotivism, and moral philosophy in general, is neutral in relation to moral judgments or conclusions.[13] Since emotivism is focused on how moral terms are used to impose one person's attitudes on those of another, it is a philosophical approach to ethics that can be used to support any set of moral attitudes and the assertions those attitudes produce. Stevenson's ideas also produce an ethical system with irresolvable arguments, or in MacIntyre's words "interminable disagreements."[14] In the background of this characterization is the idea that good is an unanalyzable property. Moore's idea produces a philosophical context in which moral disagreements cannot be rationally resolved since those disagreements are always a function of clashing subjective attitudes that contend for supremacy based on a person's psychological strength and not on the basis of reason. A victorious attitude is always at risk of being vanquished by an argument put forth by a stronger personality. MacIntyre also notes that Stevenson's method produces interminable arguments because Stevenson himself asserts that the interminable nature of moral argumentation, like the neutrality of moral philosophy, is a prerequisite to a valid approach to ethics in general.[15] A last feature of Stevenson's thought MacIntyre highlights is the fact that since human reason is not logically related to moral conclusions it is not only moral terms such as "good" that take on different meanings. Words that indicate logical relationships such as "therefore" and "because" take on different meanings as well. Such terms now support the emotive and dynamic function of moral persuasion but do not indicate a logical relationship as they do in other types of rational discourse.[16]

12. *SHE*, 258.
13. *SHE*, 258.
14. *SHE*, 258.
15. *SHE*, 259.
16. *SHE*, 259.

Beyond his summary of the characteristics of Stevenson's moral philosophy, MacIntyre also offers a number of criticisms, many of which are implied by his previous observations. Perhaps his strongest criticism from a conceptual perspective is his assertion that the primary use of moral terms for emotivism, which is influencing the attitudes of others, cannot be the primary use of moral terms. The emotivist function of moral terms is to convince or impose one's own attitudes on those of others. That is an action that must always follow, and therefore be secondary to, the original formation of the views that one is trying to impose on others. Stevenson's emotive theory offers no account of how one forms the attitudes that serve as the source of the moral manipulation that emotive statements seek to accomplish.[17] A related criticism MacIntyre offers that may be more powerful than his conceptual concern is the misery of the emotive world Stevenson describes. Emotivism posits a world of incessant and unending manipulation whenever a person utters a moral statement.[18] Moral discussions, assertions, and conclusion are always made to get another person to do or think in the same way as the one making the assertion. Ethics is reduced to being the mechanism through which each person can coerce others to conform to their views. Can anyone think of a more alienating or unattractive approach to ethics?

Common Traits of Modern Ethics as the Background to MacIntyre's Later Thinking

In MacIntyre's view, emotivism, like the other twentieth-century schools of modern moral philosophy, exhibits several distinct features. MacIntyre does us the service of describing and summarizing these common traits in the following manner:

> It is held that facts can never entail evaluations, that philosophical inquiry is neutral between evaluations, that the only authority which moral views possess is that which we as individual agents give to them. This view is the final conceptualization of the individualism which has had recurrent mention in this history; the individual becomes his own final authority in the most extreme possible sense.[19]

17. *SHE*, 259.
18. *SHE*, 259.
19. *SHE*, 264.

These features are alive and well not only in the twentieth century, but their influence has continued to the present day and are some of the most powerful ethical concepts in the moral culture of twenty-first-century Europe and America. MacIntyre also notes that these features are not without their rivals. He observes the fact that rival traditions of ethics coexist with the modern conceptions he has identified. He asserts what might be a confusing perspective when he says that there are multiple surviving moral traditions in competition with modern moral philosophy. MacIntyre lists a few of these traditions, to include Aristotelianism, ancient Christian moral tradition, Puritan ethics, the aristocratic ethics of consumption, the ethics of democratic and socialist political systems, and asserts that they too have had significant impact on contemporary moral concepts and vocabulary.[20]

In opposition to the features of modern moral philosophy MacIntyre posits a set of features that constitute or characterize some of these other ethical traditions. On the basis of these traditions, he asserts that philosophical enquiry is not morally neutral because such enquiry discovers ethical concepts and criteria that we have to acknowledge as true. In making that discovery we recognize these ideas have an authority that goes beyond an individual subjective perspective and that our use of moral language implies and manifests this recognition.[21] When a person says that an act is morally good, they are typically making an assertion that claims an objective rather than a subjective authority. To say something is good is to say something more than "I like this thing or action." Such a statement implies a standard by which an act or an object can be measured as good. In addition, MacIntyre asserts that some facts can entail moral obligations.[22] It seems that the naturalistic fallacy may itself be a fallacy.

MacIntyre describes adherents to these two sets of moral features as people that stand within a surviving moral tradition, for example a Stoic, a Catholic, or a Puritan, and those, who on the other hand, stand outside of all traditions, which includes emotivists and other schools of modern moral thought.[23] Standing outside of tradition is a mark of modern thought that is most influenced by Immanuel Kant. For the ancient Greeks of the polis moral standards were understood in the context of

20. *SHE*, 266.
21. *SHE*, 264.
22. *SHE*, 264.
23. *SHE*, 266.

a person's role within a community. For Kant and the modern thinkers that follow him, the search for moral principles takes place in the context of a person's status as a human deprived of all social context. Kant's Categorical Imperative seeks to identify moral principles that are universally applicable, that is, applicable to every person all the time. For Kant ethical principles can only be obligatory if they apply no matter the situation. Thus, we have modern moral schools that stand outside a tradition rather than inside of one.[24]

For MacIntyre, these two sets of positions, within and outside of traditions, have little hope of reconciliation. There is no court of appeal between these conceptual rivals for a number of reasons. First, the schools typically choose examples that insulate their ideas from the criticism of rival traditions or perspectives.[25] The different schools end up talking past one another because they focus on evidence that supports their position and provides little space for criticism from other perspectives. A more fundamental difference keeping the different perspectives from entering into a fruitful dialogue is the difference in methods between the adherents of a surviving tradition of morality and those of twentieth-century modern ethics. The surviving traditions have an interconnecting web of ideas that give rise to the meaning of the moral words and ethical concepts used by those traditions. Within the communities that produced these traditions there existed a consensus about rules, virtues, and goals that produced a good life for both individuals and the community in which each person lived. It was a network of ideas based on reason, where moral concepts were supported and justified through logic and rational discourse. This is not the case for the twentieth-century modern schools. The foundation of the moral theories of these schools lay in the authority of the individual and not within that individual's reason, but on the basis of a person's attitudes, feelings, likes and dislikes. The resulting dialogue between these differing perspectives is again an exercise in

24. An interesting counter to MacIntyre's description is the fact that Kant's thinking also produces a tradition in which other philosophers follow and build upon Kant's thought. Although this is likely a fair counterargument, MacIntyre might respond by noting the individualism intrinsic to Kant's thought and that of other modern moral philosophers truncates the impact a tradition might have on an individual person. This is due to the authority of the individual to legislate his or her own morality and the fact that the role of a community in shaping the thought of an individual person is ignored. A Kantian or modern tradition is therefore much reduced compared to the other traditions that boast robust sets of rules, virtues, and goals that shape a community and the individuals that comprise a community.

25. *SHE*, 264.

which one school cannot understand the moral assertions of the other. Where the members of a surviving tradition will articulate moral assertions on the basis of reason and the consensus of their community, the adherents of modern moral philosophy only see those traditionalists as a collection of individuals who are merely asserting their own feelings and failing to recognize that fact.[26]

This, MacIntyre asserts, is the present situation of the contemporary moral debate. The implications for him are twofold. First, he says one should carefully choose the community in which one wants to live because the choice of community will determine the rules, virtues, and goals that guide a person's life. The practices of a community are so fundamental they will define not only a person's conception of human nature, but the very meaning of the moral terms a person uses.[27] This is not to say that people choose their communities from a blank tablet. Every human is born into a community and that community will have great influence on the social choices a person will make as a mature moral agent. And in making the choice of a community a person will be making a choice of the type of ethics that will guide not only his or her own actions, but also the way in which the person relates to other people inside and outside of that community; how they relate to loved ones and strangers. Second, it is this divide that MacIntyre will seek to overcome in much of his work throughout the remainder of the twentieth century and into our new millennium. MacIntyre's books, to include titles such as *After Virtue, Whose Justice, Which Rationality, Three Rival Versions of Moral Enquiry*, and *Dependent Rational Animals*, attempt to untie the conceptual knots he articulates at the end of *A Short History of Ethics*. His writing is certainly one of the most important contributions to moral philosophy in the English-speaking world during the second half of the twentieth century. I hope that anyone reading this summary of his early thought is inspired to take a crack at his later, more mature thinking. Doing so will be an investment that will surely pay dividends not only to your understanding of moral philosophy, but also to your ability to live a flourishing life.

---

26. *SHE*, 266.
27. *SHE*, 268.

Enlightenment Versus Classical Ethics

Having completed our review of MacIntyre's 1960s take on the history of ethics in the Western world I will now apply some of the historical observations he offers in a twenty-first-century critique of modern ethics and its impact on leadership. Starting first with the philosophical thought of the Enlightenment, one can say that Enlightenment political theory has often been praised for its contributions to the founding documents of the United States and other Western democracies. Despite the success of enlightenment political thought and its popularity in some quarters, one might say that the legacy of Enlightenment ethics is more of a mixed bag. One can assume Enlightenment ethics are the best approach to ethics because they are articulated by the most important modern philosophers who presumably would have greater insight into ethical issues than medieval or ancient thinkers. Given Enlightenment advances in political thought and the fact that they were able to build on the good insights of their predecessors and repudiate the mistakes of earlier moral philosophers, it seems like the Enlightenment thinkers and the modern ethicists inspired by that tradition should be the most credible and indeed be the best when it comes to understanding morality. If you have made it this far in the book, you probably know that this analysis is too simplistic. While Enlightenment ethics have certainly been influential and no doubt have contributed genuine insight to our understanding of ethics, many (including MacIntyre) would question whether modern moral thinking has been an improvement to ethics in general. A significant number of contemporary philosophers see modern and postmodern ethics as a step backwards from the classical approach to ethics with its emphasis on the virtues. This is a controversial stance, but MacIntyre is not the only philosopher to hold it, and after teaching ethics for the last decade, I have come down on the side of the virtue ethics trend that has been gathering steam in the English-speaking world since the 1950s.[28] The following comments will be a brief summary of what I see as the weaknesses of modern and contemporary moral thought, why classical ethics is superior to modern and

---

28. Cf. Anscombe, "Modern Moral Philosophy," 1–19, for an early and influential critique of Enlightenment ethics that led to renewed interest in classical morality and the examination of virtue as a moral concept. Other thinkers that have focused on virtue ethics in the years since Anscombe's article include Michael Stocker, Mortimer Adler, Phillipa Foot, Stanley Hauerwas, Robert Roberts, Romanus Cessario, and many others.

postmodern ethics in view of those weaknesses, and how those strengths and weaknesses relate to our understanding of leadership.

The Weaknesses of Contemporary Moral Thought

In discussing the ethics of the Enlightenment, there are two thinkers that in my view have had the greatest impact on the moral culture of twenty-first-century America, and they are Immanuel Kant and John Stuart Mill. As MacIntyre mentions, Kant's moral thought has largely defined the nature of ethics for most people in the Western world, even though most of those people have never read Kant nor even heard of him. From my experience in teaching undergraduates, the same can be said of Mill. When asking for a definition of freedom in class I encounter many students who are able to quote Mill almost word for word from his essay *On Liberty*, and again, they have neither heard of Mill nor read any of his writings. Western culture has been permeated by the thought of these two great thinkers, and the criticism I will offer of their thinking presupposes their genius and the influence that genius has had over the centuries since they put their pens to paper. That being said, even a genius has limitations and can propose ideas that have negative effects over time. The following is a quick review of that criticism.

The moral thinking of Kant and Mill and modern ethics in general is problematic because they neglect aspects of human life that must be addressed for an accurate and effective discussion of ethics. From a Kantian perspective, that neglect ends up narrowing ethics and limiting the behavior that can be examined from an ethical perspective. In addition, Mill's thinking tends to lower the standards of morality that are applied in the narrow context of Kant's thinking.

So, what aspects of human experience does modern moral thought neglect? Thinkers like Kant and Mill do not effectively come to grips with the simple fact that humans are animals. It is such a basic aspect of human existence that it is easy to overlook when considering the rational aspects of ethics, but it is an extraordinary weakness that warps the understanding of morality. Our experience of morality, our experience of ethics, always takes place in the context of human biology. Kant's thinking is particularly weak in this area. Kant wants to establish a purely rational morality. He is proposing an approach to morality that is universally applicable on the basis of reason alone, an emphasis evident even in the title of his influential *Critique of Pure Reason*. While reason is fundamentally important to ethics, it is not the only part of human nature that is of great consequence to morality. Humans are biological creatures that live in communities and exist over time, so any approach to morality that does not adequately account for things like emotions, appetites, habits, memory, the passage of time, and the influence of relationships (i.e., communities)—all of which find their basis in the physiology of the human person—will present an account of ethics that is inaccurate, misleading, and flawed. There has never been a moral choice in the history of the world that was made on the basis of reason alone. The neurophysiology that gives rise to and affects our moral experience always includes reason, memory, appetite, and emotion. Humans are not computers when making moral decisions, yet reading Kant's and Mill's moral thought has led some of my students to that precise conclusion. Kant's blind spot with regard to biology is particularly clear in his dismissal of inclination—the rough equivalent of what Aristotle identifies as desire—from moral consideration. For Kant morality concerns only obedience to the universal moral principles a person develops on the basis of his or her own intellect. If a person does something out of love or any other emotional or physical inclination, it is not a moral act, according to Kant. The act of feeding a child, if done out of love, falls outside the realm of morality. In Kant's moral universe, one must either ignore inclinations or act against them. Not only is this unrealistic—just think of how often people follow their desires rather than choosing what is rational—it also takes a whole host of moral actions off the ethical radar. As MacIntyre points out, morality in a Kantian approach is only about what is contrary to your moral principles, about what a person should not do, and has little to say about what a person should do. For example, a young adult who is habitually unable to delay gratification will not necessarily violate a universal moral rule due to that inability, but that person is unlikely to develop the capacities necessary to live a morally good life. Kant's moral thinking is too narrow to effectively address this situation in ethical terms. Making choices that delay the gratification of inclination is a moral issue that literally every human person faces, and Kant's ethics have little to say about such decisions. Biological inclination is one example of a crucial moral issue that is off Kant's ethical playing field and thus deprives a person following Kant's ethics the guidance necessary to make numerous, daily moral choices.

Mill's utilitarianism is similarly blind to biology because it reduces moral deliberation to a calculation regarding the pleasure or suffering associated with a particular moral choice. As in my earlier comments regarding utilitarianism and virtue, utilitarianism could cover the biological aspects of morality. It is focused on pleasure and pain, which are biologically based concerns, and it could cover issues such as which desires and habits are the consequences of a person's moral choices. The problem is, these are consequences that utilitarian investigations rarely address because of the Hobbesian assumptions behind those calculations. For Hobbes, desire is static and unchanging. It is not something that can be criticized or modified by human behavior. Utilitarians often make the same assumption and therefore rarely examine the impact choices have on habits and desires. Utilitarian moral analysis thus becomes an algorithmic comparison of pleasures and pains caused by the impact a choice has on external circumstances and seldom contends with issues such as habits, memory, or experience, or what implications those biologically based phenomena might hold for future moral choices. Utilitarianism, with its focus on public reform and the happiness of the many, ends up being a calculation concerning the environmental impact of consequences and hardly ever recognizes the fact that humans are animals existing over a period of time. Those choices literally become part of human neurophysiology and have profound implications for the future moral choices a person makes. These are considerations that are simply absent from most utilitarian discussions.

A last concern about Enlightenment ethics stems from combining the moral thinking of Kant and Mill. We have seen that Kant narrows the moral zone of thinking, and Mill says the only criteria to judge moral acts comes from analyzing the consequences of a moral choice. Mill has something else to add to his analysis of consequences, however, which is his profoundly influential view of freedom. In his essay *On Liberty*, Mill asserts that the only definition worthy of the name is the idea that freedom is the ability to do what one wants.[29] Now that we have read our history of ethics, we can see that the Sophists are back on the scene. Mill does not rest with the Sophist view, though, adding to it the idea that the only thing that should cause the freedom of a person to be limited or restricted is when a person uses that freedom to hurt someone else. It is an intuitive and powerful idea. Given the dignity of each person and the rights of freedom deriving from that dignity, it makes sense to only deprive a person of those rights in cases where a person is using his or

---

29. Mill, *On Liberty*, 83.

her freedom to do something that clearly harms others. Can you really argue against supporting freedom except in a case where it hurts other people? In my view the answer to that question is no. Mill is right. The rights of individual freedom should be protected, but no one should have the freedom to hurt others.

The problem with this principle is when it becomes the primary criteria for all moral judgments. It sets up a very low standard of morality. The combination of Mill's thought on utility and liberty and Kant's restriction of ethics only to universally valid moral principles is a moral culture in which anything can be done so long as the act itself does not hurt anyone else. This combination yields an ethical culture that is concerned with very few choices. Practical choices for the most part are excluded from this field of morality, a field that also presents a terribly low standard by which to judge those few choices that remain to be examined from a moral perspective. "It's all good as long as no one loses an eye" was a funny comment I often heard growing up, but it actually reflects the narrowed moral thinking and low standards that dominate our contemporary culture.

This narrow and low standard of ethics has had an enormously detrimental impact not only on moral culture in general, but also on leadership. It is arguable that the leaders of today and the elites of American culture have never been held in lower esteem by their fellow citizens.[30] Even the writers of the leadership education industry, which has been thriving for more than four decades, recognize that leadership in the United States, despite their best and well reimbursed efforts, has never been in a greater state of disrepair.[31] While this is a complex societal problem, it is clear that the problems associated with contemporary leaders and their failures are closely linked to the ethics of those leaders. A moral toolbox that includes only Kantian duties and utilitarian consequences cannot enable leaders to make the moral choices necessary for successful leadership. The ethical choices faced by leaders are among the most difficult and vexing moral issues that are faced by any group of people. And the primary aspect of that difficulty is not connected to their complexity,

---

30. Cf. long-term polling trends regarding the moral perceptions of American chronicled by Gallup, "Moral Issues." See also the Pew Research Center's study of trends in the trust of Americans toward the federal government: Pew Research Center, "Americans' Views of Government."

31. Cf. Kellerman, *End of Leadership*, Pfeffer, *Leadership BS*, and Kolditz et al., *Leadership Reckoning*, for three recent critiques of the corporate and higher education leadership industry.

although no doubt many leadership decisions are complicated. Ethical choices of leaders are often hard because they include issues that require significant moral strength and wisdom to face and overcome. What is a leader to do when he or she is faced with a choice where the consequences pit the interests of the leader against those of the organization or its followers? What will a leader do when making the "ethical choice" in a situation where the consequences will hurt the leader or the ones she or he loves? We all know the real answer to those questions. To repeat the words of author David Brooks, "The leadership class is fundamentally self-dealing."[32] The large majority of leaders will choose what is in their own interest, which is the type of choosing that is enabled and fostered by the thinking of Kant and Mill. Kant's thinking will tell the leader that this is a practical choice and ethics are not at stake. Mill's thinking will help the leader make a choice in which pain—that is the pain of getting caught—is not likely. These are not the standards that will lead to the courageous, self-sacrificial decisions leaders must make if they are to be effective at their craft.

Leadership in the Context of Virtue-Based Ethics

The virtue-based approach of classical ethics can yield different results from the modern criteria that so often lead to self-interested behavior. Using Aristotle's approach to ethics, we can see that such an approach is more realistic because it is biologically based, it is broader and more dynamic, and it leads to higher standards for making ethical choices than do the ethics of Kant and Mill.

The realism of the virtue-based approach lies in the fact that it accounts for human biology as the context in which we make moral choices. Humans are rational animals whose appetites, emotions, and remembered experience all have an impact on each moral decision. Aristotle proposes a view of moral deliberation where reason guides the appetites and emotions to moral decisions that unavoidably become part of a person's experience and habits, which lead to similar moral choices in the future. Classical ethics recognizes the critical role habit plays in making moral choices and thus makes that role central in its analysis of ethical decisions.

---

32. Brooks, "Who Is James Johnson?"

In addition, Aristotle's method for moral choice is expansive compared to that of Kant. For a thinker like Aristotle, desire and inclination are indeed part of the equation when making moral decisions in the context of virtue because any free and informed decision, i.e., any decision that is not coerced or made in ignorance, is an ethical decision. We know they are ethical because those voluntary decisions are subject to moral evaluation. We praise people for making them if they are good and blame them for making those decisions if they are bad.[33] This leads to a significantly larger scope for ethics than is currently used in American culture. Something as simple as brushing one's teeth in this context becomes an ethical decision. Brushing your teeth is a free action made on the basis of knowledge, is a habit, and leads to the good of dental health. Of course, brushing your teeth is not the most momentous of moral decisions, and a virtue-based approach to ethics does not preclude us from seeing tooth brushing as a habit of good oral hygiene either. The habit of tooth brushing over time does contribute and even contributes significantly to a good life, thus making it a moral issue as well as an issue of oral hygiene.

This breadth leads to a more dynamic approach to moral decisions when combined with Aristotle's primary criteria for making moral decisions, which is the virtue of practical wisdom. Instead of reducing ethical complexity and trying to stuff the criteria for moral choice into one box of rules as Kant and Mill attempt to do, a virtue-based approach recognizes that the criteria for moral decisions vary on the basis of a multiplicity of factors. Circumstances, intentions, consequences, duties, a person's moral character, or a combination of all these factors can each be the primary concern in a specific situation. There is no one rule that can account for all of these factors.[34] In a virtue-based approach, practical wisdom is the habitual capacity that enables a person to sift through all of these competing factors to come to a good decision.

A virtue-based approach also ends up advocating higher moral standards than the ethics of Kant and Mill. This is the case because the primary concern is how the choice will affect one's moral habits. If we recognize that it is our moral character, our very selves, that are at stake

---

33. Cf. Aristotle, *Nicomachean Ethics*, 1109b30–1111b3 for Aristotle's description of voluntary acts and their relationship to moral evaluation.

34. Although this description leaves out absolute moral principles, the habit-based approach of classical ethics need not be relativistic. Aristotle contends that some actions can never be justified based on particular circumstances because those actions are always wrong. Cf. *Nicomachean Ethics*, 1107a8–1107a26.

when making moral choices, we will not only be careful, we will want to make excellent choices. Although the relation between choice and moral character is not always clear to people, many—even most of us—would want to be the best person they could be if confronted with that reality. Social science has demonstrated the intuition that human individuals are highly resistant to the idea that they are not a good person.[35] Although we are frail and imperfect, the desire to be good is quite prevalent. If the concern driving your moral choice is your own character, it is natural to hold higher standards than in a context where the only moral concern is not harming others.

A virtue base approach to ethics also has the merit of describing how desire affects our choices and how it can help drive excellent moral behavior. Desire in the context of our habits leads not only to applying excellence as a yard stick for our decisions; desire can also yield habitually excellent moral behavior. So how does that work? Take, for example, the idea of procrastination. For Kant, it is unlikely procrastination will fit under an ethical lens because it will often be unrelated to a universal duty. For Mill, procrastination will be right if it leads to good results and wrong if it leads to bad results. Often, I have asked my students, "Is procrastination right or wrong or neither right nor wrong?" Virtually all of them say procrastination is neither right nor wrong. When viewing procrastination from the perspective of Kant's and Mill's principles (which they do without any prodding because of the dominance of those principles in our culture), they are correct. For Kant, it's nor a moral issue, and for Mill, you need more information. If, however, I put the virtue-based lens of ethics on the question and ask if choosing to procrastinate is excellent or mediocre, they also almost universally recognize procrastination is mediocre, especially as a habit. And, while procrastination might sometimes yield a good consequence, we all know that the habit will not produce good results over time.

In the context of habit and the results a habit will yield over time, excellence becomes not only the principle guiding decisions, but also becomes a goal that is earnestly desired. This can be seen in the impact a habit has on desire. And it is in the desire of habits that we see the real power of habitual moral choices for every person, and for leaders in particular. When humans establish a habit through their choices, those

---

35. Cf. Luban, "Integrity," 279–310, for a fascinating discussion on integrity and a succinct summary of social science establishing the many ways humans will try to avoid recognizing their own corruption.

choices and the resulting habits impact the desires of a person. Aristotle makes the keen observation that gratifying an appetite makes an appetite stronger, and modern neuroscience confirms his observation.[36] Habits enlist our desires. We enjoy our habits. We want to do them. And we can see this desire at play in our moral choices. For example, if an honest person, a person in the habit of telling the truth, gets in a tough spot and tells a lie, the person feels awful. The habit of honesty pushes people to tell the truth. They want to tell the truth. They will not be flawless in their ability to tell the truth, but once they establish the habit, they will be reliable truth tellers because that is the behavior they now enjoy as the result of their habit. Honest people are not perfect truth tellers, but they can be excellent ones.

It is the dynamic of desire in excellent habits that can be so powerful for leaders. Although modern people may not recognize the importance of choice to moral habits, they still recognize the fact that they want leaders of good moral character.[37] They want people who can be trusted to lead them. A leader with excellent moral habits is trustworthy because the habit of practical wisdom enables that person to choose well, and other moral habits give a leader the strength to follow that wisdom. It is a strength born of desire. When people are in a difficult moral situation and want to do what is right (due to their habits), they are more likely to be able to rise to the occasion than a person who cannot recognize the morality of the situation or is only concerned about consequences in a self-interested manner. This is directly applicable to leaders, who inevitably encounter situations that are morally difficult. Perhaps the most difficult are situations in which leaders have to put the interests of others, whether they are the interests of their followers or of their team as a whole, above their own. Unfortunately, these decisions are as routine as they are difficult. Leaders will inevitably face these situations and will have to make difficult, even painful decisions if they are to choose what is truly good. It is only the leaders who have prepared themselves through excellent moral habituation that will have any chance to make good decisions in those situations. Without recognizing the importance of morally excellent habits to effective leadership, our culture will not be

---

36. Cf. Aristotle, *Nicomachean Ethics*, 1119b8–1119b9, and Duhigg, *Power of Habit*, for a review of the neuroscience backing up Aristotle's claim.

37. Cf. Barna, "America's Values Study: Report #6" to see a large survey indicating an overwhelming majority (more than 70 percent) of Americans that want ethical leaders.

able to correct the many failures of self-interested leaders that so often end up in the headlines.

A final thought regarding the relationship between ethics and leadership can be explored if we return to one of the initial concepts our history identified. The Greeks asserted the centrality of *areté* for the understanding of ethics. Translated into English, the term *areté* means excellence, and in the context of ethics, it is translated as virtue. Virtue refers to morally excellent habits. Ethics in this context literally means the pursuit of excellence. Leadership in the context of an ethics of excellence is nothing other than the pursuit of excellence that leaders enable by inspiring their followers. Leadership is at the service of organizational excellence, which means the object or goal of leadership is the same as ethics. They are both constituted by the pursuit of excellence. Leadership cannot be done well without an ethics of excellence. It is only by recognizing this fact that our leaders can hope to regain the mantle of leadership respect that our culture so urgently desires and needs.

Bibliography

Acton, Lord John Emerich Edward Dalberg. "Letter 1." *Acton-Creighton Correspondence*, April 5, 1887. https://oll.libertyfund.org/title/acton-acton-creighton-correspondence.
Adkins, W. H. *Merit and Responsibility in Greek Ethics*. Oxford: Clarendon, 1960.
Anscombe, G. E. M. "Modern Moral Philosophy." *Philosophy* 33 (1958) 1–19.
Aquinas, Thomas. *Summa Theologica*. Translated by Father of the English Dominican Province. New York: Benziger Brothers, 1948.
Arendt, Hannah. *Eichmann in Jerusalem: A Report on the Banality of Evil*. New York: Viking, 1963.
Ariely, Dan, et al. "Large Stakes and Big Mistakes." *Working Papers* No. 05–11. Boston: Federal Reserve Bank of Boston, 2005. https://www.bostonfed.org/publications/research-department-working-paper/2005/large-stakes-and-big-mistakes.aspx.
Aristotle. *Nicomachean Ethics*. New York: Macmillan, 1962.
Augustine. *Confessions*. Translated by Henry Chadwick. Oxford: Oxford University Press, 2009.
―――. *The Morals of the Catholic Church*. Translated by Richard Stothert. Nicene and Post-Nicene Fathers, First Series 4. Revised and edited for New Advent by Kevin Knight. Buffalo, NY: Christian Literature, 1887. http://www.newadvent.org/fathers/1401.htm.
―――. *The Trinity*. Translated by Edmund Hill. Hyde Park, New York: New City, 1991.
Baker, Patrick. *Italian Renaissance Humanism in the Mirror*. Cambridge: Cambridge University Press, 2015.
Barna, George. "America's Values Study: Report #6: The Interplay Between Belief and Values." Arizona Christian University (February 2023). https://www.arizonachristian.edu/wp-content/uploads/2023/02/Americas-Values-Study-Report-6.pdf.
Beiser, Frederick C. "Hegel and the Problem of Metaphysics." *The Cambridge Companion to Hegel*. Edited by Frederick C. Beiser. Cambridge: Cambridge University Press, 1993.
Bentham, Jeremy. *The Principle of Utility*. 1789. https://pressbooks.bccampus.ca/classicreadings/chapter/jeremy-bentham-on-the-principle-of-utility/.

Bernstein, Rebecca. "Parenting Around the World: Child Rearing Practices in Different Cultures." *Touro University Worldwide,* July 19, 2016. https://www.tuw.edu/health/child-rearing-practices-different-cultures/.

Beutel, Albrecht. "Luther's Life." In *The Cambridge Companion to Martin Luther,* edited by Donald K. Kim, 3–19. Cambridge: Cambridge University Press, 2003.

Brooks, David. "Who Is James Johnson?" *New York Times,* June 16, 2011. https://www.nytimes.com/2011/06/17/opinion/17brooks.html.

Chandler, Diane. "The Perfect Storm of Leaders' Unethical Behavior: A Conceptual Framework." *International Journal of Leadership Studies* 5 (2009) 69–93.

Churchill, Winston S. *The War Speeches Of The Rt. Hon. Winston S. Churchill.* Edited by Charles Eade. London: Cassell and Company, 1952.

Cicero. *On Duties.* Translated by Harry G. Edinger. Indianapolis: Bobbs-Merrill Educational, 1974.

Conway, Daniel. "Life After the Death of God: Thus Spoke Nietzsche." In *The History of Continental Philosophy,* edited by Alan Schrift, 2:103–36. Chicago: University of Chicago Press, 2013.

Cornwell, John. "MacIntyre on Money." *Prospect Magazine,* October 20, 2010. https://www.prospectmagazine.co.uk/essays/54612/macintyre-on-money.

Defoe, Daniel. *Serious Reflections of Robinson Crusoe.* London: W. Taylor, 1720.

Duhigg, Charles. *The Power of Habit: Why We Do What We Do in Life and Business.* New York: Random House, 2014.

Edelman. "Edelman Trust Barometer." 2023 Edelman Trust Barometer Global Report. https://www.edelman.com/sites/g/files/aatuss191/files/2023-03/2023%20Edelman%20Trust%20Barometer%20Global%20Report%20FINAL.pdf.

Figueira, Thomas J., and Gregory Nagy, eds. *Theognis of Megara: Poetry and The Polis.* Baltimore: The Johns Hopkins University Press, 1985.

Frankl, Viktor. *Man's Search for Meaning.* Boston: Beacon, 1959.

French, Shannon E. "When Teaching the Ethics of War Is Not Academic." *Chronicle of Higher Education, Chronicle Review,* March 2003. https://www.chronicle.com/article/when-teaching-the-ethics-of-war-is-not-academic.

Gable, Dan. *Coaching Wrestling Successfully.* Champaign, IL: Human Kinetics, 1998.

Gallup. "Moral Issues." https://news.gallup.com/poll/1681/moral-issues.aspx.

Goleman, Daniel, et al. *Primal Leadership: Realizing the Power of Emotional Intelligence.* Boston: Harvard Business School Press, 2002.

Goodwin, Doris Kearns. *Team of Rivals: The Political Genius of Abraham Lincoln.* New York: Simon and Schuster, 2005.

Grynbaum, Michael. "New York's Ban on Big Sodas is Rejected by Final Court." *The New York Times,* June 26, 2014. https:www.nytimes.com/2014/06/27/nyregion/city-losesfinal-appeal-on-limiting-sales-of-large sodas.html.

Guthrie, W. K. C. *The Sophists.* Cambridge: Cambridge University Press, 1971.

Heine, Heinrich. *History of Philosophy and Religion in Germany.* Translated by J. Snodgrass. New York: State University of New York Press, 1986.

Heskett, James L., et al. "Putting the Service Profit-Chain to Work." *Harvard Business Review* (July–August 2008). https://hbr.org/2008/07/putting-the-service-profit-chain-to-work.

History.Com Editors. "This Day in History: 13 November 1861, General George McClellan Snubs President Lincoln." Updated November 12, 2024. https://www.history.com/this-day-in-history/mcclellan-snubs-lincoln.

Hobbes, Thomas. *The English Works of Thomas Hobbes*. Edited by W. Molesworth. London: Bohn, 1839.

———. *Leviathan*. Edited by Richard Tuck. Cambridge: Cambridge University Press, 1999.

Homer. *The Iliad*. Edited by M. S. Silk. Cambridge: Cambridge University Press, 2004.

Hume, David. *Enquiry Concerning the Principles of Morals*. Edited by Tom L. Beauchamp. Oxford: Oxford University Press, 1998.

———. *A Treatise of Human Nature*. Edited by L. A. Selby-Bigge. Oxford: Clarendon, 1896.

Hunt, Lester. *Nietzsche and the Origin of Virtue*. New York: Routledge, 2001.

Hutcheson, Frances. *An Inquiry into the Original of Our Ideas of Beauty and Virtue*. Edited by Wolfgang Leidhold. Indianapolis: Liberty Fund, 2004.

Internet Encyclopedia of Philosophy. "William of Ockham (Occam, c. 1280—c. 1349)." https://iep.utm.edu/ockham/.

Kahneman, Daniel. *Thinking Fast and Slow*. New York: Farrar, Straus, and Giroux, 2011.

Kant, Immanuel. *Groundwork of the Metaphysics of Morals*. Translated by Mary Gregor. Cambridge: Cambridge University Press, 1997.

———. *Prolegomena to Any Future Metaphysics*. Translated by Paul Carus. Chicago: Open Court, 1912.

Kellerman, Barbara. *The End of Leadership*. United States: HarperCollins, 2012.

King, Martin Luther, Jr. *Letter From a Birmingham City Jail*. 1963. https://www.africa.upenn.edu/Articles_Gen/Letter_Birmingham.html.

Koistinen, Olli. *The Cambridge Companion to Spinoza's Ethics*. Cambridge: Cambridge University Press, 2010.

Kolditz, Thomas, et al. *Leadership Reckoning*. Houston: Monocle, 2021.

LA Times Archives. "Officer Says He Threatened Iraqi." *Los Angeles Times*, November 20, 2003. https://www.latimes.com/archives/la-xpm-2003-nov-20-fg-hearing20-story.html.

Lehrman Institute. "The War Effort: McClellan's Headquarters." http://www.mrlincolnswhitehouse.org/washington/the-war-effort/war-effort-mcclellan-headquarters/.

Levack, Brian, et al. *The West: Encounters and Transformations, Since 1550, Atlas Edition*. 2nd ed. Harlow, England: Longman, 2007.

Lewis, C. S. "The Necessity of Chivalry." *Time and Tide* 21 (August, 1940) 13–16. http://www.veritascaritas.com/wp-content/uploads/2023/03/C.-S.-Lewis-The-Necessity-of-Chivalry.pdf.

Libcom.org. "Entry on Diggers and Levellers." https://libcom.org/history/1642–1652-diggers-levellers.

Locke, John. *Essay Concerning Human Understanding*. London: T. Tegg and Son, 1836.

Luban, David. "Integrity: Its Causes and Cures." *Fordham Law Review* 72 (2003) 279–310.

Ludwig, Dean C., and Clinton O. Longenecker. "The Bathsheba Syndrome: The Ethical Failure of Successful Leaders." *Journal of Business Ethics* 12 (1993) 265–73.

Lutz, Christopher. "Alasdair Chalmers MacIntyre (1929—)." The Internet Encyclopedia of Philosophy, A Peer Reviewed Source. https://iep.utm.edu/mac-over/.

———. *Tradition in the Ethics of Alasdair MacIntyre: Relativism, Thomism, and Philosophy*. New York: Lexington, 2004.

Machiavelli, Niccolò. *The Prince*. Translated by W. K. Marriott. Philadelphia: Brandywine Studio, 2008.

MacIntyre, Alasdair. *After Virtue*. Notre Dame: University of Notre Dame Press, 1981.

———. "An Interview with Giovanna Borradori." In *The MacIntyre Reader*, edited by Kelvin Knight, 255. Notre Dame: University of Notre Dame Press, 1998.

———. *A Short History of Ethics*. New York: Macmillan, 1966.

———. *Whose Justice, Which Rationality?* Notre Dame: University of Notre Dame Press, 1988.

Marlantes, Karl. *What it is Like to Go to War*. New York: Atlantic Monthly Press, 2011.

Marx, Karl. "The Communism of the Paper Reinischer Beobachter." *Deutsche-Brusseler-Zeitung*, September 12, 1847. https://marxists.architexturez.net/archive/marx/works/1847/09/12.htm.

Mayer, D. M., et al. "How Does Ethical Leadership Flow? A Test of a Trickle-Down Model." *Organizational Behavior and Human Decision Processes* 108 (2009) 1–13.

McDonald, Duff. "When You Get That Wealthy You Start to Believe Your Own Bullshit: The Miseducation of Sheryl Sandberg." *Vanity Fair*, November 27, 2018. https://www.vanityfair.com/news/2018/11/sheryl-sandberg-harvard-business-school-leadership.

McInerney, Joseph. *The Greatness of Humility: St. Augustine on Moral Excellence*. Eugene, OR: Pickwick, 2016.

Mcintyre, Jane L. "Strength of Mind: Prospects and Problems for a Humean Account." *Synthese* 152 (2006) 393–401.

Merriam-Webster Dictionary Online. "Justice (n.)." Updated December 7, 2024. https://www.merriam-webster.com/dictionary/justice.

Mill, John Stuart. *Autobiography*. New York: Columbia University Press, 1924.

———. *On Liberty*. Edited by David Bromwich and George Kateb. New Haven: Yale University Press, 2003.

———. *Utilitarianism*. Cambridge: Hackett, 1979.

Munro, John. "Money, Prices, Wages, and 'Profit Inflation' in Spain, the Southern Netherlands, and England During the Price Revolution Era: ca. 1520—ca. 1650." *História e Economia Revista Interdisciplinar* (2008) 12–71.

Natali, Carlo, and D. S. Hutchison, ed. *Aristotle: His Life and School*. Princeton: Princeton University Press, 2013.

Nietzsche, Friedrich. *The Antichrist*. Translated by H. L. Mencken. New York: Alfred A. Knopf, 1918.

———. *Beyond Good and Evil*. Translated by Walter Kaufmann. New York: Vintage, 1966.

———. *The Gay Science*. Translated by Thomas Common. Mineola, NY: Dover, 2006.

———. *Human, All to Human*. Translated by R. J. Hollingdale. Cambridge: Cambridge University Press, 1996.

———. *The Nietzsche Reader*. Edited by Keith Ansell Pearson and Duncan Large. Hoboken, NJ: Wiley-Blackwell, 2006.

———. *On the Genealogy of Morality*. Translated by Carol Diethe. New York: Cambridge University Press, 2007.

———. *Thus Spoke Zarathustra*. Edited by Adrian Del Caro and Robert Pippin. Cambridge: Cambridge University Press, 2006.

———. *Twilight of the Idols*. Translated by R. J. Hollingdale. London: Penguin Classics, 1990.

Obicci, Peter Adoko. "Effect of Ethical Leadership on Employee Performance in Uganda." *Journal of Management and Science* 4 (2014) 1–12.

Osborne, Thomas. "Faith, Philosophy, and the Nominalist Background to Luther's Defense of the Real Presence." *Journal of the History of Ideas* 63 (2002) 63–82.

Overton, Richard. *An Arrow Against All Tyrants*. 1646. https://oll.libertyfund.org/titles/overton-an-arrow-against-all-tyrants.

Owens, Bradley P., et al. "Expressed Humility in Organizations: Implications for Performance, Teams, and Leadership." *Organization Science* 24 (2013) 1517–38.

Oxford English Dictionary. "Define." https://www.oed.com/dictionary/define_v?tab=meaning_and_use#7200064.

Paton, Nic. "Performance Related Pay Does Not Encourage Performance." *Management Issues*, June 25, 2009. https://www.management-issues.com/news/5640/performance-related-pay-doesnt-encourage-performance/.

Patterson, Thomas C. *Karl Marx, Anthropologist*. Abingdon: Routledge, Taylor, and Francis, 2020.

Pew Research Center. "Americans' Views of Government: Decades of Distrust, Enduring Support for Its Role." June 6, 2022. https://www.pewresearch.org/politics/2022/06/06/americans-views-of-government-decades-of-distrust-enduring-support-for-its-role/.

———. "Public Trust in Government: 1958–2024." https://www.pewresearch.org/politics/2024/06/24/public-trust-in-government-1958-2024/.

Pfeffer, Jeffrey. *Leadership BS*. New York: HarperCollins, 2015.

Plato. *Crito*. In *Five Dialogues*, 45–57. Edited by John M. Cooper. Translated by G. M. A. Grube. Indianapolis: Hackett, 2002.

———. *Dialogues of Plato, Volume I*. Translated by R. E. Allen. New Haven: Yale University Press, 1984.

———. *Gorgias*. Translated by Walter Hamilton and Chris Emlyn-Jones. London: Penguin, 2004.

———. *Meno*. Translated by G. M. A. Grube. Indianapolis: Hackett, 1980.

———. *Phaedo*. Translated by G. M. A. Grube. Indianapolis: Hackett, 1977.

———. *Republic*. Translated by G. M. A. Grube. Indianapolis: Hackett, 1974.

———. *Symposium*. Translated by Christopher Gill. London: Penguin, 1999.

Popkin, Richard. *The History of Skepticism From Savonarola to Bayle*. Oxford: Oxford University Press, 2003.

Porter, Burton F. *Philosophy Through Fiction and Film*. New York: Prentice-Hall, 2003.

Prichard, H. A. "Does Moral Philosophy Rest on a Mistake?" *Mind* 21 (1912) 21–37.

Rawls, John. *A Theory of Justice*. Boston: Harvard University Press, 1971.

Rist, John. *Augustine: Ancient Thought Baptized*. Cambridge: Cambridge University Press, 1994.

Schofield, Phillip. *Bentham: A Guide for the Perplexed*. London: Continuum, 2009.

Schultz, Bart. *The Happiness Philosophers: The Lives and Works of the Great Utilitarians*. Princeton: Princeton University Press, 2017.

Scruton, Roger. *Kant: A Very Short Introduction*. Oxford: Oxford University Press, 2001.

Spade, Paul, ed. *The Cambridge Companion to Ockham*. Cambridge: Cambridge University Press, 1999.

Stanford Encyclopedia of Philosophy. "Immanuel Kant." Edited July 31, 2024. https://plato.stanford.edu/entries/kant/.

Stavridis, James. *Sailing True North: Ten Admirals and the Voyage of Character*. New York: Penguin, 2019.

Steinhage, Anna, et al. "The Pros and Cons of Competition Among Employees." *Harvard Business Review,* March 2017. https://hbr.org/2017/03/the-pros-and-cons-of-competition-among-employees?ab=at_art_art_1x1.

Stern, Robert. "MacIntyre and Historicism." In *After MacIntyre: Critical Perspectives on the Work of Alasdair MacIntyre,* edited by Susan Mendus and John Horton, 146. Notre Dame: University of Notre Dame Press, 1994.

Stewart, Jon, ed. *Kierkegaard and His Contemporaries: The Culture of Golden Age Denmark.* Berlin: Walter de Gruyter, 2003.

Tan, Le, et al. "The Impact of Leaders' Passion at Work on Leader Effectiveness: The Mediating Role of Transformational Leadership." *Proceedings of International Conference on Artificial Intelligence, Management Science and Electronic Commerce (AIMSEC),* August 2011, 1681–84.

Taylor, C. C. W., and Mi-Kyoung Lee. "The Sophists." *The Stanford Encyclopedia of Philosophy* (September 30, 2011). Edited August 18, 2020. https://plato.stanford.edu/entries/sophists/.

Tennyson, Alfred. "The Charge of the Light Brigade." In *The Charge of the Light Brigade and Other Poems,* 52–53. Mineola, NY: Dover, 1992.

Thomas, David Lloyd. *Routledge Philosophy Guidebook to Locke on Government.* London: Routledge, 1995.

Thucydides. *The History of the Peloponnesian War.* Edited by M. I. Finley. Translated by Rex Warner. London: Penguin Classics, 1972.

Tolkien, J. R. R. *The Fellowship of the Ring.* New York: Harper Collins, 2008.

Vainio, Olli-Pekka. "After Relativism: Alasdair MacIntyre on Tradition and Rationalism." *Nova et Vetera* 20 (2022) 315–30.

Vile, M. J. C. *Constitutionalism and the Separation of Powers.* Indianapolis: Liberty Fund, 1998.

Weinstein, Jack Russel. *On MacIntyre.* Toronto: Wadsworth, 2002.

Wicks, Robert. *Schopenhauer's The World as Will and Representation: A Reader's Guide.* London: Continuum, 2011.

Woodson, Neal. "We Cut the Coal." https://nealwoodson.net/2016/07/06/we-cut-the-coal/.

Yerkes, Robert M., and John D. Dodson. "The Relationship of Strength of Stimulus to Rapidity of Habit-Formation." *Journal of Comparative Neurology of Psychology* 18 (1908) 459–82.

Index

"the Absolute" Hegel and, 214–15, 242
Acton, Lord, 209
Adler, Mortimer, 267n28
Aesop's fable, on the ant and the grasshopper, 234
aesthetic life, 240–41
After Virtue (MacIntyre), 72, 266
Agamemnon, 48–51
agathos
    leaders like Agamemnon and, 48–51
    word meaning, 20–21, 44–45
aischros, word meaning, 45
Albert the Great, Saint, 119
Alcibiades, 24–25
Alexander the Great, 100
American culture, 273
ancient Greek society, contrast of modern ethics and, 93–94
Anglican Church, 150
apathy, ethics of, 104–7
appetite, 67, 77, 77n16
Arendt, Hannah, 213
areté, word meaning, 2, 235, 276
Aristophanes, 30, 38
Aristotelian view of philosophy, 4, 264
Aristotle
    background of, 71
    Categories, 119
    critics of, 83–85
    De Anima, 76–77n16
    on deliberation, 76–78
    on desire, 46–47
    field of ethics, 12
    formulations, 74–75
    on good as a concept, 72–74
    on habits, 77–79
    habitual excellence, 27
    on happiness, 65
    on honor, 185–86
    human soul, understanding of, 76–77n16
    humility, human error, leadership, 88–91
    influential in history of ethics, 72
    on laws, 68
    MacIntyre on, 86–88, 148–49
    on magnanimity, 107–9
    Metaphysics, 35n18
    moral choice, criteria for, 75, 80–83, 233
    moral principles, 273nn33–34, 274–75
    moral thinking, 58, 63, 71–72
    Nicomachean Ethics, 26, 71, 104n38
    pleasure and pain terms of ethics, 226
    on Socrates, 34, 36
    on the supreme good, 74–76, 78–79
    Thomas Aquanis and, 119–20
    virtue-based approach to morality, 75n13
Ashley, Anthony, 158

Augustine of Hippo, Saint
    on Christian ethics, 116–18
    Confessions, 65
    on happiness, 117–18
    influences of, 119
    Luther's, view of sin, 127–28
authority, 159, 200
autonomy, 191–92
Ayer, A. J., 261

Bacon, Frances, 133
bad societies, 102–4
Bathsheba Syndrome, 48
beauty, 64–65
Bentham, Jeremy
    Mill family and, 222
    natural moral principles, 224
    pleasure and pain terms of ethics, 223–26
    utilitarian philosopher, 166
    utilitarianism of, 223–26
Bernstein, Eduard, 218
book burnings, example of moral thinking, 14
Boromir (character), *The Lord of the Rings*, 9–10
bourgeois economy, 216–19
Brady, Tom, 27
British ethics, eighteenth-century
    Butler, on reason in relation to ethics, 163–94
    Hume, on moral "ought," 165–70
    leadership reflections, 170–73
    Locke, on liberty, poverty, and rationality of ethics, 158–61
    overview, 157–58
    sentimental moral theorists, 161–62
Brooks, David, 5–6
bureaucracy, ethics of, 212–15
bureaucratic zoo, leadership in, 219–21
Butler, Joseph, 163–64

Cable, Dan, 188
Caesar Augustus, 130
Callicles, 42, 46
Calvin, John, 128–29
Calvinism, 150
Cambridge Platonists, 160

Candide (Voltaire), 180
Carville, James, 154
categorical imperatives, 195–96, 198, 200–202, 213, 265
Categories (Aristotle), 119
Catholicism. *see* Roman Catholic Church
Celtic literature, 3
Cessario, Romanus, 267n28
change and permanence, 63–64
Charge of the Light Brigade (Tennyson), 168
choice
    impact of, 230
    Kierkegaard on, 239–40
    moral choice, 75, 80–83, 94–95, 233–35
Christian morality
    Aquinas' contribution to ethics, 118–21
    Augustine's contribution to ethics, 116–18
    leadership reflections, 123–25
    MacIntyre on, 149
    motivation for obeying God, 113–16
    Nietzsche on, 248–54
    overview, 111–22
    unity of for Chistian ethics, 112–14
    William of Ockham, God in ethics, 121–23
Christian traditions, 147
Christianity. *see also* Roman Catholic Church
    Anglican Church, 150
    impact on modern Europe, 206, 241–43, 248–54
    Protestant Reformation, 127
    Puritan movement, 149–50
    secular reason and, 242–43
Churchill, Winston, 60–62
Cicero, 108, 129–30, 178, 186
classical morality, 233
Clinton, Bill, 154
Collingwood, R. G., 261
colonization, impact of, 24
common traits, of twentieth-century ethics, 263
Communist Party of China, 231–32

Index

community
    diversity and collaboration in leadership, 60–62
    goodness of, 82n31
    Hagel on, 207–8
    justice in, 66
    need for, 55
compassion, 247
Confessions, (Augustine), 65
consequences, utilitarian focus on, 232–37
contemplative life, 100
contemporary moral thought, 268–72
conventional persons, 33–34
corrupt leaders, 48–51
criticism, 39–40
Critique of Pure Reason (Kant), 190, 268
Crito dialogue (Plato), 40

Danish ethics, nineteenth century
    Kierkegaard, Soren, 238–43
    Moller, Poul Martin, 238
    Sibbern, F. C., 238
David, King (of ancient Israel and Judah), 48–49, 133
De Anima (Aristotle), 76–77n16
De L'Esprit (*On Minds*) (Helvetius), 178–79
Declaration of Independence, 15
DeFoe, Daniel, 150–51, 154
deliberation, 76–78, 80–81
democratic governments, separation of powers, 175
Dependent Rational Animals (MacIntyre), 266
desire
    Aristotle on, 46–47, 76–77
    Greek society on, 64–66
    Helvetius on, 179
    leadership and, 142–44
    Plato on, 46–47
    society and, 98–100
    term usage, 77n16
    Thomas Aquinas on, 119
despotism, 58–59, 176
Dewey, John, 261
Diderot, Denis, 180
Diggers and Levellers (fighting groups), 152–54
dignity, of every human being, 116
Diotema, 118
diversity and collaboration in leadership, 60–62
Dodson, John, 155
Dominic Guzman, Saint, 118
Dominican Order of priests, 118–19
Duhigg, Charles, 69–70
Dungy, Tony, 69
duty, as a concept, 94–96, 228
duty, Kant's ethics of, 190–97, 228

Eichmann, Adolph, 213
eidos, word meaning, 21–22
Either/Or (Kierkegaard), 240
emotions, in leadership, 170–73
emotive moral thought, 259–63
emotivism
    common traits, twentieth-century, 263–66
    Stevenson on, 261–63
employees, competing for honor, 188
Encyclopdie (Diderot), 180
English civil war (1642–1649), 152–54
Enlightenment era, 157
Enlightenment vs. classical ethics, 267–68
Enron, leadership failure, 124
Epicureans, 104–7
epistemology, 63
eros, meaning of, 64
ethical innovation, 34
ethics
    of apathy, 104–7
    comparison of ancient to modern, 92–94
    individualism, as focal point of, 151–52
    MacIntyre's three approaches to, 148–49
    of tranquility, 104–7
    why be ethical, 146–47
ethics, history of
    leadership reflections, 15–17
    moral concepts over time and place, 10–14
    overview, 9–10

Index

ethics, in post-medieval era
    Hobbes, 131–38
    leadership reflections, 142–44
    Luther, 126–29
    Machiavelli, 129–31
    overview, 126
    Spinoza, 139–41
eudaimonia, meaning of, 74
Euthyphro dialogue (Plato), 241
evil, meaning of, 44
excellence and ethics, 25–28
executive function of ethics, 191

Fabian socialist movement, 231
Facebook, leadership failures, 124
false consciousness, 211, 217
Fear and Trembling (Kierkegaard), 242
follower motivation, 154–56
followers
    as ends, 201–4
    honor as motivation, 201–4
    Kant on, 236–37
Foot, Phillipa, 267n28
Francis of Assisi, Saint, 118
Franciscan Order of priests, 118–19
Frankl, Viktor, 84
freedom
    Hegel on, 208
    Hegel *vs.* Marx, 216–19
    leadership and, 142–44
    in the marketplace, 145
    right to, 159
    Spinoza on, 139–41
French ethics, eighteenth-century
    Helvetius, 178–80
    human nature, 178–80
    leadership reflections, 185–88
    Montesquieu ethics, 174–78
    overview, 174
    Rousseau, 180–84
    society, relativism and, 174–78
Further Adventures of Robinson Crusoe, The (DeFoe), 150

Gable, Dan, 25–26, 28
Galileo, 133
Geneva Conventions, 16
German ethics, nineteenth century
    "anti-German" philosophers, 243–44
    Heine, 238, 244–45
    influencer thinkers, 238
    leadership reflections, 254–57
    National Socialism, 253
    Nietzsche (*see* Nietzsche, Friedrich)
    Schopenhauer, 238, 243, 245–47
    secularization of, 244
German Idealism, 205
Glaucon (older brother of Plato), 53–54
glory, 186
goal determination, 76
goals
    choice and, 80–82, 89, 98
    passion and, 254–55
GOAT (Greatest of All Time), 27
God
    on Abraham's sacrifice of Isaac, 242–43
    as the fulfillment of all desire, 120
    goodness of, 114
    holiness of, 113
    motivations for obeying, 113–16
    as nature, 140
    power of, 114–15
    sovereign power of, 122
    unity for Chistian ethics, 112–13
    William of Ockham on, 121–23
Goleman, Daniel, 171–72
good
    Aristotle on, 72–74
    common good, 44–47
    desire for, 36
    as desire for God, 123
    as an idea, 98–100
    impact of, 102–4
    Locke on, 160
    Moore on, 259–61
    Plato's description of, 41–42, 117
    Stevenson on, 261
    utilitarian context, 249
good societies, Thomas Aquinas on, 120
good things, for a happy life, 84
good will, 193
good/bad and pleasure/pain, meanings of, 45
Gorgias dialogue (Plato), 42–47, 59

Index

government, forms of, 176
Greek literature
    Agathos and *Areté*, 18–23
    colonization, impact of, 24
    historical change, 23–25
    The Iliad and *The Odyssey*, 19
    myths and, 23–24
    Theognid literature, 19–23, 53
Groundwork of the Metaphysics of Morals, The (Kant), 189

habits, 63, 68–70, 77–79, 110, 274–75
happiness
    bad societies and, 102–4
    as goal for moral evaluation, 231
    Kant on, 198
    Nietzsche on, 251
    social context and, 163–64
    Spinoza on, 139–41
    term usage, 101
    Thomas Aquinas on, 120
    virtues and, 114–15
    word translation, 74
happy life, categories of, 84
harmony, 161–62
Harvard Business Review, 142
Harvard Business School (HBS), 124–25
Hauerwas, Stanley, 267n28
Hay, John, 88
Hegel, Georg Wilhem Friedrich
    on community, 207–8
    on freedom, 208
    idealism of, 215
    individualistic context for morality, 207
    leadership reflections, 219–21
    master-serf relationship, 208–11
    on morality of Marx, 215–19
    overview, 205–6
    role of history on ethics, 206–7
    on Roman antiquity, 208
    Schopenhauer and, 245
    "spiritual zoo," 212, 219
Heine, Heinrich, 238, 244–45
Helvetius, Claude-Adrien, 174, 178–80
Herodotus, 43
history
    community impact, 206
    epicurean thought, 100–102
    impact of society, 2n1
    importance of, 2n1
    stoic, 100–102
History of Philosophy and Religion in Germany, The (Heine), 244
History of the Peloponnesian War (Thucydides), 131
Hitler, Adolf, 50, 244
Hobbes, Thomas
    approach to ethics, 147
    as an atheist, 135
    Leviathan, 14
    MacIntyre on, 148
    moral motivation, 151
    moral thought of, 131–38
    on self-interest, 154, 156
    on state of nature, 32, 152
Homer
    Agathos and *Areté*, 19–23
    Iliad, The and *The Odyssey*, 19
Homer's Achilles, 7, 18
honor, as motivation for followers, 185–88
hubris, 23, 203
human error, 89–90
human motivation, 139
human nature
    consequence to morality, 269
    corruption of society and, 180
    as determined and transformable, 178–80
human soul, understanding of
    Aristotle, 76–77n16
    Plato, 55–58
human will, importance, 254
humanism, 146
Hume, David, 13, 161–62, 165–70, 234
humility
    Cicero on, 203
    in leadership, 88–91
    Marx on, 14
    meaning of over time, 12–13
    nature of and it's value, 89n45
Hutcheson, Francis, 161–62, 222
hypothetical imperatives, 196

Iliad, The and *The Odyssey* (Homer), 19

immoral leaders, 49–51
incentive systems, 188
inclination, Kant on, 94–95
Indianapolis Colts, 70
individualism, 3, 151–52, 212, 265n24
injustice, 44–45, 53, 56
integrity, as a moral concept, 78n23
interminable disagreements, 262
Introduction to The Principles of Morals and Legislation, An (Bentham), 222
irresolvable arguments, 262
Islam, 119

Jewish population, 249–50
Jewish traditions, 147
John XXII, Pope, 121
Jordan, Michael, 27
judgments, about individual people, 20
justice
    in the community, 55–60
    Hume on, 169–70
    meaning of over time, 12, 12n12
    in modern ethics, 93
    Montesquieu on, 178
    in Plato's *The Laws*, 66
    in *The Republic*, 53–54
    in society, 102
    Sophists on, 30–32

Kahneman, Daniel, 69
kakos, word meaning, 44–45
Kant, Immanuel
    categorical imperatives, 195–96, 198, 200–202, 213, 265
    on consequences, 163
    Critique of Pure Reason, 190, 268
    duty, ethics of, 190–97, 228
    as Enlightenment thinker, 141
    on followers, 236–37
    German philosopher and ethicist, 92
    Groundwork of the Metaphysics of Morals, The, 189
    Hume and, 157, 190
    impact and power of his ethics, 197–98
    individualism, 265n24
    on justice, 93–94
    Kingdom of Ends, 218
    leadership reflections, 201–4
    MacIntyre's critique of, 199–201
    as most significant modern philosopher, 189n1
    nature of ethics, 268
    neglected aspects of his thinking, 268–69
    Newton and, 190
    overview, 189–90
    purely rational morality, 57
Kautsky, Karl, 218
Kierkegaard, Soren, 238–43
King, Martin Luther, Jr., 220–21
Kingdom of Ends, 218
knowledge, abstract *vs.* moral knowledge, 12

language, function of, 12
Laws, The, dialogue (Plato), 52, 60, 66–67
laws of nature, 25
leadership
    current failures in, 5–6
    ethics and, 5, 15–17
    excellence and ethics, 25–28
    human will, importance of, 254
    impact on organizations, 15–17
    Socrates and, 38–40
    of virtue-based ethics, 272–76
leadership reflections
    agathos and leaders like Agamemnon, 48–51
    in the bureaucratic zoo, 219–21
    consequences, utilitarian on, 232–37
    diversity and collaboration in leadership, 60–62
    ethics and impact on organizations, 15–17
    excellence and ethics of leadership, 25–28
    follower motivation, 154–56
    followers as ends, 201–4
    freedom and desire in, 142–44
    honor, as motivation for followers, 185–88
    humility, human error, and leadership, 88–91

moral corruption of leaders, 254–57
opportunity for moral development, 107–10
Plato, habits, and National Football League, 68–70
reason and emotion, 170–73
Socrates as leader, 38–40
Sophists, Thomists and modern leadership, 123–25
Left Hegelians (Hagel's followers), 215
legislative function of ethics, 191
Letter from a Birmingham City Jail (King, Jr.), 220–21
Leviathan (Hobbes), 14
Lewis, C. S., 7
liberty, right to, 159
Lincoln, Abraham, 88, 91
Locke, John
    on authority of the sovereigns, 159
    background of, 158
    Enlightenment era, 141
    ethical concepts, 153–54
    on the natural person, 159
    rationality of ethics, 158–61
    reason and emotion, 170–73
    right to property and liberty, 159
logic, use of, 56–57
Longnecker, Clinton, 48–49
long-term concerns, 234
Lord of the Rings, The (Tolkien), 9–10
love, 65
Ludwig, Dean, 48–49
Luther, Martin, 126–29, 244
lying, 84–85, 85n36, 97

Macedon, empire of, 100
Machiavelli, Niccolò
    fear as the strongest motivator, 49
    Prince, The, 130–31
    Realpolitik, of modern state, 129–31
MacIntyre, Alasdair
    After Virtue, 72, 266
    as an atheist, 111
    biographical details, 3–4
    Dependent Rational Animals, 266
    Hobbes, criticism of, 135–38
    impact of society, 14–15
    later thinking of, 263–66
    leadership reflections, 15–17
    moral concepts over time and place, 10–14
    as a moral relativist, 11
    on myths, 23–24
    Short History of Ethics, A, 1–3, 10–11, 266
    three approaches to ethics, 148–49
    Three Rival Versions of Moral Inquiry, 266
    Whose Justice? Which Rationality? 266
magnanimity, 107–9
Malone, Karl, 27
manipulators, 49–50
Marino, Dan, 27
marketplace, rights and freedom in
    Diggers and Levellers (fighting groups), 152–54
    individual, emphasis on, 151–52
    leadership reflections, 154–56
    MacIntyre's approaches to ethics, 148–49
    overview, 145
    religious to secular transition, 149–51
    why be ethical, 146–47
Marlantes, Karl, 187
marriage, 240
Marx, Karl
    background of, 215
    bourgeois economy and, 216–19
    Hegel, on morality of, 215–19
    Hegel's notion of freedom and, 211
    on humility, 14
    as a Left Hegelian, 215
    moral thought, 205–6
Marxist critique of liberal individualism, 3
Mary II, Queen of England, 159
master-serf relationship, 208–11
McClellan, George, 88, 90
McDonald, Duff, 124
"Me Too" movement, 148
Medici, Lorenzo de, 130
mendicant religious orders, 118
Meno (Plato), 36
metaphysics, 52, 63

Metaphysics (Aristotle), 35n18
military mission, example of leadership, 16
Mill, James, 222–23
Mill, John Stuart
    Bentham collaborator, 222–23
    On Liberty, 223, 268
    neglected aspects of his thinking, 268–69
    utilitarian philosopher, 166, 226–32, 234
Milton, John, 151
modern ethics
    contrast of ancient Greek, 93–94
    rival traditions, 264
Moll Flanders (DeFoe), 150
Moller, Poul Martin, 238
monarchy, 176, 185
Montesquieu, Charles-Louis de Secondat, Baron de la Bréde et de, 174–78
Montezuma, Aztec King, 177
Moore, G. E., 259–61
moral choice
    Aristotle on, 75, 80–83
    Bentham on, 224–25
    choice and habits, dynamic between, 233–35
    Kant on, 94–95
    Kierkegaard on, 239–40
    threefold criteria for, 80–83
moral concepts
    description of, 37
    over time and place, 10–14, 37
    Plato on, 37–38
moral conservatives, 34
moral corruption of leaders, 254–57
moral deliberation, 76
moral development, in leadership, 107–10
moral good, desire for, 36
moral ideas, society's impact on, 14–15
moral judgment, 197–98
moral order, overstepping of, 23–24
moral "ought" from factual "is," 165–70
moral psychology, 76–77
moral terminology and common good, 44–47

morality
    desire and habit and, 63
    virtue-based approach to, 75–76
myths, MacIntyre on, 23–24

National Football League, 69–70
natural laws, 224n7
natural moral principles, 224
natural persons, 32–33, 54, 159
natural rights, 159
naturalistic fallacy, 260–61
nature
    laws of, 25
    state of, 181
Nazi party, Germany
    Auschwitz concentration camp, 84
    book burnings, 14
    Eichmann, Adolph, 213
    genocidal actions, 230
    Hitler, Adolph, 50, 244
    Nietzsche's rejection of, 253
    truth telling in, 98, 200
New York City, on sugary soft drinks, 68
Newton, Sir Isaac, 190
Nicomachean Ethics (Aristotle), 26, 71, 104n38
Nietzsche, Friedrich
    Christian morality, 248–54
    On the Genealogy of Morality, 249
    as German thinker, 238, 243
    human will, importance of, 254
    humility, as a vice, 13
    leadership reflections, 254–57
    master and serf relations, 205
    Thus Spoke Zarathustra, 254
    Ubermensch. see Ubermensch, in Nietzsche's writing
    will to power, 247–54
Ninety-Five Theses (Luther), 127

Ockham's Razor, 121
On Liberty (J. S. Mill), 223, 268
On the Genealogy of Morality (Nietzsche), 249
Order of Preachers (Dominican priests), 118
organizations, impact of leadership ethics, 15–17

Overton, Thomas, 152
Ovid (Roman poet), 51

Paradise Lost (Milton), 151
parenting, 97
passion, goals and, 254–55
paternalism, 68
patristic authors, 116
permanence, change and, 63–64
Philip II, king of Macedon, 100
Pink, Dan, 155–56
Plato
    Agathos and leaders like Agamemnon, 48–51
    Crito dialogue, 40
    description of the good, 41–42, 117
    on desire, 46–47
    dialogues of, 41–42, 241
    Euthyphro dialogue, 241
    Glaucon (older brother of), 53–54
    Gorgias dialogue, 42–47, 59
    Laws, The, dialogue, 52, 60, 66–67
    Meno dialogue, 36
    on moral concepts, 37–38
    Republic, The. See *Republic, The,* dialogue (Plato)
    as student of Socrates, 30, 34–35
    Symposium, The, dialogue, 52, 60, 64–66, 87, 118
    Theaetetus dialogue, 30
pleasure and pain terms of ethics, 223–32
pleasure/pain and good/bad, meanings of, 45
power, 209, 247
Power of Habit, The (Duhigg), 69
powerlessness, 101
Price Revolution, 131–32
Prichard, H. A., 93–94, 261
pride, 23
Primal Leadership (Goleman), 171–72
Prince, The (Machiavelli), 130–31
Principia Ethica (Moore), 259
principle of utility, 222
productive science, 76
property, right to, 159
Protagoras, 30

Protestant Ethic and the Spirit of Capitalism, The (Weber), 150
Protestant Reformation, 127
psychological materialist, 179
psychology
    motivation for moral choice, 224–25
    Plato's understanding of, 55–58
Puritan movement, 149–50
Putney debates (1647), 152–53

Rainborough, Thomas, 153
Rawls, John, 12n12, 102
Realpolitik, Machiavelli on, 129–31
reason
    Butler on, 163–64
    deliberation and, 76–78
    importance of ethics, 42–44
    Kant on, 191
    in leadership, 170–73
    role of and failure of, 85–86
    Spinoza on, 140
relativism, 96–98, 177
religious morality, 165
religious to secular ethics, 149–51
Renaissance era, 129, 146
Republic, The, dialogue (Plato)
    bridge between ethics and politics, 52
    cave allegory, 64
    on the concept of a good, 47, 117
    diversity and collaboration in leadership, 60–62
    on justice in the community, 55–60
    overview of, 52
    question of justice, 53–54
republicanism, 176
rhetoric
    meaning of, 42–44
    a Sophist virtue, 29
rights
    individuals, 152–54
    in the marketplace, 145
Roberts, Robert, 267n28
Robinson Crusoe (DeFoe), 150, 151
Rolling Stones (rock musical group), 123
Roman Catholic Church, 4, 127, 146, 210, 244
Rousseau, Jean Jacques, 151, 180–84

Schopenhauer, Arthur, 238
Scientific Revolution, 131, 133
secular ethics, 149–51
secularization, of Germany, 244
self-interest, 246
self-love, 181–82
self-understanding, 140–41
separation of powers, in democratic governments, 175
service-profit chain, 142
Seward, William, 88
Shaftesbury, Lord (previously Anthony Ashley), 158
Shaftesbury, Third Earl of, 158, 161–62
shame, 21–22
Short History of Ethics, A (MacIntyre), 1–3, 10–11, 266
short-term concerns, 234
Sibbern, F. C., 238
skepticism, 210
slavery, 102, 210–11, 230–31, 249–50
Smith, Adam, 151
society
    bad societies, 102–4
    corruption of, 180–84
    good societies, 102
    history's impact on, 14–15
sociological moralist, 176
Socrates
    Aristotle on, 34
    Athenians and, 14
    early life of, 38
    humility of, 35
    knowledge and, 34–38
    as leader, 38–40
    on love by the female sage Diotema, 64
    Plato, student of, 30, 34–35
    teaching style, 35–36
    wisdom of, 29–34
Socratic dialogue, 35
Sophists
    approach to ethics, 147
    background of, 29–30
    on goal of rhetoric, 45–46
    on goals and desires, 207
    on greatest good, 45, 123
    on injustice, 45
    on justice, 30–32
    on meaning of rhetoric, 42–43
    on success, virtues of, 30–31
    on supreme good, 42
Spinoza, Baruch, 139–41
"spiritual zoo," 212, 219
Stanton, Edward, 91
Steinhage, Anna, 188
Stevenson, C. L., 259, 261–63
Stocker, Michael, 267n28
stoics
    citizen, each person as, 209
    history, 100–102
    schools of thought, 104–7
success, 30–31
suffering, 40
Symposium, The, dialogue (Plato), 52, 60, 64–66, 87, 118

Tacitus, 249
Tampa Bay Buccaneers, 69–70
Tennyson, Lord, 168
Theaetetus dialogue (Plato), 30
Theognid literature, 19–23, 53
Theognis of Megara, 20
theoretical thinking, 76
Thinking Fast and Slow (Kahneman), 69
Thomas Aquinas, Saint
    Christian ethics, contribution to, 118–21
    on greatest good, 123
    on honor, 185–87
    MacIntyre on, 147–48
    thoughts of, 4
Three Rival Versions of Moral Inquiry (MacIntyre), 266
Thucydides, 24, 131
Thus Spoke Zarathustra, (Nietzsche), 254
Tolkien, J. R. R., 9–10
tranquility, ethics of, 104–7
truth, 87
truth telling, 97–98, 109, 193, 196–97
twentieth-century ethics
    common traits of, 263
    contemporary moral thought, 268–72
    emotive moral thought, 259–63

Enlightenment *vs.* classical ethics, 267–68
leadership, of virtue-based ethics, 272–76
MacIntyre's later thinking, 263–66
overview, 258–59
tyrants, 49–50

Ubermensch, in Nietzsche's writing, 7–8, 243, 247–57
universe, system of
Epicureans on, 106
Greek myths on, 23–24
Plato on, 64
Spinoza on, 140
Stoics on, 104–5
University of Iowa wrestling team, 26
Utilitarianism (Mill, J.S.), 223, 226, 232
utilitarianism, baseline principle of, 45
utilitarianism, nineteenth-century
Bentham and, 223–26
leadership reflections, 232–37
MacIntyre's critique of, 226–32
Mill's defense of, 226–32
overview, 222–23

victim, transformed to agent, 141

virtue-based approach to morality/ethics, 75–76, 272
virtues
Aristotle on, 87
bad societies and, 102–4
happiness and, 114–15
short *vs.* long-term goals, 83–85
Thomas Aquinas on, 120
Voltaire, 180

Wardley, Duncan, 188
Weber, Max, 150
Welsh coal miners during WWII, 60–62
What It Is Like to Go to War (Marlantes), 187–88
Whose Justice? Which Rationality? (MacIntyre), 266
William of Ockham, 121–23, 126, 128
William of Orange, 159
writ of harem, 139

Xenophon, 30, 38

Yerkes, Robert, 155

Zeno, 104

www.ingramcontent.com/pod-product-compliance
Lightning Source LLC
Chambersburg PA
CBHW032052220426
43664CB00008B/962